WHITE-COLLAR CRIME IN IRELAND

LAW AND POLICY

Edited by

JOE McGRATH
BCL (NUI) PhD (NUI)

CLARUS PRESS

Published by
Clarus Press Ltd,
Griffith Campus,
South Circular Road,
Dublin 8.
www.claruspress.ie

Typeset by
Gough Typesetting Services, Dublin

Printed by
Sprint Print Ltd,
Dublin.

ISBN
978-1-911611-21-9

Disclaimer
Whilst every effort has been made to ensure that the contents of this book are accurate, neither the publisher, editor(s) or contributors can accept responsibility for any errors or omissions or loss occasioned to any person acting or refraining from acting as result of any material in this publication.

FOREWORD

It is often said, probably with some reasonable justification, that Ireland has been slow to put in place adequate measures for dealing with white-collar crime. However, the wide range of topics covered in this book demonstrates there are many aspects to the enforcement of the law in this area.

Indeed, as one of the articles demonstrates, the question of what constitutes white-collar crime may itself give rise to some issues on the margins. Likewise, as other papers show, the range of enforcement measures can range from a traditional criminal prosecution, through regulatory measures (including administrative penalties) to various forms of civil enforcement.

But as the current debate about whether it might be appropriate to introduce a form of criminal offence relating to the reckless management of financial institutions demonstrates, one of the questions in the past has sometimes been a disconnect between the consequences which cause understandable public concern and the specific offences of which individuals might, in principle, be found guilty.

These questions came into particular focus, hardly surprisingly, in the fall-out from the banking crisis with the profound consequences for so many that followed. But a succession of reports suggests that, at least in the main, the causes of the banking collapse were not, at least to any significant extent, attributable to a breach of the law. Rather it would seem that failed policies, both at banking, regulatory and governmental level were the main culprits. So perhaps the first port of call has to be public education and debate about where we draw the lines between what is considered to be a breach of the law capable of punishment in some form or other, on the one hand, and that which is purely an error of judgment, albeit sometimes a significant one, on the other.

An ordinary middle ranking manager in any organisation, public or private, would be most unlikely to think it fair that they could be subjected to a criminal prosecution because they made a mistake even though it might happen that the mistake had serious consequences. Most would agree that disciplinary action might follow in a proportionate way including, if justified, dismissal. But we do not ordinarily consider that making mistakes, even bad ones, gives rise to a criminal sanction. If we are to move away from that position, then we need a thorough understanding of the issues which arise and that provides one of the very many reasons for welcoming this thorough examination of the subject.

Further, as a reading of the papers demonstrates, there are issues and questions in relation to most aspects of the field. Does our 'ordinary' criminal process provide an effective means for prosecuting white-collar crime? If not, why not and what measures might be considered necessary to remedy the situation? But to what extent are there legitimate reasons for departing from the ordinary criminal process in the context of crimes such as those discussed in this book?

Do regulators have sufficient power to do their job effectively? Again, if not, what measures might be considered and would they be justified? The issue of administrative penalties also comes into play.

Furthermore, in the context both of criminal prosecution and regulatory action, there are real questions about whether, certainly in the past, there has been sufficient expertise and resources, both legal and otherwise, to enable existing law to be deployed to its maximum advantage. While one collection of essays will not solve all of the problems associated with capacity, this book must surely provide an invaluable source for those charged both with ensuring that there is sufficient expertise and those who are required to take appropriate measures.

While civil remedies can provide an effective enforcement mechanism in certain areas they may not be considered adequate in others not least because the normal consequence of a civil remedy is simply to put the parties back into the position in which they would have been had wrongdoing not taken place so that the only detriment to the wrongdoer is that they do not retain any ill-gotten gains. In at least some areas this may not be considered to be an adequate deterrent. Furthermore, the question of the likelihood of civil litigation being capable of being effectively pursued may depend on whether the scale of any claim is likely to justify the expenditure. Where there is a single, or a small number, of claimants and where the claim is likely to be significant, this may not prove a problem. However, the absence of a class action jurisdiction in Ireland makes it a lot less likely that civil claims will be brought where there are a large of number of claimants with relatively small claims. On the other hand, the question of class actions can itself be a matter of some controversy given that it is sometimes said that the US class action model more often benefits lawyers than those who have suffered wrongdoing.

These comments are intended to demonstrate, as I think each of the articles in this book shows, that there are often no easy answers to the problems posed by dealing with white-collar crime. But one thing is certain: solutions adopted without a thorough understanding of the issues and the problems are much more likely to make things worse rather than better. With that in mind there can be no doubt whatsoever that this book will make a hugely valuable contribution to increasing knowledge and understanding of the wide range of questions which surround the enforcement of white-collar crime in Ireland.

It should be a must read not only for practitioners (and in that category I include judges, lawyers and regulators who are likely to be directly involved in the process) but also, vitally, policy makers. All of our thanks are due to the many authors for their careful and thoughtful contributions and it is to be hoped that their collective work will lead to improved policy formation, the allocation of appropriate resources and an enhanced ability of those at the coalface in regulation and litigation to deal with the often complex issues which arise.

Mr Justice Frank Clarke
Chief Justice
Supreme Court
3 December 2018

PREFACE

White-collar crime has become a significant area of interest for academics, practitioners and policy makers. This was not always so. Traditionally, researchers who specialised in issues related to criminal justice and punishment were usually more interested in 'real' or 'serious' crimes, neglecting the study of regulatory crimes that were often considered technical, victimless, and enforced by specialist agencies, if at all. This emphasis was also reflected in the leading Irish criminal law textbooks and continues to be reflected in contemporary Irish criminal law education at third level, which emphasises the importance of 'real' crimes, involving violence against the person, like homicides, assaults and sexual offences, or conventional property-related offences, like theft.

Regulatory criminal law has, however, become increasingly influential and is now a prominent method of enforcing corporate obligations in a diverse range of regulatory domains, including company law, health and safety law, and competition law, among others. Some regulatory agencies have extensive powers and may summarily prosecute crime in their respective areas, colonising ground once held by conventional police and prosecutors. Moreover, these administrative agencies need not always fulfil procedural requirements previously necessary under paradigmatic criminal law. The more frequent employment of strict liability mechanisms and 'reverse onus' provisions, for example, reflects the instrumental approach underpinning much of the emerging regulatory framework. In other instances, punitive civil sanctions are blurring the distinctions between criminal and civil jurisdictions.

Moreover, the compliance-orientated 'responsive' model of corporate enforcement in Ireland, when adopted by regulators, meant that the harsh criminal regime was not always implemented in practice, except as a last resort, when other methods had failed. In some instances, it appeared that there remained a tendency to 'manage' corporate wrongdoing through strategies such as guidance, persuasion and negotiation rather than criminally punish it. Since the financial crisis, however, a more stringent approach to enforcement has emerged. Politicians have condemned white-collar criminals, calling them terrorists and accusing them of treason. New laws were introduced to facilitate the detection, investigation and prosecution of white-collar crime, in recognition of the systemic economic harm that it may cause in the financial and corporate sectors. These initiatives recently culminated in the prosecution and conviction of some of Ireland's most senior bankers.

Given the trend towards the increased use of robust criminal legislation, an increased willingness to prosecute white-collar crime, and sustained calls for more laws to combat corporate wrongdoing, it is reasonable to assume that more Irish legislation will be forthcoming. The Irish Law Reform Commission, for example, recently finalised its Report on Regulatory Crime and Corporate Offences, which recommends enhancing the regulatory powers of regulators and the introduction of new offences. Though published after the completion of the chapters in this collection, it reflects some of the issues canvassed here, and puts further pressure on the Government to legislate in this field. Drawing on the work of leading scholars and practitioners, this collection is ideally placed to contribute to the discourse on the future of regulatory enforcement in Ireland. It will be of significant interest to policy makers, researchers and practitioners in this field.

Joe McGrath
January 2019

SHORT TABLE OF CONTENTS

DETAILED TABLE OF CONTENTS

ABOUT THE CONTRIBUTORS

David Carson is the Partner in charge of Deloitte's Forensic practice in Ireland with over 30 years' experience in providing investigation and dispute services and giving evidence as an Expert Witness. He has extensive experience in corporate restructuring, corporate investigations and M&A. David has been appointed to a number of high profile, complex insolvency and restructuring cases in recent years. He is a Fellow of Chartered Accountants Ireland and holds a LLB from Queen's University Belfast.

Remy Farrell is a senior counsel practicing in the area of criminal, regulatory, disciplinary and extradition law. He is co-author of *The European Arrest Warrant in Ireland* (2011).

Kenan Furlong is a partner in A&L Goodbody where he leads their White-Collar Crime Group. He has advised on many of Ireland's most high profile corporate crises in recent years. Kenan is Chairman of the International Bar Association's Business Crime Committee. He has presented to the Irish Government on draft legislation, lectures at a number of Irish universities, and has chaired international conferences across the globe.

Cathal Grennan is a Senior Associate in A&L Goodbody specialising in white-collar and regulatory crime. He has advised on a number of Ireland's most high profile corporate crises in recent years. Cathal is a graduate of NUI Galway, the Law Society of Ireland and the Honourable Society of Kings Inns. Cathal lectures regularly on a number of areas of Irish law including money laundering, the regulation of lobbying and whistle-blower protection.

Claire A Hill is the James L Krusemark Chair in Law at the University of Minnesota Law School. She is a member of the American Law Institute and an associate reporter on its Compliance, Risk Management, Governance, and Enforcement project. Claire has published numerous articles and book chapters in journals and books in the US and Europe, in the fields of corporate governance, law and language, and behavioural economics, including on the role of culture, personality and identity in banks and other organisations, as well as edited volumes and books, one with Richard Painter, Better Banks, Better Bankers (University of Chicago Press), and one with Brian Quinn and Steven Davidoff Solomon, and a textbook on Mergers & Acquisitions (West).

Mary Catherine Lucey is Associate Professor in UCD Sutherland School of Law and is a Non-Governmental Adviser to the Competition and Consumer Protection Commission. She received her D. Phil from the London School of Economics and Political Science. Her research on competition law appears in leading international academic journals. She is a member of the International Competition Network's Agency Effectiveness Working Group.

Joe McGrath has a PhD in corporate and financial regulation and is a lecturer at the Sutherland School of Law, University College Dublin. His first monograph, *Corporate and White Collar Crime in Ireland: A New Architecture of Regulatory Enforcement*, was published by Manchester University Press in 2015. He coordinates the Advanced Diploma in Corporate, White-Collar and Regulatory Crime at the Honorable Society of King's Inns.

Tom O'Malley is a Senior Lecturer in Law at NUI Galway, a practising barrister and a member of the Law Reform Commission. He has extensive experience of both research and practice in the areas of criminal justice, sentencing and constitutional law. His many publications include *Sentencing Law and Practice,* 3rd ed (2016), *Sexual Offences*, 2nd ed (2013), *Sentencing: Towards a Coherent System* (2011) and *The Criminal Process* (2009). He is currently Chair of Working Group appointed by the Minister for Justice and Equality to review the treatment of vulnerable witnesses in the investigation and prosecution of sexual offences.

Declan O'Reilly is the Bureau Legal Officer of the Criminal Assets Bureau. He is a solicitor qualified in Ireland, Northern Ireland, England and Wales. He sits on the Irish Anti-Money Laundering Steering Committee, the CARIN Steering Group, and represents Ireland at the EU Asset Recovery Offices forum. He holds an LLM in Commercial Law and an Advanced Diploma in White Collar and Regulatory Crime.

Barry Robinson is a Director in Deloitte's Forensic practice in Ireland. He has worked on global large-scale, complex, corporate investigations and is experienced in the preparation of expert witness reports in commercial disputes. He is an Associate of Chartered Accountants Ireland and holds a Diploma in Forensic Accounting and holds a BSc (Accounting with French) from Queen's University Belfast and is undertaking an MSc (Forensic Accounting) at the University of Portsmouth.

Eimear Spain is a Senior Lecturer at the University of Limerick. A graduate of the BA in Law and Accounting, her PhD was funded by the Irish Research Council. She worked as a Research Coordinator in Macquarie University in Sydney and as a Senior Lecturer in the University of Northumbria in England.

Ciaran Walker is a Consultant, in the Financial Services Regulation & Governance group, at the Dublin office of the international law firm Eversheds Sutherland. He advises firms and lectures regularly on governance and culture issues in financial services. He was previously Deputy Head of Enforcement at the Central Bank of Ireland.

Chapter 1

WHITE-COLLAR CRIME: CONTEMPORARY ISSUES IN POLICING, PROSECUTION AND PUNISHMENT

*Joe McGrath**

The term 'white-collar crime' is notoriously ambiguous and definitionally problematic.[1] It was first used in 1939 by Sutherland in a speech to the American Sociological Society, as it was then known. He subsequently defined it as wrongdoing 'committed by a person of respectability and high social status in the course of his occupation.'[2] It has been suggested, however, that

> '[i]f Sutherland deserved a Nobel prize, as Mannheim thought, for pioneering this field of study, he certainly did not deserve it for the clarity or serviceableness of his definition. … The apparent success of the label in finding public acceptance may testify less to its coherence than to its capacity to name a supposed threat.'[3]

In particular, difficulties arise because Sutherland focused on the identity of the offender in the definition, rather than the nature of the offence. This raises ambiguities because the same criminal offence might or might not be a white-collar crime depending on who has committed the wrong. Others, however, like Edelhertz, provided an offence-based definition, defining white-collar crime as 'an illegal act or a series of illegal acts committed by nonphysical means and by concealment or guile to obtain money or property, to avoid the payment or loss of money or property, or to obtain personal or business advantage'.[4] Some scholars have argued that the definitional approach adopted by scholars depends on whether the perspective of a populist or a patrician is adopted; the former is the offender-based approach which 'situates white-collar crime in the struggle against socio-economic inequality' while the latter is more likely to be an offence-based approach which 'takes a narrower, more technical, and less reform-oriented view of white-collar crime'.[5]

---

* Lecturer, Sutherland School of Law, University College Dublin.

1 David Nelkin, 'White collar and corporate crime' in Mike Maguire *et al* (eds) *The Oxford Handbook of Criminology* (4th edn, Oxford University Press 2007) 733.

2 Edwin Sutherland, *White Collar Crime* (Dryden Press 1949) 9.

3 David Nelkin, 'White collar and corporate crime' in Mike Maguire *et al*, eds. *The Oxford Handbook of Criminology* (4th edn, Oxford University Press 2007) 733, 738.

4 Herbert Edelhertz, 'The nature, impact and prosecution of white-collar crime' (National Institute of Law Enforcement and Criminal Justice 1970) 3.

5 Neal Shover and Francis T Cullen, 'Studying and Teaching White-Collar Crime: Populist and Patrician Perspectives' (2008) 19(2) Journal of Criminal Justice Education 155, 156.

Nevertheless, conceptual difficulties remain as to its unifying core especially when white-collar crime involves a whole range of misconduct including financial offences (like false accounting), offences against consumers (like selling adulterated food), offences arising from the employment relationship (like breaches of health and safety laws) and offences against the environment (like pollution).[6] In one instance, urinating in public was considered a white-collar crime because the perpetrators were more likely to be stock brokers from Manhattan than homeless people.[7] However, white-collar crime is rarely so trivial; research has shown that it often costs the State far more in financial terms than conventional forms of crime.[8] The Global Economic Crime and Fraud Survey conducted by PWC in 2018, for example, determined that 49% of global organisations reported experiencing white-collar crime in the previous two years and that nearly two thirds of respondents found that the most disruptive of these cost up to a million dollars.[9] Furthermore, though often defined as merely economic in nature,[10] white-collar crime can also cause significant social and physical harm when it causes violence through unsafe work places and defective products.[11] Less tangibly, it may undermine the social trust in business and in the power of government to regulate business effectively.[12]

Despite some definitional ambiguities, it is clear that the Irish landscape addressing white-collar criminality has changed significantly in the last two decades.[13] In 1998, the McDowell Report concluded that Ireland was

> 'characterised by a culture of non-compliance …those who are tempted to make serious breaches of company law have little reason to fear detection

---

6 Steve Tombs, 'Corporate Crime' in Chris Hale *et al* (eds), *Criminology* (Oxford University Press 2005) 267, 269.

7 Eric A Posner and Dan M Kahan, 'Shaming White-Collar Criminals: A Proposal for Reform of the Federal Sentencing Guidelines' (1999) 42 JL & Econ 365.

8 The Whitaker Committee estimated that the losses incurred through white-collar crime in 1984 were ten times the value of all stolen property investigated by the Gardaí, see: *Committee of Inquiry into the Penal System* (Stationery Office 1985) 55. More recently it has been noted that the costs of crimes investigated by the Revenue Commissioners far exceed the costs of street crime. See: Shane Kilcommins *et al*, *Crime Punishment and the Search for Order in Ireland* (Institute of Public Administration 2004) 130.

9 PWC, *Pulling Fraud Out of the Shadows; Global Economic Crime and Fraud Survey* (2008), available at: <https://www.pwc.com/gx/en/services/advisory/forensics/economic-crime-survey.html> (accessed: 30 May 2018).

10 Micahel Levi, 'Economic Crime' in Mike McConville and Geoffrey Wilson (eds), *The Handbook on the Criminal Justice Process* (Oxford University Press 2002) 424.

11 Joe McGrath and David Doyle 'Attributing Criminal Responsibility for Workplace Fatalities and Deaths in Custody: Corporate Manslaughter in Britain and Ireland' in Kate Kitz-Gibbon and Sandra Walklate (eds), *Homicide Gender and Responsibility: International Perspectives* (Routledge 2016); Russell Mokhiber, *Corporate Crime and Violence: Big Business Power and the Abuse of the Public Trust* (Sierra Club Books 1989); James Gobert and Maurice Punch, *Rethinking Corporate Crime* (Butterworths 1993).

12 Susan Shapiro, 'Collaring the Crime not the Criminal: Reconsidering "White-Collar Crime"' (1989) 55 American Sociological Review 346.

13 Joe McGrath, 'Twenty Years since the McDowell Report: A Reflection on the Powers and Performance of the Office of the Director of Corporate Enforcement' (2018) 60 Irish Jurist 33.

> or prosecution. As far as enforcement is concerned, the sound of the enforcers footsteps on the beat is never heard.'[14]

It largely echoed the sentiments in the Cox Report forty years earlier which concluded that companies were careless about complying with their legal obligations and that breaches of the law were seen as trivial and technical.[15] The persistent under-policing of the corporate sector was arguably a natural reflection and consequence not just of the political and social inertia regarding corporate regulation at that time, but also of the institutional architecture of enforcement which existed. Though enforcement of the Companies Acts was supplemented by some specialist agencies, white-collar crimes were often addressed by the same police and prosecutors that addressed ordinary crimes, even though they lacked the skills, training and resources to detect and investigate complex cases of corporate wrongdoing.[16]

As Ireland gradually transitioned from a rural State, with relatively low levels of corporate activity, to a highly open and global centre for commerce and finance, a process which commenced in the late 1950s but which only really crystallised in the 1990s, a new model of corporate and financial regulation emerged. Since the 1990s, the conventional crime monopoly became fragmented because a variety of specialist, interdisciplinary agencies with enhanced powers now address corporate wrongdoing. The near exclusive dominance of conventional crime methods has also faded because corporate wrongdoing is now specifically addressed by a much more sophisticated and 'responsive' corporate enforcement architecture: taking compliance orientated and sanctioning approaches, using both civil and criminal enforcement mechanisms, where criminal law is now often the sanction of last resort.[17] More recently, however, since the financial crisis, the architecture seems to have shifted again. In the past white-collar crime had been marginalised from crime debates,[18] but now corporate and financial crimes are increasingly politicised and new laws are regularly passed to make it easier to hold wrongdoers to account.[19] In addition to resolving problems in enforcing the law, they also had ostentatiously political purposes. They reflected

---

14 Report of the Working Group on Company Law Compliance and Enforcement (Stationery Office 1998) para. 2.4-2.5.

15 Report of the Company Law Reform Committee (Stationery Office 1958).

16 Joe McGrath, 'The Prosecution of White-Collar Crime in a Developing Economy: A Case Study of Ireland in the 20th Century' in Judith van Erp *et al*, eds. *Handbook on White-Collar Crime in Europe* (Routledge, 2015) 399.

17 Joe McGrath, Corporate and White-collar Crime in Ireland: A New Architecture of Regulatory Enforcement (Manchester University Press, 2015); Ian Ayres and John Braithwaite, *Responsive Regulation: Transcending the Deregulation Debate* (Oxford University Press, 1992).

18 Joe McGrath, 'The traditional court of crime approach to the definition of a crime' in Shane Kilcommins and Ursula Kilkelly, *Regulatory Crime in Ireland* (Lonsdale 2010) 29.

19 Joe McGrath, 'Instrumental and expressive governance: corporate and white-collar crime in contemporary society' Law and Financial Markets Review (2017) 11 (2-3), 96.

the political desire to 'tool up' executive power and 'act out' for public approval, to 'govern through' white-collar crime.[20]

In this collection, Kilcommins and Spain argue that these developments have emerged due to a greater awareness, particularly since the financial crash, that white-collar crimes can affect the economic security of the State in ways that are at least as serious as so-called 'ordinary crimes'. This recognition has disrupted settled features of the landscape of regulatory enforcement. While traditionally the State generously granted special rights to accused persons to protect them from abuses of unjust processes, in recognition that the State was so much stronger than the accused, this is gradually being unravelled in order to counter the economic threats to the State caused by potentially powerful corporate actors. They state:

> 'It is clear that the landscape has changed almost beyond recognition. Our understanding of white-collar crime as relatively benign, with weak enforcement mechanisms and little will to investigate or punish, has not survived. A wide variety of civil, administrative and regulatory mechanisms are now being utilised alongside criminal law instruments in the prosecution of such crimes, crimes which are being investigated and prosecuted by specialist agencies. In addition to a growing decentralisation of investigative and prosecutorial powers, there has also been a decline in the relative power of sovereign nations when ranged against large and/or sophisticated corporations and this has reshaped how we understand the state/accused relationship.'

While there may be a greater recognition of the harms now posed by serious corporate irresponsibility, much remains unknown or under explored about the causes of white-collar crime. The standard theory in the study of 'street crime' maintains that crime is caused by social deprivation and lack of opportunity but this does not fit the white-collar crime paradigm so a variety of theories have formed a patchwork explanation of sorts. Strain theory suggests that company directors seek to realise their desire to personally excel and be promoted or maximise success for the business but if the achievement of these goals is constrained by legal rules, they may employ 'innovative' techniques which may operate outside the law.[21] In recessions, for example, where profits are squeezed and economic performance is uncertain, companies and their officers may engage in illegality because they strain to achieve their objectives through legitimate means.[22] It may also be the case, however, that a pronounced period of

20 Jonathan Simon, *Governing Through Crime: How the War on Crime Transformed American Democracy and Created a Culture of Fear* (Oxford University Press 2007).

21 Robert K Merton, 'Social Structure and Anomie' (1938) 3 Am Sociol Rev 672.

22 Sally Simpson and Melissa Rorie, 'Economic Fluctuations and Crisis' in Shanna R Van Slyke, Michael L Benson and Francis T Cullen (eds), *The Oxford Handbook of White-Collar Crime* (Oxford University Press 2016), 326; Marshall Clinard and Peter Yeager, *Corporate Crime* (New York Free Press 1980); Carl Keane, 'Impact of Financial Performance on Frequency of Corporate Crime: A Latent Variable Test of Strain Theory' (1993) 35 Canadian J Criminology 293; Stephen Box, *Recession, crime and punishment* (Macmillan 1987).

economic success could increase corporate activity in the State with a consequent increase in opportunities for white-collar crime.[23] Similarly, a period of lax regulation may lead to a period of corporate scandal which in turn prompts stiff regulation which eventually fades.[24] Broader social and technological changes may also generate new opportunities for committing more crimes and new types of crimes.[25] Other theorists suggest that crime is the logical weighing of benefits and burdens. If the benefits (wealth, power etc) outweigh the burdens (the risk of getting caught, convicted and imprisoned), then the rational person will supposedly commit the crime.[26] Others contest the idea that white-collar criminals mindfully weigh costs and benefits because '[t]hey seem to have reached their decisions to commit crimes with little thought or reflection. In many cases it was difficult to say that they had ever really 'decided' to commit a crime at all.'[27] Hodges, meanwhile, argues that sanctions have a limited effect in curbing corporate misbehaviour; it is suggested that people are less likely to break the law when it is fairly applied and maps on to the values systems of those who are required to comply with it.[28]

Some literature suggests that criminal activity is learned behaviour.[29] Company directors are informed by the mores of the people they work with and become loyal to the company over a period of time, depending on it economically and perhaps socially. They replicate the existing patterns of behaviour within the firm which may include illegal conduct. The employees may then develop techniques of neutralisation to rationalise and justify behaviour that they would otherwise not commit.[30] These techniques are particularly appropriate in corporate settings where corporate offenders can deny that there is a victim or argue that they were just following orders from management.[31] In this collection, Hill also analyses complex issues of causation and motivation, combining behavioural and legal

[23] Paul Povel, Rajdeep Singh, and Andrew Winton, 'Booms, busts, and fraud' (2007) 20(4) The Review of Financial Studies 1219.

[24] Erik F Gerding, 'The next epidemic: Bubbles and the growth and decay of securities regulation' (2005) 38 Conn L Rev 393.

[25] Tamara D Madensen, 'Opportunities for White-Collar Crime' in Shanna R Van Slyke, Michael L Benson and Francis T Cullen (eds), *The Oxford Handbook of White-Collar Crime* (Oxford University Press 2016) 382; Marcus Felson and Ronald V Clarke 'Opportunity Makes the Thief: Practical Theory for Crime Prevention (London Home Office, 1998); Neal Shover and Andrew Hochstetler, *Choosing white-collar crime* (Cambridge University Press 2005).

[26] Richard A Posner, *Economic Analysis of Law* (Little, Brown and Company 1972) 365.

[27] Eugene Soltes, *Why they do it: inside the mind of the white-collar criminal* (Public Affairs 2016).

[28] Chris Hodges, *Law and Corporate Behaviour; Integrating Theories of Regulation, Enforcement, Compliance and Ethics* (Hart 2015) 15-43.

[29] Edwin Sutherland, 'White Collar Criminality' (1940) 5 Am. Sociol. Rev. 1; Ross L Matsueda, (1988) 34 'The current state of differential association theory. Crime and Delinquency', 277; Ross L Matsueda, 'Differential social organization, collective action, and crime' (2006) 46(1-2) Crime, Law and Social Change 3.

[30] Gresham M Sykes and David Matza, 'Techniques of Neutralisation: A Theory of Delinquency' (1957) 22 Am. Sociol. Rev. 664.

[31] Robert Jackall, *Moral Mazes: The World of Corporate Managers* (Oxford University Press 1988).

analyses to consider individual group and cultural dynamics at play in the commission of white-collar crime. She tentatively concludes:

> 'Notwithstanding the voluminous scholarship on why people do what they do (including committing crimes and near-crimes) we apparently don't know enough to prevent the creation, use and concealment of emission-disguising software and ghost accounts, or many other types of problematic behavior. More research is of course, and always, needed. I argue here for more work that has practice and theory meet and become better acquainted. Costs and benefits beyond the canonical ones must be identified, and theories as to how, when, and why people's assessments of such costs and benefits might lead towards, or away from, criminal and other problematic behavior must be formulated.'

Perhaps, however, it is easier to commit this kind of problematic behaviour when it is unlikely to be detected. White-collar crime has often been considered to be invisible because it typically occurs behind closed doors and is difficult to discover. For example, traditional policing techniques like walking the beat are ineffective when the beat does not circle the boardroom table.[32] It may also be considered invisible because the victims are rarely aware that they have been victimised and therefore do not report the crime.[33] For example, victims of price fixing may not be aware that they are paying more than they should for a product. In addition, white-collar crimes may occur across multiple jurisdictions, through complex webs of companies, over a period of many years, creating distance in time and space between the perpetrator and the victim which enhances the authorless of the wrongdoing.[34] The nature of the corporate form is partially responsible for ambiguity also. Large corporations have organisational structures that can obscure the responsibility of the individual actors therein, resulting in the fragmentation of knowledge and culpability. Intention itself becomes ambiguous. Corporate personality can become a 'Gyges ring' for company officers, giving them a convenient cloak of invisibility.[35] In the past, the invisibility of white-collar crime was heightened when media coverage focused on more traditional forms of conventional crime, like homicides and sexual offences. When corporate wrongdoing was covered, it was sometimes labelled an accident or a disaster, something for which no one can or should be held responsible. This may have been a result of an unwillingness to see it as 'real' crime, a lack of investigative journalism, the fear of litigation, or a fear of losing advertising revenue from companies.[36] More recently, however, it has been argued that this is a cliché because the media considers white-collar crime

32 Joe McGrath, 'The Prosecution of White-Collar Crime in a Developing Economy: A Case Study of Ireland in the 20th Century' in Judith Van Erp, Wim Huisman, Gudrun Van de Walle (eds), *The Routledge Handbook of White-Collar and Corporate Crime in Europe* (Routledge 2015) 399.

33 Steven Box, *Power, Crime, and Mystification* (Tavistock 1983) 16 and 30.

34 James Coleman, *The Criminal Elite: The Sociology of White-collar Crime* (3rd edn, St. Martin's Press 1994) 83.

35 Elizabeth Wolgast, *Ethics of an Artificial Person: Lost Responsibility in Professions and Organisations* (Stanford University Press 1992).

36 Maurice Punch, *Dirty Business: Exploring Corporate Misconduct: Analysis and Cases* (Sage Publications 1996) 266.

a form of 'infotainment'.[37] Media coverage of white-collar crime prosecutions in Ireland, for example, particularly those relating to former bank executives most associated with the financial crash, has been extensive.[38]

Moreover, detection is now increasingly likely because internal corporate investigations are becoming increasingly sophisticated. These investigations more frequently employ data analytics and machine learning techniques to a greater extent than before, technologies which are facilitating the detection of wrongdoing with greater ease. Large complex corporations no longer provide immunity when forensic analytics clearly identify relationships, behaviours and money trails. In this collection, Carson and Robinson provide an overview of the different forms of fraud that often generate corporate investigations and detail how these frauds are investigated and by whom. They conclude:

> 'The landscape in which investigations are conducted is evolving. The volume of data, and how a company stores and processes data in the future, will have a significant impact on how an investigation is conducted. This will undoubtedly involve an increase in the use of data analytics and machine learning tools and techniques. The process followed, regardless of the tools and techniques employed, will remain the most important component of any investigation.'

Detection is also increased as regulation and policing are increasingly 'decentred', extending beyond traditional State-centred forms to include third parties, like legal and accounting professionals who are also increasingly required to act as gatekeepers to prevent and detect wrongdoing.[39] They do so either by acting as 'bouncers', who exclude wrongdoers from a market or business, or as 'chaperones', who exercise ongoing supervision to detect and disrupt misconduct.[40] In particular, they are increasingly required act as 'information reporters' who report their suspicions that criminal offences may have been committed.[41] Detection may also be facilitated by increasing protections for whistle-blowers who may disrupt misconduct. In this collection, Grennan and Furlong analyse the evolution of the Irish law on whistle-blowing,

---

[37] Michael Levi, 'The media construction of financial white-collar crimes' (2006) 46(6) British Journal of Criminology 1037.

[38] Joe McGrath, 'Twenty Years since the McDowell Report: A Reflection on the Powers and Performance of the Office of the Director of Corporate Enforcement' (2018) 60 Irish Jurist 33.

[39] Colin Scott 'The Regulatory State and Beyond' in: Peter Drahos (ed) *Regulatory Theory: Foundations and Applications* (ANU Press 2017) 265; Colin Scott 'Private Regulation of the Public Sector: A Neglected Facet of Contemporary Governance' (2002) 29 Journal of Law and Society 56; Julia Black, 'Decentring regulation: Understanding the role of regulation and self-regulation in a 'post-regulatory' world' (2001) 54(1) Current legal problems 103; Joe McGrath, *Corporate and White-collar Crime in Ireland: A New Architecture of Regulatory Enforcement* (Manchester University Press 2015).

[40] Reinier H. Kraakman, 'Gatekeepers: the anatomy of a third-party enforcement strategy' (1986) 2(1) Journal of Law, Economics, & Organization 53.

[41] Shane Kilcommins, Ian O'Donnell, Eoin O'Sullivan, and Barry Vaughan, *Crime, Punishment and the Search for Order in Ireland* (Institute of Public Education 2004) 166.

analysing in particular the strengths and weaknesses of the Protected Disclosures Act 2014. This Act, they note,

> 'aims to provide a comprehensive suite of protections for a broad category of people who would seek to 'blow the whistle' on wrongdoing discovered at work. Alongside other legislative reforms regarding the regulation of lobbying and bribery and corruption, the Act represents a credible attempt by the Irish legislature to address a culture wherein Ireland has been perceived as a 'cold house' for whistle-blowers.'

Even when detected, there is considerable debate as to the best method of addressing white-collar criminality within the legal system. In particular, there is some debate as to the usefulness of criminal law in addressing corporate wrongdoing. In an early leading article on regulatory offences, Sayre warned against the criminalisation of morally neutral conduct because 'Once it becomes respectable to be convicted, the vitality of the criminal law becomes sapped.'[42] Corporate wrongdoing, it is sometimes suggested, does not 'fit' within the criminal law; it is less damaging because 'public order is not violated in business offences as it is in conventional crime' and because such deviancy 'has a less threatening character'.[43] Accordingly, if corporate wrongdoing is to be addressed by the criminal law then there must be a new 'clarity of criminal justice purpose'.[44] Gopalan also warned that

> 'it undermines the coercive power of the criminal law, dilutes its expressive power, over-deters otherwise desirable business activities, conflates blameworthiness with imprisonment, creates incentives for prosecutors to abuse their powers, fuels an appetite for enhancing prison terms, and increases social costs.'[45]

In this collection, Walker is also cautious about the role that sanctions should play in securing compliance and is particularly sceptical that strong criminal justice responses will deter misconduct in the financial services sector but he does not dismiss such approaches entirely. He states:

> 'Overly-focusing on sanctions as a tool of deterrence may actually be counter-productive. It may result in a 'blame' culture in which firms and individuals in the firms are unlikely to engage constructively with the regulator about regulatory issues (other than in accordance with minimum legal requirements) and may be consciously or unconsciously disinclined to 'speak up' or carry out investigations of potential issues as to do so may result in evidence being produced which may be used by the regulator to sanction the firm and/or individual. This would simply result in many unethical behaviours/breaches not being effectively addressed.'

---

42 Francis B Sayre, *Public Welfare Offences* (1933) 33 Colum L Rev 55, 79-80.

43 Michael Clarke, *Business Crime: Its Nature and Control* (Polity Press 1990) 20.

44 Michael Levi, 'Economic Crime' in Mike McConville and Geoffrey Wilson (eds), *The Handbook on the Criminal Justice Process* (Oxford University Press 2002) 424.

45 Sandeep Gopalan, 'Skilling's Martyrdom: The Case for Criminalization Without Incarceration' (2009-2010) 44 USF L Rev 459, 461.

Instead, he ambitiously argues for overhauling the broader culture in banks within which decisions are made, re-engineering thought processes and behaviours as they relate to risk-taking, and to routinise consumer-centred strategies. This work, he argues, can be achieved, in part, through the advocacy work undertaken by the Central Bank communicating what kinds of behaviours are acceptable, as well as through its enforcement work when this fails. The goal must ultimately be to make corporate actors internalise governance norms so that they obey the law because they recognise that it is both the right thing to do and in their interests, though sanctions will be necessary when they don't.

Lynch Fannon has suggested, however, that civil strategies are preferable to criminal law for pragmatic reasons. Criminal trials are expensive and lengthy, convictions are difficult to secure, and defendants are more likely to have the resources to resist prosecution and challenge any weaknesses in the laws.[46] The arguments in favour of civil liability are well supported. A former Director of Public Prosecutions called for the increased use of administrative sanctions because regulatory criminal offences with small penalties do not stigmatise, effectively punish or deter corporate offenders and therefore do not belong in the criminal law.[47] The Macrory Report in the UK concluded that flexible, risk-based tools are more likely than criminal sanctions to repair damage and change behaviour.[48] Clarke has also argued that white-collar crime is better addressed by compliance orientated sanctions because unlike conventional criminals they can easily be found at their workplace and encouraged to obey the law, and because the criminal process does not compensate the victim or improve work practices.[49] The Law Commission in the UK also determined that the criminal law should only address the most serious 'harm-related moral failings' and that civil and administrative sanctions could address less serious regulatory issues.[50] Meanwhile, the Law Reform Commission in Ireland is seeking views as to whether civil financial sanctions ought to be more widely used as a means of regulatory enforcement in Ireland.[51]

In this collection, Lucey explores the civil enforcement arsenal available to the Central Bank of Ireland and the Competition and Consumer Protection Agency (CCPC). In particular, she examines how advocacy and transparency initiatives work with civil pragmatic measures, like settlements and administrative fines, to address corporate wrongdoing. She notes that similar tools can differ in

---

46 Irene Lynch Fannon, 'Controlling Risk Taking: whose job is it anyway?' in Shane Kilcommins, and Ursula Kilkelly (eds) *Regulatory Crime in Ireland* (First Law 2010) 113.

47 James Hamilton, 'Do we need a system of administrative sanctions in Ireland' in Shane Kilcommins and Ursula Kilkelly (eds), *Regulatory Crime in Ireland* (First Law 2010), 15.

48 Rory Macrory, *Regulatory Justice, Making Sanctions Effective* (Better Regulation Executive 2006).

49 Michael Clarke, *Business Crime: Its Nature and Control* (Polity Press 1990).

50 Law Commission of England and Wales, *Consultation Paper: Criminal Liability in Regulatory Contexts* (LCCP 195-2010) 68.

51 Law Reform Commission (LRC IP 8 – 2016) *Issues paper: Regulatory enforcement and corporate offences* (LRC 2016).

their effectiveness when applied differently by enforcers, noting how the tools available to the Central Bank highlight the shortcomings of their comparators applied by the CCPC. She argues in favour of enhancing the civil enforcement toolkit, welcoming more 'biting competences, such as civil fines':

> 'It is to be hoped that the fruits of the Law Reform Commission's project on regulatory enforcement will encourage the legislature to fortify the general civil toolkit by broadly conferring stronger civil enforcement competences more broadly on to agencies. Even if, notwithstanding the opportunities available under Art 37 of the Constitution, agencies are not granted power to impose civil fines, there are cogent grounds to support the introduction of civil fines by *courts* in civil proceedings initiated by a public enforcement agency.'

Of course, the choice between compliance and sanctioning approaches, and between civil and criminal sanctions is not a stark one. Regulation is most likely to be effective when regulators are 'benign big guns' that 'speak softly and carry a big stick'.[52] Under this model, they must have punitive weapons, like criminal sanctions, but work best when disposed to use a variety of little sticks to achieve compliance with the law.[53] Crucially, however, enforcers must, when necessary, be willing to invoke these sanctions, or fire the 'big gun'. It is this willingness to criminally prosecute that gives regulatory agencies credibility and makes the use of lesser sanctions and compliance-strategies possible. After all, if companies know they will not be sanctioned then they may be less inclined to comply with the law. Hawkins, for example, has noted that the compliance-orientated approach only really works when the sanctioning approach sits in the background as a threat. In his opinion:

> '… it is the device which that makes all other law enforcement possible by granting credibility to more private and informal practices and thereby, in the great majority of cases, foreclosing the possibility of costly prosecution and trial.'[54]

Corporate criminal liability is not, however, without its problems. Khanna, for instance, has suggested that the development of information gathering powers and diverse and effective systems of civil liability means that the desirability of corporate criminal liability has disappeared in all but the most exceptional circumstances.[55] The complexity of the company as an artificial legal person may also make corporate criminal liability even less useful. For example, a more

---

52 John Braithwaite, 'Convergence in Models of Regulatory Strategy' (1990-1991) 2 Current Issues Crim Just. 59

53 Joe McGrath, *Corporate and White-collar Crime in Ireland: A New Architecture of Regulatory Enforcement* (Manchester University Press 2015) 151-153.

54 Keith Hawkins, *Law as Last Resort: Prosecution Decision-Making in a Regulatory Agency* (Oxford University Press 2002) 13.

55 Vikramaditya S Khanna, 'Corporate Criminal Liability: What Purpose Does it Serve' (1996) 109 Harv L Rev 1477. See also: Wilson Meeks, 'Corporate and White-Collar Crime Enforcement: Should Regulation and Rehabilitation Spell an End to Corporate Criminal Liability' (2006-2007) 40 Colum JL & Soc Probs 77.

limited range of punishments may apply to corporate entities. Companies can be prosecuted but not imprisoned which can make corporate criminal liability 'inferior as a practical matter to an appropriate corrective measure on the civil side.'[56] Companies can be fined but 'severe penalties flow through the corporate shell and fall on the relatively blameless' through lower levels of profits for shareholders and increased prices for consumers.[57] Substantive and procedural difficulties also arise as different models of ascribing intent to the company continue to cause problems in law. Should the company be liable for the actions of its employees (vicarious liability), where the board of directors are culpable (identification doctrine), or where corporate decision-making procedures are to blame (organisational liability)?[58] Additionally, the Irish Constitution applies to natural persons so to what extent can corporations enjoy due process rights if they are prosecuted?[59] Therefore, in addition to problems raised by the efficacy of the criminal law generally, corporate personhood raises particular problems relating to criminal procedure, constitutional rights and the 'spill-over' effect of punishment.

In the chapter on individual and corporate criminal liability in this collection, Farrell observes that there are very different considerations at play when companies are prosecuted, as against when natural persons are prosecuted. He observes that these considerations are not merely technically legal and procedural, but that the prosecution of companies poses different moral considerations and enforcement objectives that ought to be considered. Noting the many legal difficulties that go with prosecuting a legal entity that has no body, he observes:

> 'One of the remarkable features of our criminal justice process is the extent to which it remains resolutely focused on the prosecution of individuals as opposed to corporate bodies. The procedural machinery that has been put in place to deal with the prosecution of companies is limited in scope and effect. Persistent basic procedural problems remain. This simply underlines the extent to which a prosecution against a company is imbued with the quality of exceptionality. Given the pre-eminence of limited liability companies as the primary means by which regulated businesses are transacted it begs the question as to why this should be so – if companies commit most white-collar offences then why does it remain so difficult to prosecute them?'

Moving to the post-conviction phase of the criminal process, O'Malley examines the application of sentencing principles to individuals and companies convicted

---

56 Daniel R Fishel and Alan O Sykes, 'Corporate Crime' (1996) 25 J Legal Studies 319.

57 John Coffee, 'No Soul to Damn: No Body to Kick: An Unscandalized Inquiry into the Problem of Corporate Punishment' [1981] Michigan Law Review 386, 387.

58 John Gobert, 'Corporate Criminality: Four Models of Fault' (1994) 4 Legal Studies 393.

59 Joe McGrath and David Doyle, 'Attributing Criminal Responsibility for Workplace Fatalities and Deaths in Custody: Corporate Manslaughter in Britain and Ireland' in Kate Kitz-Gibbon and Sandra Walklate (eds), *Homicide Gender and Responsibility: International Perspectives* (Routledge 2016).

of offences in the criminal courts. The courts, he notes, must have regard to the constitutional imperative of proportionality, whereby each sentence must reflect the particular circumstances of the offence and the personal circumstances of the offender, considering the mitigating and aggravating factors that apply in each case. This analysis is considered against the backdrop of the penal purposes of sentencing and the extent to which punishment may deter white-collar crime. Noting that significant reforms have been advanced to reform the law on regulatory enforcement since the financial crisis, involving the creation of new offences and harsher sentences, he cautions that new reforms should be evidence-based, and that much can be done to fight white-collar crime by strengthening the expertise and resources of the existing institutions of enforcement. He states:

> 'Punishment for those convicted must be proportionate and dissuasive. It is important that sentencing should not be treated as an afterthought, much less ignored, in any law reform exercise. The range and severity of available penalties, and the principles according to which offenders are sentenced may well influence both individual and corporate behaviour. More formal guidance than currently exists would also be welcome, not least because it would increase public confidence in the criminal justice system.'

O'Reilly cautions, however, that even in the absence of criminal conviction for white-collar criminality, the proceeds of financial crimes may be confiscated and forfeited. Moreover, he argues that professionals in receipt of money earned from breaching regulatory laws are potential money launderers, a reflection he describes as a 'heart arresting moment' for lawyers and others who might be aware that their clients are not observing all necessary regulatory requirements. His message is stark:

> 'Confiscating and forfeiting the proceeds of regulatory crime is an incredibly new, fast paced and emergent area of law. Those who treat regulatory offences as merely a cost of doing business may one day receive a visit from officers of the Criminal Assets Bureau, amongst others. At that point the die may be cast and the short term financial benefits once gained will be confiscated and forfeited with ignominy. The white-collar perpetrators of regulatory crime will suffer the same fate as thieves, fraudsters and drug dealers.'

This collection gathers together the scholarship of researchers, regulators and practitioners to provide an important account of the key theoretical debates regarding white-collar crime, while also shedding light on the substantive and procedural law on policing, investigation and punishment of white-collar criminality. Most of this scholarship finds its origins in lectures delivered by the authors on the Advanced Diploma in Corporate, White-Collar and Regulatory Crime at the Honourable Society of King's Inns. The editor thanks the contributors for generously supporting this project and also the peer-reviewers for reviewing each of these chapters. This collection is likely to stimulate an extensive conversation on corporate regulation and governance in Ireland.

Chapter 2

DEFINING CORPORATE, WHITE-COLLAR AND REGULATORY CRIME: OFFENCES, DEFENCES AND PROCEDURE

Shane Kilcommins and Eimear Spain***

Introduction

New approaches adopted to tackle white-collar crime have unsettled traditional commitments and assumptions about the operation of the criminal process. More nuanced understandings of harm and 'systems risks', for example, are emerging[1] including a growing recognition of the harm done to ordinary citizens through misconduct in the financial and corporate sectors and through misconduct in the political arena. A new governmental approach has emerged in light of the changing nature and perception of security risks, employing a variety of mechanisms (civil, administrative and regulatory) in tandem with criminal law instruments. Technological changes and a recognition that the disequilibrium in power between the State and the accused is no longer as pronounced are also impacting on constructions of State-accused relations. New investigative and prosecutorial networks are also emerging that in part rely on information gathering and information transfer beyond the traditional reach of the police and prosecution agencies. These changes are occurring against the backdrop of a delegation of power to an extensive range of specialist agencies with wide investigative powers and supported by a wide range of criminal sanctions available summarily and on indictment. There is also evidence of an increasing willingness to imprison individuals convicted of serious corporate crime.[2] In this chapter we begin by examining the concept of white-collar crime, including its scope, cause and consequences, before exploring some of the changes which are impacting upon traditional understandings of the criminal process and the changing nature of the power used by the State in its battle against white-collar crime.

---

* Professor Shane Kilcommins is the Head of the School of Law at the University of Limerick.

** Dr Eimear Spain is a senior lecturer at the School of Law, University of Limerick.

1 Jurgen Habermas, *Between Facts and Norms* (Polity Press 2008 repr) 432-435.

2 Joe McGrath, 'Sentencing White-Collar Criminals: Making the Punishment fit the White-collar Crime' [2012] 3 Irish Criminal Law Journal 71, 75; Dara Robinson, 'Collared' [2014] 180(1) Gazette of the Law Society Ireland 40.

Identity

The concept of white-collar crime is ill-defined with attempts to accommodate it within the traditional discourse on crime proving challenging in light of the contested nature of the concept and the tendency to define crime 'according to a 'real crime' perspective'.[3] Edwin Sutherland, a pioneer of white-collar criminology, suggested that white-collar crime was 'a crime committed by a person of respectability and high social status in the course of his occupation',[4] thus challenging the stereotypical assumptions about all crime being committed by the lower classes. This understanding of white-collar crime maintains currency today, despite criticism.[5] Shapiro suggests that it 'rests on a spurious correlation between role-specific norms and the characteristics of the occupants of these roles',[6] conflating the perpetrators with their misdeeds and ultimately leading to 'an unfortunate mixing of definition and explanation'.[7] Other elements which may be included in a definition of white-collar crime might include 'a violation of trust'[8] and the 'organisational' or 'economic' attributes of white-collar crime. It is clear that considerable disagreement exists about the range of misconduct that would fall within the definition. In order to avoid the straight-jacket of overly prescriptive accounts, some commentators have accordingly attempted to develop typologies of the forms of crime that may fit under the general penumbra of white-collar crime. These include: financial offences (from share dealing to bribery to tax evasion); offences against consumers (price fixing, illegal sales, unfit goods); crimes against employees; and crimes against the environment.[9] Green has suggested that the uncertainty surrounding this group of crimes can be attributed to the moral complexity and ambiguity in such offenses:

> 'what is interesting and distinctive about this group of crimes is that, in a surprisingly large number of cases, there is a genuine doubt as to whether what the defendant was alleged to have done was in fact morally wrong…[T]he question is whether the conduct engaged in was more or less acceptable behavior, at least in the realm in which it was performed, and therefore, should not have been subject to criminal sanctions in the first place.'[10]

---

3 Joe McGrath, *Corporate and White-collar Crime in Ireland: A New Architecture of Regulatory Enforcement*, (Manchester University Press 2015) ch 1.

4 Edwin Sutherland, *White Collar Crime* (Dryden Press 1949) 9.

5 See David Friedrichs, *Trusted Criminals: White Collar Crime In Contemporary Society* (2nd edn, Wadsworth/Thomson Learning 2004) 4-12; Stuart P Green, 'Moral Ambiguity in White-collar Criminal Law' (2014) 18(2) Notre Dame Journal Of Law, Ethics And Public Policy 501.

6 Susan P Shapiro, 'Collaring the Crime, not the Criminal: Reconsidering the Concept of White-Collar Crime [1990] 55(3) American Sociological Review 346.

7 John Braithwaite 'White collar crime' [1985] 11 Annual Review of Sociology 1, 3.

8 See Katherine Williams, *Criminology* (Oxford University Press 2001) 64.

9 See Steve Tombs, 'Corporate Crime' in Chris Hale *et al*, eds *Criminology* (Oxford University Press 2013) 267, 269.

10 Stuart P Green, 'Moral Ambiguity In White-collar Criminal Law' (2014) 18(2) Notre Dame Journal of Law, Ethics And Public Policy 501, 502.

If there are tensions in relation to the definition of white-collar crime, it is also the case that there is no settled agreement on causation. Whilst there is consensus that 'theories of crime' that focus on poverty or poor socialisation cannot account for the phenomenon of white-collar crime, no criminological approach has emerged to dominate the landscape. Instead, a variety of approaches can be employed, the merits of which may vary depending on ideological standpoint or the circumstances of individual cases. To begin with, one can refer to 'classicism or rational choice theory'. This approach presupposes that crime is based on calculative reasoning, in which the actor coldly weighs up the perceived benefits and ranges them against the expected costs (likelihood and consequences of detection). As Charles Murray, for example, notes: '...offenders are extremely pragmatic. Their calculations seemed to be based on a hard headed appreciation of the facts'.[11] Proponents of this theory suggest that weak regulation or non-enforcement provides a fertile ground for white-collar criminality.

Some criminologists would suggest that white-collar crime can be explained by 'differential association', i.e. criminal behaviour is learnt behaviour. If an individual is in an environment where there is a surplus of favourable dispositions to law violation over unfavourable dispositions, this may contribute to his or her involvement in crime.[12] Sykes and Matza, argue that criminals also learn 'techniques' that enable them to 'weaken' the hold society places over them, and to justify their wrongdoing. These techniques act as defence mechanisms that discharge the wrongdoer from the constraints associated with moral order.[13] Some also support the view that white-collar crime is caused by 'strain'. Structurally induced strain in society is created through an emphasis on economic success, the pursuit of individual self-interest, competitiveness, and materialism. Aware of the disjunction between institutionalised aspirations (pressures to maximise profit, growth, efficiency) and the availability of legitimate opportunities, white-collar criminals will 'innovate' in order to achieve institutional goals.[14] Research has also indicated many characteristics associated with psychopathy may be beneficial in the business domain[15] and that white-collar offenders score higher on some measures of psychopathology and psychopathic traits compared with non-white-collar offenders.[16]

---

11 Charles Murray, 'The Physical Environment and Community Control of Crime' in James Q Wilson (ed), *Crime and Public Policy* (ICS Press 1983) 107, 115.

12 See Edwin Sutherland, 'White-collar Criminality' [1940] 5(1) Am Sociol Rev 1, 10-11.

13 See Gresham M Sykes and David Matza 'Techniques of Neutralisation: a theory of delinquency' (1957) 22 Am Sociol Rev 664-670.

14 ibid.

15 Paul Babiak, 'From darkness into the light: Psychopathy in industrial and organizational psychology' in Hugues Herve and John C Yuille (eds), *The psychopath: Theory, research, and practice* (Lawrence Erlbaum Associates 2007) 411.

16 Laurie L Ragatz, William Fremouw and Edward Baker 'The Psychological Profile of White-collar Offenders Demographics, Criminal Thinking, Psychopathic Traits, and Psychopathology' (2012) 39(7) Criminal Justice and Behaviour 978; Tage Alalehto, 'Economic crime: Does personality matter?' (2003) 47 International Journal of Offender Therapy and Comparative Criminology 335; Paul Babiak, Craig S Neumann and Robert D Hare (2010) 28 'Corporate psychopathy: Talking the walk' Behavioral Sciences and the Law 174.

Another distinguishing feature of white-collar crime is the impact of such crime on society. It is accepted, and recent experience in Ireland would support the contention, that the '...financial cost of white-collar crime is probably several times as great as the financial cost of all the crimes which are customarily regarded as the 'crime problem...'.[17] More significantly perhaps, Sutherland also emphasised the impact of such crime on society:

> 'The financial loss from white-collar crime, great as it is, is less important than the damage to social relations. White-collar crimes violate trust and therefore create distrust, which lowers social morale and produces social disorganisation on a large scale. Other crimes produce relatively little effect on social institutions or social organisation.'[18]

Despite this, it has long been felt that the rich and powerful who commit white-collar crime are relatively immunised from the full reach of criminal law. Carson notes:

> '...The behaviour of persons of respectability and upper socio-economic class frequently exhibits all the essential attributes of crime but it is only very rarely dealt with as such. Systems of criminal justice favour certain economically and politically powerful groups and disfavour others, notably the poor and unskilled who comprise the bulk of the visible criminal population'.[19]

The crimes of the powerful remain at the margin of attention with censure aimed at a 'disproportionate number of those who are poor, uneducated and unskilled'.[20] As Norrie suggests: 'The cunning of the law lies in its ability to mask the one-sidedness of its instrumental content through its formal character as a logic of universal individualism'.[21]

The Hegemony of State-Accused relations and 'Crime in the Streets' Justice

New approaches to tacking white-collar crime unsettle traditional commitments and assumptions about the operation of the criminal process. These commitments and assumptions focused largely on 'street crime', emphasising a 'police – prosecutions – prisons' way of knowing the justice system. Such

---

17 Edwin Sutherland, 'White-collar Criminality' (1940) 5(1) Am Sociol Rev 1, 5; Shane Kilcommins *et al*, *Crime, Punishment and the Search for Order in Ireland* (IPA 2004) 131.

18 Edwin Sutherland 'White-collar Criminality' [1940] 5(1) Am Sociol Rev 1, 10-11.

19 William G Carson 'White-collar Crime and the Enforcement of Factory Legislation' (1970) 10(4) Brit J Criminol 383, 384.

20 Ciaran McCullagh, 'Getting the Criminals We Want: the social production of the criminal population' in Patrick Clancy (ed), *Irish Society: Sociological Perspectives* (IPA 1995) 410, 411-412.

21 Alan Norrie, *Crime, Reason and History: A Critical Introduction to Criminal Law* (Cambridge University Press 2001) 23.

an understanding has a long history. Beginning in the nineteenth century, a State-accused model of justice emerged which significantly shaped how crime conflicts were presented, addressed, legitimated and concluded. It had a number of telling features. To begin with, it was organised around a *centralised (constitutional) state* and the 'institutionalised fiction' of the 'public sphere as the central principle of its organisation',[22] both of which helped to promote the sense of 'civilized association' and an 'objectivated' criminal process.[23] The adversarial criminal trial — involving 'a contest morphology' that included oral presentation of evidence, lawyer led questioning, cross-examination by counsel, relative 'judicial passivity' during the guilt determining phase of the trial, and informational sources secured by both the prosecution and defence — exemplified this objective representation.[24]

The crime itself was no longer viewed as a *personal altercation*, but a phenomenon that required an institutional response demarcated from emotive, subjective and personal references. In creating this 'buffer zone between system and person [by establishing a] zone of indifference'[25] between the lived ontological experiences of the crime conflict and its effective administration, new imperatives could be foregrounded, particularly those that emphasised procedure, the ideological neutrality and rationality of the process, and its objectivated nature.[26] Facticity, objectivity, rationality, and neutrality — coalescing with the filtering fiction of the 'public interest' — facilitated this drive from personal to institutional referents.[27]

In addition, the focus of *criminal law* moved away from the notion of 'manifest criminality' based on the disposition of the accused to a more formalised conception of criminal liability. As Habermas noted: '[t]he positivization, legalization, and formalization of law meant that the validity of law can no longer feed of the taken-for-granted authority of moral traditions'.[28] This more codified approach to law also impacted on the image of the human subject who increasingly came to be constituted as a rational, autonomous and self-governing being.[29] The criminal law itself became preoccupied with structuring the criminal

---

22 Jurgen Habermas, *The Structural Transformations of the Public Sphere: an inquiry into a category of Bourgeois Society* (Polity Press 2010 repr) 125.

23 Jurgen Habermas, *The Theory of Communicative Action: reason and the rationalisation of society* (Polity Press 2004 repr) 148.

24 Mirjan Damaska, *The Faces of Justice and State Authority* (Yale University Press 1986) 88.

25 Jurgen Habermas, *The Theory of Communicative Action: the critique of functionalist reason* (Blackwell 2006 repr), 308.

26 For a fuller analysis, see Shane Kilcommins, 'The victim in the Irish criminal process: a journey from dispossession towards partial repossession' (2017) 68(4) NILQ 505.

27 More generally, see Shane Kilcommins, Susan Leahy, Eimear Spain and Kathleen Moore Walsh, *The Victim in the Irish Criminal Process* (Manchester University Press 2018).

28 Jurgen Habermas, *The Theory of Communicative Action: reason and the rationalisation of society* (Polity Press 2004 repr) 148.

29 Martin Wiener, *Reconstructing the Criminal: Culture, Law, and Policy in England: 1830-1914* (Cambridge University Press 1990) 54-55.

law in terms of voluntary conduct, responsibility, and excusing conditions — the 'analytic framework of actus reus/mens rea/defence'.[30]

The State could draw upon the *power* of a centralised police force and a public prosecutor's office which would gather and present evidence in the public interest. As States grew stronger in relation to the criminal process, an increased emphasis was placed on centralised bureaucracy and on the fairness and objectivity of the investigation, prosecution and adjudication. Garland succinctly captures this phenomenon[31]:

> 'The offender is defined as a legal subject, a citizen inscribed with rights and duties, entitled to equal treatment before the law. The State which punishes does so by contractual right in accordance with the terms of a political agreement. Its power to punish has its source in the offender's action — it is the agreed consequences of a contractual breach. The State has here no intrinsic or superior right. It meets the citizen on terms of equality and must not encroach upon his or her rights, person or liberty except in circumstances which are rigorously and politically determined in advance–*nulla poena sine lege*.'

As a consequence, in part, of this process of State monopolisation, a discourse and practice of liberal legalism emerged (emphasising the universality, liberty and sameness of the individual person) to rebalance power relations in the justice arena. For the accused, this meant that the justice network was restructured to incorporate a clearer and more substantive body of due process rights that would guarantee, as far as practicable, both substantive and procedural justice. It also ensured that the State increasingly dissociated itself from local and informal networks of power.

A State-accused logic of action thus came to cast a long shadow over criminal process relations in the nineteenth and twentieth centuries. It defined the accused as the primary (exclusive) rights-bearer, with institutional practice heavily coordinated in accordance with this feature. The criminal law itself increasingly focused on a *relatively narrow range of offences*, constructing a very narrow view of criminal typology, giving the impression that it is only certain socio-economic classes that commit crime. This inevitably contained a 'disproportionate number of those who are poor, uneducated and unskilled'.[32] Indeed it has long been felt that the rich and powerful are relatively immunised from the full reach of criminal law.[33] Criminal law teaching itself helped to inculcate a set of attitudes

30 Nicola Lacey, 'Contingency, Coherency and Conceptualism: Reflections on the Encounter between Critique and the Philosophy of the Criminal Law' in Anthony Duff (ed), *Philosophy of the Criminal Law* (Cambridge University Press, 1998) 23; Finbarr McAuley and Paul McCutcheon, *Criminal Liability: A Grammar* (Round Hall, Sweet and Maxwell 2000) 1-32.

31 David Garland, *Punishment and Welfare: a history of penal strategies* (Gower 1985) 18.

32 Ciaran McCullagh, 'Getting the Criminals We Want: the social production of the criminal population' in Patrick Clancy (ed), *Irish Society: Sociological Perspectives* (IPA 1995) 411-412.

33 See William G Carson, 'White-collar Crime and the Enforcement of Factory Legislation'

towards the legal system in society, exhorting in particular its legitimacy on the basis of its neutral nature, whilst ignoring the underlying structural inequalities of power which are imbricated in the cross-currents of society. The ideology of objectivity, egalitarianism and the strict application of rules can mask and mystify law's partiality, particularly its capacity to preserve and maintain the status quo for those in power.[34]

The modern State-accused model of justice might also be described, in part, as an *1861 Offences against the Person* way of knowing criminal wrongdoing. Such an approach focuses on 'personal references' — assaults, homicides, sexual offences, criminal damage. It was therefore very much rooted in 'crime in the street' harms to individuals. Regulatory wrongdoing was more 'apersonal' in nature, and thus construed as having comparatively benign effects.[35] The argument was that 'these were not real crimes to which stigma should attach, but were rather in the nature of administrative regulations with non-stigmatising penalties such as fines'.[36] Late modernity is challenging many of these assumptions. In the next section we explore some of the changes which are impacting upon traditional commitments and understandings of the criminal process.

Perceptions of Harm

To begin with, more nuanced understandings of harm and 'systems risks' are emerging.[37] As a result, distinctions traditionally drawn between crimes which are *mala prohibita* and *mala in se* are not as clear cut.[38] Misconduct in the banking and corporate sectors, in the workplace, in the environment, in the political arena and in the distortion of competition in the market poses as much, if not more, of a threat to our everyday lives as ordinary crime, with the potential to affect more people. Our security can be affected in a myriad of different ways by misconduct of this nature including, among other things, workplace injuries, loss of equal opportunity, loss of competition, loss of jobs, loss of reputation

(1970) 10(4) Brit J Criminol 383, 384; Michel Foucault, *Discipline and Punish: the birth of the prison* (Penguin 1991 repr) 276.

34 See Martin Horowitz, *The Transformation of American Law, 1780-1860* (Oxford University Press 1992) 266; Alan Norrie, *Crime, Reason and History: a critical introduction to criminal law* (Cambridge University Press 2001) 23. More generally, see Shane Kilcommins, Susan Leahy and Eimear Spain 'The Absence of Regulatory Crime from the Criminal Law Curriculum' in Kris Gledhill (ed), *Criminal Law Pedagogy* (Routledge 2016) 195.

35 Richard A Wright and David O Friedrichs, 'White-collar crime in the criminal justice curriculum' (1991) 2 *Journal of Criminal Justice Education* 95, 105.

36 Nicola Lacey, 'Criminalization and Regulation: the Role of Criminal Law' in Christine Parker, Colin Scott, Nicola Lacey, John Braithwaite (eds), *Regulating Law* (Oxford University Press 2004) 161.

37 Jurgen Habermas, *Between Facts and Norms* (Polity Press 2008 repr), 432-435.

38 Joe McGrath, 'The Colonisation of Real Crime in the Name of All Crime' in Shane Kilcommins and Ursula Kilkelly (eds), *Regulatory Crime in Ireland* (First Law 2010) 60-61; Steve Tombs and David Whyte, 'Crime, harm and corporate power' in John Muncie, Deborah Talbot and Reece Walters (eds), *Crime: Local and Global* (Willan Publishing 2009) 137.

and the consequent devaluation of share prices and pension funds, threats to the environment, increased taxation, and increased costs for consumers. As a result, harm is now increasingly interpreted to include system references in addition to personal references.

New Modes of Governance

There is also a new governmental approach involving the changing nature and perception of security risks and the emergence of more 'networked governance' strategies that employ civil, administrative and regulatory mechanisms alongside criminal law instruments. This extended, somewhat fluid, institutional arrangement is very different from the traditional bifurcated representation of wrongs as either civil or criminal harms, with almost mutually exclusive formal processes for knowing and handling conflicts.[39] These strategies are supported by a wide range of criminal sanctions available summarily and on indictment. Durkheim neatly captures this expansion in criminalisation, juxtaposing it with the decline in severity in penal punishments[40]:

> 'Seeing with what regularity repression seems weaker the further one goes in evolution, one might believe that the movement is destined to continue without end; in other words, that punishment is tending towards zero… For there is no reason to believe that human criminality must in its turn regress as have the penalties which punish it. Rather everything points to its gradual development; that the list of acts which are defined as crimes of this type will grow, and that their criminal character will be accentuated. Frauds and injustices, which yesterday left the public conscience almost indifferent, arouse it today and this insensitivity will become more acute with time.'

The emergence of this regulatory criminal framework is significantly different from the unified monopolies of centralised control underpinning policing and prosecution in the modern State. Arguably these new techniques and strategies can be seen as part of a pattern of more, rather than less, governance, but taking 'decentred', 'at-a-distance' forms.[41] The number of administrative agencies that have entered the criminal justice arena, colonising the power to investigate regulatory crimes in specific areas and to prosecute summarily, has increased dramatically in Ireland in recent years. They include: the Revenue Commissioners, the Competition Authority, National Employment Rights Authority, the Director of Consumer Affairs, the Environmental Protection Agency, the Food Safety Authority, the Health and Safety Authority, and the Office of the Director of Corporate Enforcement. Moreover, very wide powers

---

39 Colin Scott, 'Regulatory Crime: History, Functions, Problems, Solutions' in Shane Kilcommins and Ursula Kilkelly (eds), *Regulatory Crime in Ireland* (First Law 2010) 69.

40 Emile Durkheim, 'Two Laws of Penal Evolution' in Mike Gane (ed), *The Radical Sociology of Durkheim and Mauss* (Routledge 1992 repr) 46-47.

41 John Braithwaite, 'Neoliberalism or Regulatory Capitalism' Occasional Paper 5 (National University of Australia 2005); John Braithwaite, 'The New Regulatory State and the Transformation of Criminology' (2000) 40 Brit J Criminol 225.

of entry, inspection, examination, search, seizure and analysis are given to some of these agencies.

This enlargement in scope, however, is fragmented and heterogeneous in nature, occupying diverse sites and modes of operation. Governance therefore is no longer defined by centralising tendencies. Rather it is much more dispersed: 'it flows through a network of open circuits that are rhizomatic and not hierarchical'.[42] Information trails and information gateways cut across civil, administrative, criminal and regulatory domains of action, no longer limiting or fixing the reach and potential for effective intervention. In the same way that these new governance strategies seek to move beyond the limiting effects of over centralisation in policing and prosecution functions — and the fixity of traditional criminal law — they also cut across territorial boundaries. All of this involves a trend away from a hierarchical command and control apparatus of State policing and prosecution. It constitutes a new form of 'networked governance' involving the increasing 'regulation of civil society'.[43]

The Decline in Power of the Leviathan State

The perception of the strong State ranged against a weak accused is also no longer as clear cut. When the State came to dominate the crime conflict, positioning itself as the only legitimate means of coercion, it imbalanced the equilibrium in power relations. Monopolisation of this kind recalibrated the circuits of governance, resulting *inter alia* in the construction of *l'égalité des armes* to rebalance dissymmetries in power relations. The focus of the power — the subject accused of particular types of crime — was seen as vulnerable in that he or she was pitted against the unlimited resources of the Leviathan State. In this context, it is not surprising that a whole corpus of exclusionary rules and fairness of procedure rights emerged to ensure that the accused was afforded the best possible defence against unfair prosecution and punishment. Since, and to paraphrase Stephen, the State was so much stronger than the individual citizen, and was capable of inflicting so very much more harm on the individual than the individual could inflict upon society, it could afford 'to be generous'.[44]

This disequilibrium in power is no longer as pronounced. Sovereign nations are no longer the only large influential entities in the geo-political sphere. The rise of technology, the effects of globalisation and the relative autonomy of transnational corporations has also limited their power to have the last word on policy and strategic choices.[45] Moreover, when the State accuses a corporation

---

42 Nikolas Rose, *Powers of Freedom: reframing political thought* (Cambridge University Press 2008 repr) 234.

43 ibid. See also Andrew Crawford, 'Networked Governance and the post regulatory state?: steering, rowing and anchoring the provision of policing and security' (2000) 10 Theoretical Criminology 449.

44 James Fitzjames Stephen, *A History of the Criminal Law of England* (Vol I. Routledge/ Thoemmes Press 1883) 354.

45 Martin Van Creveld, *The Rise and Decline of the State* (Cambridge University Press 1999) 419-420.

or corporate actor of white-collar wrongdoing, it is often facing a party that is possessed with excellent resources, often better than the State investigation/ prosecution unit itself.[46] There is therefore a resource parity that is not accounted for in traditional constructions of State-accused relations.

Information Leverage and Information Access

Prior to the centralisation of power in State police and prosecution forces, the old system of law enforcement was heavily reliant on local networks involving rewards, victims, thief-taking and accomplice driven prosecutions. As the State increasingly began to monopolise investigative and prosecutorial functions during the nineteenth century, recourse to local networks was minimised. Where these practices continued — for example, with informants — they were downplayed. In an industrialised setting, this system of enforcement was increasingly viewed as a 'badly regulated distribution of power'.[47] It was replaced with 'public power' which could be 'distributed in homogeneous circuits capable of operating everywhere, in a continuous way, down to the finest grain of the social body'.[48] The centralised state apparatus — as expressed through the police and public prosecutors — thus completely monopolised the crime conflict. Though it remains largely true of the investigation and prosecution of 'ordinary' offences, new regulatory approaches are beginning to throw up investigative and prosecutorial networks that in part rely on information gathering and information transfer beyond the traditional reach of the police and prosecution agencies.

Aside from the fact that many regulatory agencies have very strong powers to compel the production of information,[49] legislation increasingly permits authorities including the Competition Authority, the Revenue Commissioners, the Insolvency Service of Ireland, the Director of Corporate Enforcement and the Irish Takeover Panel to share information with each other. In some instances, individuals are also required to become 'information reporters'.[50] Auditors, tax advisers, lawyers, accountants and liquidators are all bound by

46 Vincenzo Ruggiero and Michael Welch, 'Power Crime' (2008) 51 (3-4) Crime, Law and Social Change 297; Michael Benson and Francis Cullen, *Combating Corporate Crime* (NorthEastern University Press 1998) 27.

47 Michel Foucault, *Discipline and Punish: the birth of the prison* (Penguin 1991 repr) 79.

48 ibid 80.

49 Very wide powers of entry, inspection, examination, search, seizure and analysis are given to some of these agencies. See, for example, s 64 of the Health and Safety Act, 2005; s 779 of the Companies Act 2014; s 787 of the Companies Act 2014; s 30 of the Competition Act 2002; s 905 of the Tax Consolidation Act 1997; s 905(2A) of the same Act provides for the issuance of search warrants to search any premises and s 900 provides very broad powers to require the production of books, records, other documents, which may contain information relevant to liability

50 Shelley Horan, *Corporate Crime* (Bloomsbury Professional 2011); Barry Vaughan and Shane Kilcommins, *Terrorism Rights and the Rule of Law* (Willan Publishing 2008) 138-146.

statutory requirements[51] to report information to the relevant authorities.[52] As McGrath notes[53]:

> 'The use of legal and accounting professionals reflected a significant orientation of who is expected to police corporate and white-collar crime. Auditors, for example, were traditionally required to realign information asymmetries by providing investors with independent verification of the companies' financial information....Recent initiatives, however, suggest that accounting and other professionals have transitioned from private watchdogs , reporting to shareholders and directors, to public 'information reporters', private police who either prevent wrongdoing or report it after the fact for public protection.'

Very broad and generic obligations to disclose information have also recently been enacted in Ireland.[54] Section 19 of the Criminal Justice Act 2011, for example, makes it an offence for a person to fail to disclose information to An Garda Síochána as soon as practicable and without reasonable excuse, which the individual knows or believes might be of material assistance in preventing the commission or securing the apprehension of any other person for offences relating to banking and finance, company law, money laundering, theft, fraud, bribery, corruption, competition, consumer protection, cybercrime and tax collection.

In addition to facilitating exchange of information and compelling certain parties to become information reporters, the authorities are increasingly also seeking to protect and encourage witnesses to come forward and provide evidence. 'Whistleblowers' have been crucially important in Ireland on lifting the lid on various abuses such as the care of the elderly and corruption in banks. Encouraging such witnesses to provide information ordinarily takes two forms: protection and/or immunity. The Protected Disclosures Act 2014, for example, provides extensive protection for public sector workers in Ireland in respect of wrongdoings such as health and safety threats, misuse of public monies, mismanagement by a public official, damage to the environment, or

---

51 See s 447 of the Companies Act 2014, s 59 of the Criminal Justice (Theft and Fraud Offences) Act 2001. Certain persons involved in administering a Pensions Scheme are required to report to the Pensions Board reasonable suspicions of fraud or misappropriation as provided for under the Pensions Act 1990.

52 See, for example, s 42 of the Criminal Justice (Money Laundering and Terrorist Financing) Act 2010; s 931(4) of the Companies Act 2014; s 392 of the Companies Act 2014 Act; s 447 of the Companies Act 2014; and s 59 of the Criminal Justice (Theft and Fraud Offences) Act 2001.

53 Joe McGrath, *Corporate and White-collar Crime in Ireland: A New Architecture of Regulatory Enforcement,* (Manchester University Press 2015) 128.

54 s 57 of the Criminal Justice Act 1994.

concealment or destruction of information relating to any of the foregoing.[55] Immunity programmes also exist.[56]

These new circuits of information gathering are designed to overcome the challenges posed by white-collar crime, which overwhelmingly occurs in private.[57] They rely on new techniques and strategies — particularly the emphasis on legal compulsion — which are often beyond the reach of traditional State/accused relations. There is an increasing tendency through these strategies to compel or facilitate disclosure. They are supported by the less restrictive information access that is available to many regulatory agencies via the civil process[58] which also brings significant pressure to bear on the production of information.

The Flow of Power in to the Civil Sphere

Finally, another striking feature of the changes occurring in the late modern criminal process is the proliferation of hybrid enforcement mechanisms that can be employed by the agencies or, on occasion, by private parties. These mechanisms have conflated the functional distinctions that exist between criminal and civil law.[59] For example, and apart from the possibility of a criminal prosecution by the Competition Authority, private parties can seek to initiate civil enforcement of competition law under s 14(1) of the Competition Act 2002. Section 8(10) of the same Act provides that an action under s 14 may be brought whether or not there has already been a criminal prosecution in relation to the matter concerned and, in addition, a 's 14 action' will not prejudice the initiation of any future prosecution. Similarly, the Office of the Director of Corporate Enforcement can take civil or criminal enforcement actions. Civil enforcement actions include the use of restriction and disqualification orders.[60]

The increasing use of the civil jurisdiction as part of an array of strategies for contending with misconduct is well illustrated through the following vignette

---

55 Other relevant statutes include: s 6 of the Unfair Dismissals Act 1977, s 27 of the Safety, Health and Welfare at Work Act 2005, s 87 of the Consumer Protection Act 2007, s 26 of the Employment Permits Act 2006, s 50 of the Competition Act 2002, s 24A of the Communications Regulation Act 2002, ss 55A-55T of the Health Act 2004, s 61 of the Charities Act 2009, s 222 of the National Asset Management Agency Act 2009, and s 20 of the Criminal Justice Act 2011.

56 Paul Gorecki and David McFadden, 'Criminal Cartels in Ireland: The Heating Oil Case' (2006) 11 European Competition Law Review 631; Conor Talbot, 'The Protected Disclosures Act 2014 and the Cartel Immunity Programme' (2015) 7 Commercial Law Practitioner 178.

57 Daryll Brown, 'The Problematic and Faintly Promising Dynamics of Corporate Crime Enforcement' (2004) Ohio St J Crim L 521.

58 Joe McGrath, *Corporate and White-collar Crime in Ireland: A New Architecture of Regulatory Enforcement* (Manchester University Press 2015) 140.

59 Andrew Ashworth, 'Is the Criminal law a lost cause?' (2000) 116 Law Quarterly Review 225.

60 Joe McGrath, *Corporate and White-collar Crime in Ireland: A New Architecture of Regulatory Enforcement* (Manchester University Press 2015).

involving Thomas 'Slab' Murphy.[61] Though never convicted of terrorist activity, he was allegedly an important figure in the South Armagh Brigade of the IRA in the 1970s and 1980s before being elected Chief of Staff of the IRA in 1997.[62] His farm straddles County Armagh and County Louth, the border between Northern Ireland and the Republic of Ireland. The British army observation towers along the Border hills were allegedly constructed, in part, to keep surveillance on Murphy's IRA operations.[63] In March 2006, it took 400 British and Irish soldiers, PSNI and Garda officers and officials from the Criminal Assets Bureau and HM Revenue and Customs to mount a dawn raid on his farm which is located on both sides of the border. The fortune he allegedly amassed through fuel laundering and smuggling pigs, cattle, grain and cigarettes has been estimated by the BBC's Underworld Rich List at between £35 million and £40 million. Almost £200,000 in mixed currencies had been found on the land, in the house and in sheds, along with 30,000 cigarettes and 8,000 litres of fuel. It also emerged that black bags hidden among hay bales in a cow shed contained cash of €256,235 and £111,185 and uncashed cheques worth €579,270, £80,000 and 24,000 in old Irish Punts. More than 30 archive boxes of documents, ledgers and cheques were seized on the farm along with computers and separate hard drives. In the yards, three tankers and a truck with a fourth tanker concealed inside it were impounded along with an oil laundering unit. Ultimately more than €625,000 in cash and cheques confiscated by Revenue chiefs in Ireland. Nine properties in north-west England, worth £445,000, were recovered by UK authorities. An agreed legal settlement took place in October 2008.[64] In December 2015, Murphy was found guilty on nine counts of tax evasion following a lengthy investigation by the Criminal Assets Bureau. In February 2016, he was jailed and sentenced to 18 months in prison.

What is evident in this vignette is a mix of enforcement mechanisms, but with the civil tool acting as a very powerful instrument of control. It is premised on efficiency and as few restrictions as possible on fact finding.[65] In raising a tax assessment, authorities in various jurisdictions have developed considerable

---

61 For a fuller analysis, see Raymond Friel and Shane Kilcommins, 'Taxing Crime: a new power to control' in Colin King, Clive Walker, and Jimmy Gurule (eds), *The Palgrave Handbook of Criminal and Terrorism Financing Law* (Palgrave 2018). See also Barry Vaughan and Shane Kilcommins, *Terrorism Rights and the Rule of Law* (Willan Publishing 2008) 134.

62 Ed Moloney, *A Secret History of the IRA* (Penguin Books 2007) 160.

63 Toby Harnden, *Bandit Country: The IRA and South Armagh* (Hodder and Stoughton 2000).

64 Gerry Moriarty, 'Thomas 'Slab' Murphy jailed over tax like Chicago gangster' *The Irish Times* (26 February 2016), available at: <http://www.irishtimes.com/news/ireland/irish-news/thomas-slab-murphy-jailed-over-tax-like-chicago-gangster-1.2550298> accessed 1 March 2018; Elaine Carty, 'Thomas 'Slab' Murphy's conviction began with enormous CAB operation' *Irish Independent* (26 February 2016), available at: <http://www.independent.ie/irish-news/background-thomas-slab-murphys-conviction-began-with-enormous-cab-operation-34488827.html> accessed 1 March 2018.

65 Jonathan Simon, 'The Ideological Effects of Actuarial Practices' (1988) 22 Law and Society Review 771; Malcolm Feeley and Jonathan Simon, 'Actuarial Justice: the emerging new criminal law' in David Nelken (ed), *The Futures of Criminology* (Sage 1994) 173; Herbert Packer, *The Limits of the Criminal Sanction* (Stanford University Press 1968).

powers to require a taxpayer to furnish details of earnings and assets, to obtain orders freezing monies and assets, and to seek information from third parties and financial institutions.[66] Its appeal lies in its permanency and low visibility efficiency. This is copper fastened by the disequilibrium in power relations — the onus is very much on the subject of a tax audit to demonstrate compliance.

The Murphy vignette also, however, displays another important difference from traditional criminal law and correctionalist criminology outlooks. Provisions that employ civil techniques — such as confiscation or taxation of the proceeds of crime — are not designed to re-orientate human behaviour or to reintegrate those that are deviant. The civil tools employed against him dismantled the enterprise by removing money, property, laundering units, and equipment. This was further buttressed by a tax demand. Taxation practices in a criminal setting are largely agnostic to the wrongdoer's personality, environment, associations, family background, opportunities, or to the State's complicity in his or her wrongdoing.[67]

This approach to wrongdoing manages disturbances according to risk principles. It attempts to permanently alter the social, financial and physical structures around the individual — the enterprise, its financial structures, its working capital, and the proceeds arising therefrom. It assumes that the transformative individual effects of criminal law are quite limited. It is in this sense an adaptive response, a recognition that traditional crime enforcement agencies can no longer win the 'war on crime'.[68] It accepts that crime is a normal social phenomenon, something which is with us, and which needs to be managed as efficiently as possible. Moreover, by not seeking to change the individual, and by using civil and regulatory strategies, there is minimal potential for resistance.[69]

This approach to wrongdoing also bypasses professional social expertise. Taxing the proceeds of crime does not require the knowledge of social experts such as probation officers, psychiatrists, counsellors, psychologists, educationalists, correctionalist criminologists, or social workers.[70] It embraces instead new forms of expertise — accountants, auditors, tax consultants, lawyers, estate agents, data analysts, bankers, and financial consultants. None of these forms of expertise are orientated to 'normalising' the wrongdoer.[71]

---

66 Michelle Gallant, 'Tax and the proceeds of crime: a new approach to tainted finance' (2013) 16(2) *Journal of Money Laundering Control* 123.

67 Nikolas Rose, *Powers of Freedom: reframing political thought* (Cambridge University Press 2008 repr) 234; see Raymond Friel and Shane Kilcommins, 'Taxing Crime: a new power to control' in Colin King, Clive Walker and Jimmy Gurule (eds), *The Palgrave Handbook of Criminal and Terrorism Financing Law* (Palgrave 2018).

68 See David Garland, *The Culture of Control* (Oxford University Press 2001) 113.

69 Raymond Friel and Shane Kilcommins, 'Taxing Crime: a new power to control' in Colin King, Clive Walker, and Jimmy Gurule (eds), *The Palgrave Handbook of Criminal and Terrorism Financing Law* (Palgrave 2018).

70 For the use of experts in the modern criminal process, see David Garland, *The Culture of Control* (Oxford University Press 2001).

71 Raymond Friel and Shane Kilcommins, 'Taxing Crime: a new power to control' in Colin

Exculpatory Criminal Law

Many aspects of this new regulatory regime operate in opposition to the general trend of paradigmatic criminal law which permits general defences and demands both conduct and fault elements. The system of justice that applies in the regulatory realm is thus more exculpatory in orientation than its ordinary criminal counterpart. The attachment of subjective mental element to wrongdoing in conventional criminal law is often severed in the regulatory criminal arena where objective standards of culpability apply. Section 223(1) of the Companies Act 2014, for example, states that it is the duty of each director of a company to ensure that the company complies with all the requirements of the Act. As such officers are personally responsible for ensuring compliance. If it is demonstrated that a company has committed a criminal offence and the officer was aware of the basic facts, s/he must prove that s/he has not permitted the breach and has taken all reasonable steps to prevent it under s 271(2) of the Companies Act 2014. Similarly, s 58 of the Criminal Justice (Theft and Fraud Offences) Act 2001 provides that any company officer or any person purporting to act in that capacity may be convicted of an offence under the Act (such as false accounting, suppression of documents) if it is proved that the offence was carried out with his/her consent, connivance, or is attributable to his/her neglect.

Moreover, any defences that might exist in the regulatory area are also more specialised than might be the case in the general defences that apply in criminal law. For example, in competition law, it is a specific defence to show that the agreement, decision or concerted practice complained of, benefited from a declaration from the Competition Authority that the practice complained of contributes to improvement in the production or distribution of goods and services; or promotes technical or economic progress. Similarly, s 78 of the Consumer Protection Act 2007 provides a defence where the accused 'exercised due diligence and took all reasonable precautions to avoid commission of the offence' and where, in a variety of ways, the matter was not wholly within the control of the accused. Finally, some of the general duties placed on employers under the 2005 Safety, Health and Welfare at Work Act are qualified by the term 'reasonably practicable'. This means that employers have exercised all due care when, having identified the hazards and assessed the risks at their workplaces, they have put into place the necessary protective and preventive measures, and where further measures would be grossly disproportionate (having regard to unusual, unforeseeable and exceptional circumstances).

The Expressive Power of the Leviathan State

Another feature of the transformation has been the creation and increased use of specialist agencies in the detection and prosecution of white-collar crime and the grant of extensive powers to such agencies. Despite the existence of an extensive catalogue of criminal offences focused on white-collar crime in

King, Clive Walker, and Jimmy Gurule (eds), *The Palgrave Handbook of Criminal and Terrorism Financing Law* (Palgrave 2018).

Ireland in the twentieth century,[72] perpetrators had 'little reason to fear detection or prosecution. As far as enforcement is concerned, the sound of the enforcer's footsteps on the beat is simply never heard.'[73] The State response has been varied and has included the delegation of power to a wide range of specialist agencies. These agencies have been endowed with wide investigative powers, including very wide powers of entry, inspection, examination, search, seizure and analysis to some of these agencies. For example, under the Companies Act 2014 the Director of Corporate Enforcement has the power to require a company to produce for inspection specified books and documents in circumstances which suggest that fraud, illegality, or prejudice may have occurred,[74] and to obtain a search warrant to enter and search premises and seize and retain any material information found on the premises or in the custody or possession of any person found on the premises.[75] This expansion of power to decentralised and powerful specialist administrative agencies is occurring at a time when the sanctions available for regulatory breaches also appear to be gaining strength.

There is some evidence of a possible drift towards a more punitive approach to regulation in this jurisdiction.[76] Traditionally it had been said that the focus of the sanctions for many of these regulatory offences was more 'apersonal' in nature than their ordinary counterparts. The argument was that 'these were not real crimes to which stigma should attach, but were rather in the nature of administrative regulations with non-stigmatising penalties such as fines'.[77] The traditional lack of a mens rea requirement operated as the 'doctrinal marker of these defendants less than fully criminal status from a social point of view'.[78] But regulatory agencies have increasingly grown considerable teeth as regards prosecution. For example, s 78 of the Safety, Health and Welfare at Work Act 2005 now imposes on conviction on indictment for an offence under the Act a fine not exceeding €3 million or imprisonment for a term not exceeding two years, or both.[79] Following an extensive review by the Company Law Review

---

72 For example, over 280 separate offences contained in the Companies Acts 1963-2000.

73 Working Group on Company Law Compliance and Enforcement, Report of the Working Group on Company Law Compliance and Enforcement (1998) para 2.4- 2.5, available at: <https://djei.sharefile.eu/share/view/9a19aabd0ab64297> accessed 2 February 2018; See also Company Law Reform Committee, Report of the Company Law Reform Committee (1958) <http://www.clrg.org/publications/cox%20report.pdf> accessed 2 February 2018; Joe McGrath 'The Prosecution of White-Collar Crime in a Developing Economy: A Case Study of Ireland in the 20th Century' in Judith Van Erp, Wim Huisman and Gudrun Vande Walle (eds), *The Routledge Handbook of White-Collar and Corporate Crime in Europe* (Routledge 2014) 399.

74 s 779 of the Companies Act 2014. The constitutionality of a similar provision in s 19 of the Companies Act 1990 was upheld in *Dunnes Stores Ireland Co v Ryan* [2002] 2 IR 60.

75 s 787 of the Companies Act 2014.

76 Robert Baldwin, 'The New Punitive Regulation' [2004] 67(3) MLR 351.

77 Nicola Lacey, 'Criminalisation as Regulation: The Role of Criminal Law' in Christine Parker *et al*, eds, *Regulating Law* (OUP 2004) 161.

78 ibid.

79 In *DPP v O'Flynn Construction Company Limited* [2007] 4 IR 500, the Circuit Court imposed a fine of €200,000 on O'Flynn Construction Company Limited which pleaded guilty to two offences contrary to the Safety, Health and Welfare at Work Act 1989. Similarly, on conviction on indictment for competition law offences, undertakings are liable to a fine not exceeding whichever of the following amounts is the greater, namely

Group and the Director of Corporate Enforcement of the several hundred criminal offences contained in the Companies Acts, s 871 of the Companies Act 2014 created a four-tier categorisation of company law criminal offences.[80] When prosecuted on indictment, category 2 offences are punishable by a fine of up to €50,000 and/or imprisonment for up to five years and category 1 offences will be punishable by a fine of up to €500,000 and/or a sentence of imprisonment of up to ten years.[81] The approach evidences both a streamlining of the process and a strong punitive response.

However, the trends towards the extension of State power and increased punitiveness are not universal as demonstrated by the failure of successive governments to implement legislation on corporate manslaughter despite calls for legislation for over a decade. The Law Reform Commission published a report on corporate killing in 2006 and called for the introduction of two new offences: a statutory offence of corporate manslaughter for corporate entities; and, a secondary offence (grossly negligent management causing death) for corporate officers who play a role in the commission of the offence.[82] Despite successive attempts,[83] the legislature has yet to enact legislation giving effect to this recommendation, signalling that the commitment of the legislature to the punitive ideal is not complete.[84]

While the general trend has been towards an increase in the sanctions available against those guilty of crime of this nature, there is also evidence of a change in judicial attitudes to the application of those sanctions, particularly the imposition of custodial sentences upon those convicted. McGrath noted in 2012 that '[c]orporate crime is rarely considered to be as harmful as ordinary crime'.[85] However, a series of recent cases may indicate an increasing willingness to imprison individuals convicted of serious corporate crime.[86] In late March of 2009, Mr Justice McKechnie, in a judgment in the Central

€5 million or ten per cent of the turnover of the undertaking in the financial year ending in the 12 months prior to conviction.

80 This categorisation encompasses the majority of criminal offences, to the exclusion of just the most serious offences relating to market abuse, transparency and the law of prospectuses.

81 Category 3 and 4 offences will be prosecutable on a summary basis only.

82 Deirdre Aherne, 'Corporate Killing in Ireland – a new paradigm' [2004] 22 Irish Law Times 235.

83 Corporate Manslaughter Bill 2001; Criminal Justice Bill 2004; Corporate Manslaughter Bill 2007; the Corporate Manslaughter Bill 2011; the Corporate Manslaughter Bill 2013; and the Corporate Manslaughter Bill 2016. See, David Doyle and Joe McGrath 'Attributing Criminal Responsibility for Workplace Fatalities and Deaths in Custody: Corporate Manslaughter in Britain and Ireland' in Kate Kitz-Gibbon and Sandra Walklate (eds), *Homicide Gender and Responsibility: International Perspectives* (Routledge 2016).

84 Corporate Manslaughter and Corporate Homicide Act 2007 in the UK created a new homicide offence in 2007.

85 Joe McGrath, 'Sentencing White-Collar Criminals: Making the Punishment fit the White-collar Crime' [2012] 3 Irish Criminal Law Journal 71, 72.

86 Joe McGrath, 'Sentencing White-Collar Criminals: Making the Punishment fit the White-collar Crime' [2012] 3 Irish Criminal Law Journal 71, 75; Dara Robinson, 'Collared' [2014] 180(1) Gazette of the Law Society Ireland 40.

Criminal Court which considered competition law abuses by an association of Citroen car dealers, noted:

> 'If previously our society did not frown upon this type of conduct, as it did in respect of more conventional crime, that forbearance or tolerance has eroded swiftly, as the benefits of competition law become clearer... Therefore it must be realised that serious breaches of the code have to attract serious punishment [which included imprisonment]'.[87]

In the case of *Paul Begley v DPP*[88] the CCA rejected the contention that cases involving tax evasion should be categorised separately from other offences for sentencing purposes.[89] Instead, 'there will be some cases where an immediate sentence is justified and others where it will not be.'[90] Ultimately, Mr Begley's six year sentence for offences relating to the fraudulent evasion of customs duty was reduced to two years by the CCA.[91] There have been other notable high profile cases in recent times in which lengthy custodial sentences have been imposed including a case involving former solicitor, Thomas Byrne, who was convicted of 52 offences including theft, forgery and using a false instrument and sentenced to 16 years imprisonment, with four years suspended.[92] More recently, in 2015, three former Anglo Irish Bank officials were jailed for between three years and 18 months for conspiring to conceal or alter bank accounts being sought by the Revenue Commissioners.[93] In reaching his decision, the judge noted the difficulty in dealing with defendants of previously impeccably good character and stated that the challenge to the court was to balance the interests of the accused and the public interest.

Despite this trend towards imprisonment, a custodial sentence was not imposed in the high profile case in 2014 involving two former Anglo Irish Bank directors,

---

87 See *DPP v Duffy and Duffy Motors* (Unreported, Central Criminal Court, 23 March 2009). See also *DPP v Manning* (Unreported, High Court, 9 February, 2007)

88 *Paul Begley v DPP* [2013] IECCA 32.

89 ibid, 43. Following a consideration of the case of *DPP v Paul Murray* [2012] IECCA 60, a case concerning social welfare fraud, Finnegan J, delivering judgment for the court, emphasized the importance of deterrence in sentencing decisions in cases involving revenue fraud. It was suggested 'for the future guidance of sentencing courts that significant and systematic frauds directed upon the public revenue — whether illegal tax evasion on the one hand or social security fraud on the other — should generally meet with an immediate and appreciable custodial sentence'.

90 [2013] IECCA 32 [43].

91 As the trial judge had failed to properly consider or weigh the mitigating factors in respect of which Mr Begley was entitled to credit. In a subsequent case, *DPP v Campbell* [2014] IECA 15, the CCA applied the principles set out in the Begley case and sentenced the defendant to 12 months imprisonment in respect of each of nine sample counts representing various revenue and VAT offences, each sentence to run concurrently.

92 'Thomas Byrne sentenced to 16 years for theft and fraud' *The Irish Times* (2 December 2013), available at: <https://www.irishtimes.com/news/crime-and-law/thomas-byrne-sentenced-to-16-years-for-theft-and-fraud-1.1614282> (accessed: 30 November 2018).

93 Paul Cullen, 'Three Anglo officials jailed for hiding accounts linked to Seán FitzPatrick' *The Irish Times* (31 July 2015), available at: <https://www.irishtimes.com/business/financial-services/three-anglo-officials-jailed-for-hiding-accounts-linked-to-seán-fitzpatrick-1.2303179> (accessed: 30 November 2018).

Pat Whelan and Willie McAteer. Upon conviction of offences relating to the illegal purchase of Anglo Irish shares under s 60 of the Companies Act 1963 the men were sentenced to 240 hours community service.[94] Similarly, in Ireland's first bid-rigging cartel case, the Central Criminal Court imposed a fine of €7,500 (or three weeks wages) on an individual responsible for a bid-rigging cartel in the commercial flooring industry which continued for over two years. The undertaking was also fined €10,000 in circumstances where the value of the rigged tenders were over €500,000. The maximum fine available to the court was €5 million or 10% of turnover (whichever was the higher) and/or a maximum gaol sentence of 10 years. The DPP has lodged an appeal against these sentences on grounds of undue leniency and Groneki has suggested that the

> 'sentences seriously undermines the effective enforcement of competition law in Ireland....If the sentences imposed by the Central Criminal Court are not successfully appealed as being unduly lenient and appropriate sentencing guidelines developed, then the prospect for competition law enforcement in Ireland is grim.'[95]

Though all of this constitutes evidence of a drift towards the greater use or threatened use of criminal sanctions, it should not be pushed too far. The area of regulatory crime still, by and large, remains predominantly orientated towards a compliance model of enforcement.[96] This is facilitated by a wide range of strategies that favour the employment of negotiation, consultation and persuasion, rather than an exclusively sanctioning approach that would potentially polarize the various parties involved. These strategies include audits, warning letters, notices, injunctions, guidance, binding directions, and the suspension and revocation of licences. The Consumer Protection Act 2007, for example, permits the National Consumer Agency to issue prohibition orders to businesses, to take undertakings of compliance, to issue compliance notices and fixed payment penalties, in addition to prosecution functions.[97] Many agencies resolve most issues of non-compliance without the need for further enforcement actions. For example, in the years 2009-2012, there were on average 900 court prosecutions brought and 12,000 enforcement actions each year by the Environmental Protection Agency (EPA).[98]All of these ensure

---

94 Tom Lyons, 'McAteer and Whelan sentenced to 240 hours community service' *The Irish Times* (31 July 2014), available at: <https://www.irishtimes.com/news/crime-and-law/mcateer-and-whelan-sentenced-to-240-hours-community-service-1.1883662> (accessed: 30 November 2018). Judge Nolan decided that '[i]t would be most unjust to jail these two men when I feel that a State agency [the financial regulator] had led the two men into error and illegality.'

95 Paul Gorecki, 'Sentencing in Ireland's First Bid-Rigging Cartel Case: An Appraisal' (MPRA, 11 August 2017), available at: <https://mpra.ub.uni-muenchen.de/80787/1/MPRA_paper_80787.pdf> accessed 17 February 2018.

96 Joe McGrath, *Corporate and White-collar Crime in Ireland: A New Architecture of Regulatory Enforcement* (Manchester University Press 2015).

97 See Ailbhe O'Neill, 'The Consumer Protection Act 2007 – Enforcing the New Rules' (2008) 26 Irish Law Times 46.

98 EPA, *Focus on Environmental Enforcement in Ireland: a report for the years 2009-2012* (EPA 2014) 2. In 2008, the Office of the Director of Corporate Enforcement (ODCE) issued 24,000 copies of their publications, closed 850 cases on an administrative basis, made

that prosecutions remain relatively rare, employed as a last resort mechanism. As Scott has recently noted:

> 'The enforcement strategies of agencies have been arrayed in a pyramidal approach to enforcement in which the object is to maintain as much enforcement activity as possible at the base of the pyramid. This approach is said to be effective not only with businesses which are orientated to legal compliance, but also with the 'amoral calculators' for whom compliance becomes the least costly path when they know there is a credible threat of escalation to more stringent sanctions.'[99]

Conclusion

It is clear that the landscape has changed almost beyond recognition. Our understanding of white-collar crime as relatively benign, with weak enforcement mechanisms and little will to investigate or punish, has not survived. A wide variety of civil, administrative and regulatory mechanisms are now being utilised alongside criminal law instruments in the prosecution of such crimes, crimes which are being investigated and prosecuted by specialist agencies. In addition to a growing decentralisation of investigative and prosecutorial powers, there has also been a decline in the relative power of sovereign nations when ranged against large and/or sophisticated corporations and this has reshaped how we understand the State/accused relationship. Sharing of information between government agencies involved in the investigation of crime and the ability of investigative agencies to compel the production of information, alter the investigation of such crimes and mark them out for the investigation and prosecution of 'traditional' crime. All of this has occurred at a time when the evidence of a more punitive approach to regulation in this jurisdiction has emerged and suggests that the white-collar criminal will not be able to escape notice and sanction quite so easily in the future. However, these changes are meaningless in the absence of political will and necessary resources for proper enforcement.

---

a final determination on 280 initial liquidator reports, secured 20 summary convictions, secured 20 disqualifications, and one case was successfully prosecuted by the DPP following an ODCE investigation. See Paul Appleby, 'Compliance and Enforcement – the ODCE perspective' in Shane Kilcommins and Ursula Kilkelly (eds), *Regulatory Crime in Ireland* (Firstlaw 2010) 186.

99 Colin Scott, 'Regulatory Crime: History, Functions, Problems, Solutions' in Shane Kilcommins and Ursula Kilkelly, (eds), *Regulatory Crime in Ireland* (Firstlaw 2010) 73.

CHAPTER 3

TOWARDS (MORE OF) AN UNDERSTANDING OF CRIMINAL — AND MERELY BAD — CORPORATE CONDUCT

Claire A Hill[*]

INTRODUCTION

Wells Fargo and Volkswagen are just two of the companies in the news for illegal conduct. Their conduct was not just illegal — it was also shocking. Wells Fargo bankers opened 'ghost' bank accounts for real customers — accounts that the customers had not authorised and of which they were not aware.[1] Volkswagen created and used 'defeat devices' to make its vehicles pass emissions tests. The devices could detect when a vehicle was being tested, and lower emissions sufficiently during that time that the vehicle was deemed to comply. When driven, those same vehicles emitted pollutants at illegal levels.[2] There are many other examples of deeply problematic corporate behaviour. Besides Wells Fargo and VW, Takata and GM are among the best known for their recent scandals. Takata tried to make airbags more cheaply, and falsified data showing that the airbags were unstable and could be extremely dangerous and indeed, deadly, when inflated during a crash.[3] GM secretly used faulty ignition switches, which could shut off unexpectedly while people were driving.[4] Other examples include

---

* Professor James L Krusemark, Chair in Law, University of Minnesota. Some of the material in this chapter is adapted from Claire A Hill and Richard W Painter, *Better Banks, Better Bankers: Promoting Good Business Through Contractual Commitment* (University of Chicago Press 2015) and Claire A Hill 'A Personality Theory of White-collar Criminals, Near-Criminals, and Others Involved in Bad Corporate Action (And What Law Should Do About It),' (2017) 11 (2-3) Law and Financial Markets Review 75. I also wish to acknowledge very useful conversations with Bill Black and very useful comments from an anonymous referee.

1 Matt Egan, 'Wells Fargo Wells Fargo Uncovers up to 1.4 Million More Fake Accounts' *CNN* (8 August 2017), available at: <http://money.cnn.com/2017/08/31/investing/wells-fargo-fake-accounts/index.html> accessed 6 April 2018.

2 Clifford Atiyeh, 'Everything You Need to Know about the VW Diesel-Emissions Scandal' (*Car and Driver,* 24 October 2017), available at: <https://www.caranddriver.com/news/everything-you-need-to-know-about-the-vw-diesel-emissions-scandal> accessed 6 April 2017.

3 Charisse Jones and Nathan Bomey, 'Timeline: How Takata's Air-bag Scandal Erupted' *USA Today* (25 June 2017), available at: <https://www.usatoday.com/story/money/2017/06/25/takata-air-bag-scandal-timeline/103184598/> accessed 6 April 2018.

4 Alexander Stoklosa, 'GM Settles with U.S. Attorney over Ignition-Switch Case, Will Pay at Least $900 Million' *Car and Driver* (17 September 2015), available at: <https://www.

the many banks fined for rigging interest and exchange rates, money laundering, and assisting clients to evade taxes, as well as the many companies involved in violations of statutes prohibiting bribes to foreign government officials.[5] These are actual crimes, highly publicised, alleged and in many cases, admitted to and/or as to which sizeable settlements have been paid.

There is considerable other problematic corporate behaviour, some of which is most likely criminal and some of which may be in a gray area, and some of which simply causes grave societal harm. Some companies' businesses may have been built on criminal or near-criminal conduct. One company was allegedly in the business of tricking people receiving structured settlements into selling those settlements for a low lump sum. The settlements were given for exposure to lead paint; those getting the settlements might therefore very well have been cognitively impaired. The company maneuvered around the requirement that an independent person recommend the sales by steering sellers to someone who purported to be independent but was not.[6]

Bad corporate behaviour is of course actually done by individuals.[7] Some of the behaviour is ostensibly for the benefit of the corporation. Some of it may be expressly or implicitly required or encouraged by the corporation. Some of it may be done by employees going 'rogue,' for instance by taking kickbacks or trying to 'come back' from huge losses in trading positions.

Why do people commit corporate white-collar crimes — that is, crimes intended to benefit the person's employer, or intended to benefit the person at the expense of her employer? Why do they do other things that are near or at the line of criminality — and that implicate many of the same societal concerns as criminal acts do?

These are not crimes (or near-crimes) of passion — they are crimes (or near-crimes) of calculation, broadly construed.[8] People must have concluded,

---

caranddriver.com/news/gm-settles-with-u-s-attorney-over-ignition-switch-case-will-pay-at-least-900-million> accessed 6 April 2018.

5 Claire A Hill and Richard W Painter, *Better Banks, Better Bankers: Promoting Good Business Through Contractual Commitment* (University of Chicago Press 2015) Introduction and Chapter 1. US Securities and Exchange Commission, *SEC Enforcement Actions: FCPA Cases*, available at: <https://www.sec.gov/spotlight/fcpa/fcpa-cases.shtml> accessed 6 April 2018.

6 Carrie Wells, 'Attorney General's Office and Attorneys Spar over Settlement for Lead Paint Victims' *Baltimore Sun* (24 July 2017); Terrence McCoy, 'Federal Agency Accuses Settlement-Purchasing Company of Violating Consumer Protection Act' *Washington Post* (21 November 2016).

7 That being said, we are rapidly approaching a time when 'corporate' action may be taken by non-human actors. For purposes of this Chapter, I assume that all actions are ultimately attributable to human actors, as is inaction in the form of, for instance, not reporting wrongdoing.

8 Calculation is of course not necessarily done explicitly or purposively. (Hence 'broadly construed.') A person who observes that her colleagues, who have managed to reach extremely high sales targets, and promotions by lying to buyers, might 'calculate' that doing so would be worthwhile for her, or, if she found lying personally costly, might 'calculate'

implicitly or explicitly, that the expected benefits would exceed the expected costs. This formulation sounds simple, but masks considerable complexity, namely how people assess benefits and costs. The remainder of this chapter takes up this task, going beyond the simple and canonical benefits — money on the one hand, and prison on the other — to a more realistic and useful approach that can better inform policy. There is of course voluminous work done on the determinants of white-collar crime, what policies might be effective against it, and other related matters.[9] Here we focus on a particular type of white-collar crime, corporate white-collar crime, and consider the individual, group, and cultural dynamics at issue. This focus also encompasses a considerable penumbra — behaviour that may or may not be criminal, and behaviour that is not criminal but implicates many of the same sorts of societal concerns as criminal behaviour does. My vantage point is to combine psychological, legal, economic and business perspectives, and trying to explain how it arises and how particular business and legal practices might encourage or discourage it.

The Penumbra of Corporate White-Collar Crime

My account addresses the question 'why do people behave in ways they surely know or should know are illegal?' But it also addresses a far broader question— why do people in the corporate sphere behave in ways that are illegal, are close to the line of illegality, or contribute, actively or passively, to a culture in which illegal and near-illegal, or highly unethical, behaviour is encouraged or condoned? (this behaviour will be referred to as being within the penumbra of corporate white-collar crime, or as being near-criminal.) Accounts of day to day operations at GM, VW and Wells Fargo reveal some straightforwardly criminal conduct, but also much conduct that served to facilitate crime, as well as conduct that was clearly problematic whether or not it constituted a crime.[10] According to some Wells Fargo bankers, meeting the 'eight is great' sales goals (to sell eight products to each customer or household):

> 'loomed large when supervisors threatened salespeople who failed to meet [the goals]. Former employees [said that they had] 'managers in [their]

that doing so would not be worthwhile for her. The characterisation of white-collar crime as being more about net benefit then impulse is of course not novel, although it is not universal. I articulate it in this way in order to encourage a focus on specific costs and benefits, and how people might compute them. Finally, none of this is to say that 'being carried away' is never part of the story.

9 Among the recent work are edited volumes, Shanna R Van Slyke, Michael L Benson and Francis T Cullen (eds), *The Oxford Handbook of White-Collar Crime* (Oxford University Press 2016) and Judith van Erp, Wim Huisman and Gudrun Vande Walle (eds), *The Routledge Handbook of White-Collar and Corporate Crime in Europe* (Routledge 2015). A recent book on the subject is Eugene Soltes, *Why They Do It: Inside the Mind of the White-Collar Criminal* (Public Affairs 2016).

10 Anton R Valukas, '*Report to Board of Directors of General Motors Company Regarding Ignition Switch Recalls*' (29 May 2014), available at: <http://www.beasleyallen.com/webfiles/valukas-report-on-gm-redacted.pdf> accessed 7 April 2018; Jack Ewing, *Faster, Higher, Farther: How One of the World's Largest Automakers Committed a Massive and Stunning Fraud* (WW Norton 2017).

> face yelling at [them]' and that 'the sales pressure from management was unbearable.' 'We were constantly told we would end up working for McDonald's... If we did not make the sales quotas ... we had to stay for what felt like after-school detention, or report to a call session on Saturdays.'[11]

Allegedly, those not meeting their sales quotas were demoted or fired. The managers' lives apparently weren't much better. Some reported that they were:

> 'asked not only to meet but to exceed daily quotas passed down by regional bosses. Branch managers [were] expected to commit to 120% of the daily quotas, according to the former Pacific Northwest branch manager, who said results were reviewed at day's end on a conference call with managers from across the region.'[12]

It appears that there was knowledge at the lower levels—that the behaviour was illegal, by those engaging in it, and probably, their managers—and willful blindness at higher levels, culminating perhaps, in willful ignorance at the level of the more senior leaders – 'don't ask don't tell.'

Another example, of clearly enormously problematic behaviour that may or may not be a crime (and will not yield criminal sanctions) involves Moody's Investor Services' willingness to give inflated ratings to subprime securities in the years leading up to the 2008 financial crisis. What follows is from a Moody's employee's testimony before a governmental commission formed to prepare a report on the crisis, the Financial Crisis Inquiry Commission:

> 'Brian Clarkson quadrupled Moody's market share in the residential mortgage back securities (RMBS) group by simply firing (or transferring) nearly all the analysts in the group and replacing them with analysts willing to apply a new rating methodology. ...[A]rriving at an accurate answer was never objectionable, so long as that answer did not threaten market share and revenue.... Wherever Moody's encountered material market share pressure (rating competition), we can expect to see that its ratings become indistinguishable from the ratings of its competitors.
>
> There were two ways that Moody's senior management imposed the new culture on Moody's analysts. First, they 'reeducated' Moody's rating

[11] Elizabeth C Tippett, 'How Wells Fargo Encouraged Employees To Commit Fraud' *AP News* (6 October 2016), available at: <https://apnews.com/0ad359de45df4e8aa5e3a9666380319c/how-wells-fargo-encouraged-employees-commit-fraud> accessed 13 April 2018. I quoted this passage in Claire A Hill, 'A Personality Theory of White-collar Criminals, Near-Criminals, and Others Involved in Bad Corporate Action (And What Law Should Do About It),' (2017) 11 Law and Financial Markets Review 75.

[12] E Scott Recard, 'Wells Fargo's Pressure-Cooker Sales Culture Comes At A Cost,' *Los Angeles Times* (21 December 2013), available at: <http://www.latimes.com/business/la-fi-wells-fargo-sale-pressure-20131222-story.html> accessed 13 April 2018. I quoted this passage in Claire A Hill, 'A Personality Theory of White-collar Criminals, Near-Criminals, and Others Involved in Bad Corporate Action (And What Law Should Do About It),' (2017) 11 Law and Financial Markets Review 75.

> analysts – primarily structured finance analysts – that cooperation with the new culture would be rewarded and opposition punished. ...Second, they emboldened investment bankers, gave them confidence that they could stand up to Moody's analysts and gave them reason to believe that Moody's management would, where necessary, support the bankers against its own analysts. ...
>
> Moody's campaign of intimidation included all the run-of-the-mill techniques you might find at any company. Cooperative analysts got good reviews, promotions, higher pay, bigger bonuses, better grants of stock options and restricted stock. Uncooperative analysts got poor performance evaluations, no promotions, no raises (or effective pay cuts), smaller bonuses and fewer grants of stock options and restricted stock.
>
> But Moody's primary tool for implementing the culture change was a person not a technique, Brian Clarkson. In this task, Brian was especially adept at threats of employment termination. ...I think I can say, with only a little exaggeration, that I have heard Brian conjugate the verb 'to fire' in moods and tenses most grammarians do not even know exist. In my ten years at Moody's, I do not think I had three consecutive encounters with Brian in which he did not threaten to fire someone, describe someone he had fired or identify someone he should have fired.... Brian even threatened to fire people before he had hired them. ..
>
> Brian was not a rogue manager running amok while Moody's Board and CEO/President were deceived about his conduct. They recognized in Brian the character of someone who could do uncomfortable things with ease and they exploited his character to advance their agenda.'[13]

Thus, my answer to the 'why they do it' question will treat the definition of 'it' broadly, to include some behaviour that: is in a grey area or exploits a loophole in the law, facilitates or encourages white-collar crime, or yields harms of the sort that criminal law is trying to address. In this regard, consider the purchases by a purportedly sophisticated investor, IKB Deutsche Industriebank, of subprime securities in the years leading up to the crisis. Another investor in the market for these securities was quoted as saying that 'IKB was known to be a patsy. IKB had an army of Phd types to look at CDO deals and analyze them .... But Wall Street knew that they didn't get it. When you saw them turn up at conferences there was always a pack of bankers following them.'[14] IKB was bailed out, at considerable (German) taxpayer expense.[15]

---

13 Testimony of Mark Froeba before The Financial Crisis Inquiry Commission (2 June 2010) 4–9, available at: <http://fcic-static.law.stanford.edu/cdn_media/fcic-testimony/2010-0602-Froeba.pdf> accessed 7 April 2018. Clarkson also provided written testimony, and was scheduled to speak at the same panel as Froeba, but 'was unable to appear because of a medical emergency.' I quoted this passage in Claire A Hill, 'A Personality Theory of White-collar Criminals, Near-Criminals, and Others Involved in Bad Corporate Action (And What Law Should Do About It),' (2017) 11 Law and Financial Markets Review 75.

14 William D Cohan, 'SEC Should Free 'Fab' Tourre, Target Big Fish,' Opinion, Bloomberg View (20 June 2011), available at: <https://www.bloomberg.com/view/articles/2011-06-21/sec-should-free-fab-tourre-target-big-fish-william-d-cohan> accessed 14 April 2018.

15 'Lone Star to buy IKB, the German Subprime Casualty' *New York Times* (21 August

Why They Do It: Beyond Canonical Costs (and Benefits)

The behaviour explained here is a product of calculation — of an assessment, not necessarily formal and indeed, often implicit, that the expected benefits exceed the expected costs. What gets included in the calculation? Let us start with what we will call the law's view. The law establishes a cost, in the form of prison and/or fines, and devotes resources to enforcement so that a person will conclude there is sufficient likelihood of the cost being imposed. This cost is intended to offset the benefit, which is implicitly hypothesized to be money, and/or perhaps improved professional prospects.

The money benefit the behavior yields can come through many different routes. There could, of course, be direct bribes, or gaming of bonus formulas by booking fictitious profits. Insofar as the crime at issue is for the benefit of, or even on behalf of, the company, there could be company money: the company might reward meeting aggressive sales or loan targets, probably knowing that there would be sales or loans to vulnerable buyers (to whom express or implicit lies might be told). The money (and other) benefit might be avoiding a loss: it might simply be protection from being fired, as was apparently the case for the bankers at the lowest rung as to Wells Fargo's 'requirement' that eight accounts be sold to each customer. Here, the criminals presumably include those coming up with the compensation schemes — both the immediate supervisors, and up the chain, to the people to whom those supervisors and their supervisors reported.

Moreover, there could be general professional good favor (from supervisors, including bonuses or promotions) from being thought of as loyal, where loyalty takes the form of silence, willful blindness or even a cover-up in the face of questionable practices. Again, those rewarding cover-ups and the like also are getting their own benefits, perhaps by retaining their jobs or getting promotions and bonuses as well.

This simple view has the advantage of tractability — it suggests a way to proceed — and common sense. As a starting point, we might say that the prospect of jail or a fine deters criminal behaviour, and the prospect of more jail or a larger fine probably deters more. (Of course, this assumes that the criminal herself will actually pay the fine, rather than being reimbursed by her corporation. It also makes certain assumptions about how people value increments of time and money.[16] A more accurate starting formulation would hence be 'all else equal' — which it never is.)

2008), available at: <https://www.nytimes.com/2008/08/21/business/worldbusiness/21iht-21ikb.15493131.html> (accessed: 30 November 2018).

16 See generally Sally S Simpson, Melissa Rorie, Mariel Alper, Natalie Schell-Busey, William Laufer, and N Craig Smith, 'Corporate Crime Deterrence: A Systematic Review (2014) 10 Campbell Systematic Reviews. Regulators have sometimes noted that going to jail serves as far more of a deterrent than paying fines. See Belinda A Barnett, 'Criminalization of Cartel Conduct – The Changing Landscape' Joint Federal Court of Australia/ Law Council of Australia (Business Law Section) (Workshop 3 April 2009), available at: <https://www.justice.gov/atr/criminalization-cartel-conduct-changing-landscape> accessed 17 July 2018. ('As a corporate executive once told a former Assistant Attorney General of

If we could readily do better using law — higher punishments, increasing the probability of successful detection of the 'offense' and imposition of the punishment — we would. Among the challenges to doing so are difficulties in specifying what should be illegal, and difficulties in getting the appropriate enforcement. Consider in this regard that the highest-level people, people who gain significantly from their firms' commission of white-collar crime, may be particularly well-situated to avoid punishment, including by ex ante creation of a favorable evidentiary trail, and by ex post arguments and other responses fueled by resources that significantly exceed those of the enforcers.

Moreover, the explanation is clearly incomplete. The benefits from white-collar crime or near-criminal behaviour apparently aren't always or fully pursued — people don't take advantage nearly as much as there is advantage to be taken. Why not? Perhaps for some people, the expected benefits are notably low: their jobs do not readily allow them ways to benefit from white-collar crime? But white-collar crime and behaviour that is near enough to crime, while somewhat more concentrated in some fields than others, is not nearly so concentrated that 'lack of opportunity' can be a big part of the explanation. Many businesses can pressure salespeople and appraisers to be too aggressive to the point of criminality, but not all do so. Within firms, some people respond to incentives that encourage at least sharp dealing if not criminality, but some do not. Many businesses could benefit from cheating to meet regulatory requirements, but not all do so. And within businesses engaging in this activity, some individuals may be eager participants, others willing, and others completely averse. Many individuals could game bonus formulas, but not all do so. Moreover, consider those people who at enormous professional risk 'blow the whistle' because they find the wrongdoing unbearable.

Finally, what is illegal may be both over — and under-inclusive as to what should be illegal, where the law is meant to minimize or eliminate certain harms to society. Given that harm is the ultimate focus, what makes a person, group of people, or corporation act in a way that harms, even if that is technically not illegal, ought to be part of one's focus — especially since the line between illegality and such conduct may be blurry indeed. Insofar as an affirmative state of mind is needed, what about willful blindness? And if willful blindness is illegal, what about recklessness in not learning the facts? Sensible inquiries to understand why people commit white-collar crimes can and should encompass why they do things that are near the line, violate the spirit of a law (or the law,

ours: '[A]s long as you are only talking about money, the company can at the end of the day take care of me . . . but once you begin talking about taking away my liberty, there is nothing that the company can do for me.' Executives often offer to pay higher fines to get a break on their jail time, but they never offer to spend more time in prison in order to get a discount on their fine.') Finally, some work argues that going to jail is experienced very differently by different offenders (as well as by different would-be offenders), although that argument probably has far more applicability for crimes other than corporate white-collar crimes. See Adam Kolber, 'The Subjective Experience of Punishment,' (2009) 109 Columbia Law Review 182.

where law is viewed broadly as attempting to limit harm) while abiding by the letter, or passively or actively facilitate others' doing so.

Thus, we must complicate the picture. The obvious complication takes into consideration that different people are different in the way they make their cost-benefit computations. The incremental complexity of a more nuanced understanding of people is enormous. But the societal damage done by law's limits in this area is enormous as well, and new strategies to research and potentially address why people actually commit white-collar crime and how to make them less likely to do so, or at least, how to make firms be better able to identify people who are apt to do so, are increasingly being developed, as are strategies regarding what makes corporate cultures particularly conducive, or not, to white-collar crime.[17] Near-criminal behavior can and should also be addressed using these same strategies.

I will use a cost/benefit framework expansively, considering a far broader range of possible costs and benefits a person might consider in making her assessment than the canonical such costs and benefits.[18] What people consider costs and benefits depends in significant part on their personalities, motivations, temperaments, and senses of identity. To one person, making a sale by lying or nearly lying to a customer may be a cost; to another, it may not be, or it may even be a benefit, as the person gets to view herself as a skilled salesperson willing and able to do anything to close a deal. Of course, an individual's consideration of costs and benefits also takes into account the person's view of others' views – a person may want to 'fit in' or 'be thought to be a contrarian,' for instance.

The account to be constructed must consider differences among people, but must do so parsimoniously. We need a middle ground between the same story for everyone and a different story for each person — a tractable number of categories, as few as is feasible, but enough to be sufficiently realistic to provide guidance for policy.[19]

---

17 See, eg, the volumes cited in fn 9. As to culture, attention to the subject has increased on account of the 2008 financial crisis, including with analyses commissioned by companies that experienced serious criminal and otherwise bad behaviour. See, eg, Anthony Salz, *Salz Review: An Independent Review of Barclays' Business Practices* (2013), available at: <http://online.wsj.com/public/resources/documents/SalzReview04032013.pdf> accessed 17 July 2018. See also William C Dudley, 'Enhancing Financial Stability by Improving Culture in the Financial Services Industry' (20 October 2014), available at: <https://www.newyorkfed.org/newsevents/speeches/2014/dud141020a> accessed 17 July 2018. One fascinating area of research has used natural language processing, textual analysis, and content analysis. For instance, a Google search on 6 April 2018 for natural language research on corporate culture yielded 163,000,000 hits. See also <http://starlingtrust.com/> (accessed 6 April 2018), which describes ways to measure levels and networks of trust within firms.

18 This is also the approach we use in Chapter 3 of Hill and Painter, cited above. My approach is also in keeping with Herbert Simon's approach to rationality more broadly. Herbert A Simon, 'Rationality in Psychology and Economics', in Robin M Hogarth and Melvin W Reder (eds), *Rational Choice: The Contrast between Economics and Psychology* (University of Chicago Press 1986).

19 This is not to say that we want to sell short the lures of money or the deterrent effects of

Getting More Specific: Some Suggestions

Our starting point is thus that different people make different cost benefit computations, and do so for reasons relating to who they are.[20] Let us try on for fit an alternative story: that people's cost and benefit computations might differ because of different levels of accuracy or access to information. After all, the task is scarcely mechanical, and the range of estimates is likely to be broad. Of the amounts involved, the most knowable are the 'official' punishment for the crime and its payoff, but even these are not knowable with precision. The probability that particular behaviour might lead to the payoff is less knowable in many cases, and the probability that one will be caught, as well as the actual punishment that will be imposed if one is caught, is less knowable still.

I hope the reader finds this reasoning, that differences in access to accurate information explains differences in behavior, unsatisfying — I certainly do, for two reasons. The first is that while different people can make different estimates for no particular reason, people's estimates and assessments are not infrequently 'motivated' and reflect their underlying worldviews. Think of entrepreneurs willing to start a new business notwithstanding statistics that 9 out of 10 new businesses fail; think of people horrified at the prospect of being entrepreneurial for this and many other reasons. Indeed, in many of the examples described in Eugene Soltes' book *Why They Do It: Inside the Mind of the White-Collar Criminal*, faced with seemingly low (from an 'objective' perspective) expected benefits and relatively high expected costs, people 'did it' anyway.[21]

Many people seem to significantly underestimate (again, from an 'objective' perspective) the expected costs of the crimes they committed.[22] But others seem to spurn possible opportunities to make big profits through crime even though the chance of getting caught is minimal. This wouldn't seem to be just random 'differences' in how people make computations — they would seem to be anchored to and reflect, something else about the people: it strains credulity

jail time and fines. Indeed, one promising approach has been to encourage employers not to reward criminal or near-criminal behaviour. Wells Fargo should not be incentivizing 'sales' that it should know can only be made by fraud, and Goldman Sachs should not be offering 'ginormous' sales credits to salespeople who sell securities the bank thinks are of low quality. These are dramatic examples, but the principle can, and should, and increasingly is, being applied to lower-voltage inducements and expressions of approval of criminal and near-criminal behaviour. This holds promise, in part because of its expressive force.

20 In this regard. one extensive and fascinating area of research has been the relationship between personality traits and criminal conduct. See, eg, Mikael Goossen, Ingemar Johansson Sevä, Daniel Larsson et al, 'Basic human values and white-collar crime: Findings from Europe' (2016) 13(4) European Journal of Criminology 434; Marilyn Price and Donna M Norris, 'White-Collar Crime: Corporate and Securities and Commodities Fraud'(2009) 37(4) Journal of the American Academy of Psychiatry and the Law 538.

21 Eugene Soltes, '*Why They Do It: Inside the Mind of the White*-Collar Criminal' (Public Affairs 2016). Of course, 'getting it wrong' ex post does not mean that one's computation was incorrect ex ante. But these computations really do seem to have been wrong — the expected benefits were quite small relative to the expected costs.

22 Eugene Soltes, '*Why They Do It: Inside the Mind of the White*-Collar Criminal' (Public Affairs 2016) 6.

past the breaking point to ignore how people's differing priors — about their own 'luck' or 'skill,' about the aptitudes and motivations of those who might catch them, and so on — might affect their computations.

The second reason why this alternative story can't be right is that the expected cost of punishment, computed precisely, surely could not have such an important role in the computation: Crime x is worthwhile given a 10% chance of going to jail for eight years. It seems hard to imagine that the computation might change if the numbers were, say, 15 and 10. My intuition is that there is a great deal more going on — that, other than at the extremes of reward or punishment, small differences are apt to be swamped by other considerations.

What other considerations might be relevant to determining the cost benefit computation for criminal and near-criminal conduct? Increasing research on this subject is being done, sufficiently voluminous that it can only be described here in broad brush and occasional depth.[23] Let us start with the most canonical benefits and costs, money as a reward and jail or fines as a punishment. Even in these respects, different people are different. Different people have, for instance, very different valuations of money. Money is valued both for what it can buy (its instrumental use) and for what it signals (relative status). Beyond a certain point, money has a declining marginal utility in its instrumental use: people acquire what they need, and then what they want, and presumably, at some point, they run out of wants. But there is no marginal decline in money's ability to help people measure their comparative level of 'points.' Some of the people committing white-collar crime do want money for its instrumental value, but some (top executives at banks, for instance) want it more for its 'points' value – for its value in achieving higher standing, in their or, they think, others', minds, than those with fewer 'points.'

Some people value professional advancement far more than others. Some people's 'life portfolios' are more diversified than others — successful home

[23] See Claire A Hill, 'A Personality Theory of Sophisticated Investor Decision-Making (in the 2008 Financial Crisis), With Some Policy Implications' 2017/2 Revue Internationale Des Services Financiers/International Journal for Financial Services 7, Claire A Hill, 'A Personality Theory of White-collar Criminals, Near-Criminals, and Others Involved in Bad Corporate Action (And What Law Should Do About It)', (2017) 11 Law and Financial Markets Review 75, and sources cited therein, Aiyesha Dey, Robert Davidson and Abbie Smith, 'Executives' 'Off-the-Job' Behaviors and Financial Reporting Risk,' (2015) 117 Journal of Financial Economics 5, and Aiyesha Dey *et al*, 'Bank CEO Materialism: Risk Controls, Culture and Tail Risk,' (2018) 65 Journal of Accounting and Economics 191. Of particular note and importance is Tory Higgins' work on prevention vs. promotion focus and locomotion vs. assessment. The seminal work as to prevention vs. promotion is E Tory Higgins, '*Beyond pleasure and pain: How motivation works*' (Oxford University Press 2012). The seminal work as to locomotion vs. assessment is Arie Kruglanski *et al* 'To do the right thing! or to just do it!: Locomotion and Assessment as Distinct Self-Regulatory Imperatives' (2000) 79 Journal of Personality and Social Psychology 793. See also Chapter 3 of Claire Hill and Richard Painter and sources cited therein. Among other relevant considerations in cost-benefit analyses are people's inclinations towards risk, their proximity to money 'primes,' and how they view themselves in relation to their professional identity.

life, variety of outside interests, versus people for whom work is what they do and who they are. Moreover, some people are better situated to pay large fines or be barred from some professional prospects than others. (It is probably also true that some people mind time in jail less than others but I will assume away this complexity for present purposes).

What other differences might be relevant? As noted above there are differences in beliefs, personality types,[24] senses of identity (including as to individual and society identity, as to who is in the in-group and who is in the out-group, and as to who is more or less group-identified) as well as aptitudes and inclinations regarding competition, status, empathy and perspective-taking, risk, concentration, impulsiveness and deliberation. More specifically, there are extremes and middle grounds on many relevant dimensions: people who can focus narrowly and unquestioningly on tasks versus those who ask not just 'how' something can be done but also 'whether' the thing should be done; people who are motivated more or less strongly by 'points' awarded by some third party, in the form of compensation, promotion, or status; people who have different attitudes towards risk; people who believe more or less in caveat emptor; relatedly, people who have narrower and broader in-groups and out-groups; people who forge ahead versus people who are more inclined to assess alternatives and consequences, and so on. An employee may, or may not, be willing to break the law, push the envelope, or otherwise take risks to advance his own well-being at the expense of his employer's, or his employer's well-being at the expense of the broader society. A person may, or may not, be able to persuade himself that behaviour that is on the edge of criminality or enables it, or even behaviour that is clearly criminal, is acceptable or even laudatory. A person may find herself doing in small steps things she would never do in fewer (large) steps — making business connections that turn out to need facilitating and 'greasing' that progresses to bribes, or taking desperate measures to dig herself out of previous decisions that led to losses by making a huge seriously risky and irresponsible if not illegal decision. That being said, while there is literature supporting these characterizations, as well as many examples, there is much we don't know. There is clearly a doubling down pathology – but under what conditions does it arise? Perhaps more importantly, when, notwithstanding what might seem to be its precursors, does it might not arise?[25] How much of a factor is the 'slippery slope'? There is significant disagreement.[26]

Complicating matters, there are important differences in degree and kind involving the kinds of behaviour at issue. Creating and installing a defeat device

---

24 See sources cited in fn 20.

25 See John Coates, *The Hour Between Dog and Wolf: How Risk Taking Transforms Us, Body and Mind* (Penguin Books 2012).

26 Compare, for instance, William K Black, *The Best Way to Rob a Bank is to Own One: How Corporate Executives and Politicians Looted the S&L Industry* (2nd edn, University of Texas 2014) with Richard Bistrong's account available at <https://richardbistrong.com/> accessed 17 July 2018. Bistrong is a convicted FCPA violator who now runs programs instructing companies on how to detect and prevent such violations. Black's account has bad behaviour springing from 'nowhere' whereas Bistrong emphasizes more the role of a gradual trajectory.

is clearly bad. But is designing software that could in principle be used to create the device necessarily pernicious if the software has other non-deceitful uses? It might seem sensible to encourage salespeople to work their hardest and best, but when does being a forceful salesperson become 'taking advantage'?[27] A business model of lending money to people with great need for immediate cash and limited ability to repay presents considerable opportunities for problematic and perhaps illegal conduct. But, with appropriate safeguards, it also can provide a needed service. When does a company decide that it has sufficiently investigated parties whom it may contract with to act on its behalf in countries that may have less fealty to the rule of law than the US does?

Group dynamics need to be taken into account as well. For instance, groups can develop or bolster an ethical ethos, a 'look the other way/don't be a rat' ethos, an ethos of competition for better craft in regulatory arbitrage, an ethos for more (sales, hours worked, cunning or even heartlessness), an ethos promoting profits (or 'meeting one's numbers') no matter the cost, and/or many others. Groups — and 'group members' — can do what individuals would not do were they not in a group. Groups can, for instance, embolden members to take more risks.

Providing examples for all of these potential differences is beyond the scope of this chapter and indeed, would warrant a long book in its own right. A few help motivate further inquiry. My book with Richard Painter, *Better Bankers, Better Banks* recounts the examples of Enron, Greece, and Lehman Bros, which all used elaborate machinations to make themselves seem far financially healthier than they were. Some of the conduct was almost certainly illegal, and some of it was in a gray area. But gussying up financial statements is commonplace, and there is no clear line where criminality and fraud begins.

Internal documents about the three situations reveal attention to and pride in craft (including, arguably, pride in manipulating regulators), some jocularity, and definitely awareness of the greater effect of what they were doing. From an email between some of Enron's bankers:

> 'Why do they want to hedge with gas where it is now?'
> 'They're not hedging . . . they do the back-to-back swap.'
> 'This is a circular deal that goes right back to them.'
> 'It's basically a structured finance–'
> 'It's a financing?'
> 'Yeah, it's totally a financing'

From an email between some Lehman personnel:

> 'So, what's up with Repo 105? Why are we doing less next quarter end?'

27 Indeed, successful marketers and salespeople have a deep understanding of psychology. It is easy to see how the knowledge could be harmful, but the knowledge can also be neutral or even positive from a societal perspective. An understanding of how to impart a sense of urgency could be very bad for an extravagant product, but very good for car recalls or preventive measures to head off a health crisis.

> 'It's basically window-dressing. We are calling repos true sales based on legal technicalities. The exec committee wants the number cut in half.'
> 'I see . . . so it's legally do-able but doesn't look good when we actually do it? Does the rest of the street do it? Also is that why we have so much BS [balance sheet] to Rates Europe?
> 'Yes, No and yes. :)'[28]

Some people structuring mortgage-backed securities expressed qualms along the way:

> 'The real issue is that the loan requests do not make sense. $900k in combined loans to a renter with no prior mtg history stated making $16k a month as a manager of a knock off gold club distributor via the internet and mailings, a borrower that makes $12k a month as an operations manager of an unknown company – after research on my part I reveal it is a tarot reading house. Compound these issues with the fact that we are seeing what I would call a lot of this type of profile.'[29]

But they still managed to proceed with this deal and others presenting similar issues.

For some people, proceeding this way — doing 'what it takes' to move a problematic deal along — is consistent with their identity and values, and they are able to do so easily; for others, it is a considerable cost. There are also many examples along these lines of appraisers pressured to give inflated appraisals to support large mortgages, about which one could say the same thing. Indeed, recall the Moody's example discussed above. At the most senior levels, managers decide that they want to retain market share even if that sacrifices the firm's reputation for accuracy. As Froeba depicts the situation, the managers are willing to hire someone who seems to enjoy threatening to fire people. Froeba presumably could not have been made to do this task for all the money in the world.

Other examples including bankers' fixing of various benchmark interest and currency rates. Bankers spoke quite freely in chatrooms with one another:

> '[A] broker commented to a UBS trader after a Yen Libor fix on June 10 2009: 'mate yur getting bloody good at this libor game . . . think of me when yur on yur yacht in monaco wont yu'
>
> In another conversation with a UBS trader after a Libor Yen fix on August 22 2008, a broker, identified as A1, commented about another broker, A2: 'think [broker-A2] is your best broker in terms of value added :-)'. The trader replied: 'yeah . . . i reckon i owe him a lot more', to which broker-A1 responded: 'he's ok with an annual champagne shipment, a

[28] Chapter 1 of *Better Bankers, Better Banks*.

[29] Quoted on p 55 of *Better Bankers, Better Banks*.

few [drinking sessions] with [his supervisor] and a small bonus every now and then."[30]

The banker examples are so good that it's impossible to resist the temptation to include another:

> 'Swiss Franc Trader: 'can u put 6m swiss libor in low pls?'
> Primary Submitter: 'NO'
> Swiss Franc Trader: 'should have pushed the door harder'
> Primary Submitter: 'Whats it worth'
> Swiss Franc Trader: 'ive got some sushi rolls from yesterday?'
> Primary Submitter: 'ok low 6m, just for u'.
> Swiss Franc Trader: 'if u did that i would come over there and make love to you[,] your choice"[31]

These traders presumably not only made money – they also seem to have enjoyed the camaraderie. And for whatever reason, knowing that they were effectively lying to benefit themselves, in ways that could significantly adversely affect others, did not weigh sufficiently heavily on them to cause them to refrain from rate fixing. Why not?

We can't know, but there is evidence that how people characterize – one could say, justify and rationalize (or 'neutralize') – what they do relates importantly to their underlying worldview.[32] For instance, it seems that some people get enormous personal benefit from figuring out how to do end-runs around regulations. Perhaps this reflects some prior belief that regulations generally are too onerous or, more atomistically, having no particular view about regulations or government but priding themselves on their ability to be cleverer than regulators.[33] Such a sentiment might even lead people to justify participating in the development, use and concealment of defeat devices. Others pride themselves on their good citizenship and may have faith in the good intentions and aptitudes of those in government, which may mean taking a more maximal view of abiding by regulations. For the first set of people, engaging in certain sorts of criminal or near-criminal behaviour would, all else equal, be a benefit while for the second

30 Mark Odell, 'Trader transcripts: 'If You Ain't Cheating, You Ain't Trying" *Financial Times* (20 May 2015), available at: <https://www.ft.com/content/eac637ae-fefb-11e4-84b2-00144feabdc0> accessed 11 April 2018.

31 Vic Daniels, 'They Really Wrote It: The Best of the Worst Libor Emails / Instant Messages' HITC Business (1 November 2013), available at: <http://www.hitc.com/en-gb/2013/11/01/5-firms-21-astonishing-emails/> accessed 14 April 2018.

32 See citations in fn 20.

33 Indeed, relatedly, to what extent reactions to law are part of why people do what they do? Some people seek to maximally comply, out of duty, fear, or some combination of the two; some seek to minimally comply, perhaps abiding by the letter by not the spirit; some seek simply not to be caught, or even pride themselves on what they can get away with. Claire A Hill, 'Tax Lawyers are People Too: Commentary on Victor Fleischer's Options Backdating, Tax Shelters and Corporate Culture,' (2007) 26 Virginia Tax Review 1065 (reprinted in Monthly Digest of Tax Articles 2007); Jeffrey N Gordon, '*What Enron Means for the Management and Control of the Modern Business Corporation: Some Initial Reflections*' (2002) 69 University of Chicago Law Review 1233.

set, engaging in such behaviour would be a cost. The benefits and costs can be magnified by the reactions of a person's peers.

Consider the example of VW's defeat device. One account blames the development and concealment of the device on intense pressure from the top, opportunity to conceal the software at issue, and rationalization that the device would not be discovered or that punishment would be light.[34] There might also be benign use for the software, and one can imagine engineers and software coders focusing narrowly on the task and conveniently not thinking of the broader and more sinister possibilities. (The craft of focused structuring is nicely illustrated by the line in the Tom Lehrer song about Wernher von Braun: once the rockets are up who cares where they come down; it's not my department, says Wernher von Braun). Consider as well the Wells Fargo ghost accounts. Again, one can imagine an understanding of good leadership in which people are pushed to 'excel' and meet and exceed even ambitious goals.

Consider as well those targeting nominally sophisticated but actually unsophisticated purchasers for sales of 'dog' securities. How would they have explained what they were doing? They might perhaps say 'if the law says these people are sophisticated, I am entitled to treat them as such.' What about those designing and carrying out the business practice of buying structured settlements from possibly cognitively-impaired people at less than fair value? A strong form caveat-emptor, where everyone is chargeable with being able to look after themselves, or everyone is entitled to do what's best for themselves without regard to others? Or maybe somehow managing to avoid any sort of self-reflection? What about supervisors hectoring salespeople to meet unrealistic sales goals, or those above them pushing the supervisors to develop such goals and force those below them to meet them 'whatever it took'? This clearly warrants study.

As ever, group dynamics are part of the story. Some people might experience particularly keenly the cost of exclusion and loss of professional possibilities for not being willing to 'go along' with whatever the conduct is — selling overpriced 'dog' securities or buying underpriced structured settlements — while others might get caught up in the competition (to sell or buy). Individuals' accounts of what they are doing also may be influenced by the group: there may be a group narrative ('countries always game their borrowing; we're just doing that for our client.')

A final observation should be made. The costs and benefits of particular actions importantly also reflect societal values. Some of the most pernicious pathologies discussed above — the extremes of the salesperson persona, the glorification of heartlessness, and the craft of focused structuring — are sometimes depicted as impressive and laudatory. A Google search for 'movies about great salespeople'

---

[34] Luann J Lynch and Carlos Santos, 'VW Emissions and the Three Factors That Drive Ethical Breakdown' University of Virginia Darden School of Business Darden Ideas to Action (17 October 2016), available at: <https://ideas.darden.virginia.edu/2016/10/vw-emissions-and-the-3-factors-that-drive-ethical-breakdown/> accessed 11 April 2018.

yielded a link entitled '26 movies that will teach and inspire you to sell anything to anyone.'[35]

Conclusion

Notwithstanding the voluminous scholarship on why people do what they do (including committing crimes and near-crimes) we apparently don't know enough to prevent the creation, use and concealment of emission-disguising software and ghost accounts, or many other types of problematic behaviour. More research is of course, and always, needed. I argue here for more work that has practice and theory meet and become better acquainted. Costs and benefits beyond the canonical ones must be identified, and theories as to how, when, and why people's assessments of such costs and benefits might lead towards, or away from, criminal and other problematic behaviour must be formulated. Providing examples, as I have done here, is a necessary starting point, albeit one severely lacking in parsimony.[36] Bottom-up identification of examples, middle-ground detection of patterns and markers, and top-down formulating and trying on theories for fit, can all add considerably to the effectiveness of law and extra-legal forces in dealing not only with white-collar crime, but also, equally significantly, with white-collar crime's broader penumbra.

35 The search was done on 15 April 2018.

36 Ideally, 'it takes a theory to beat a theory,' but if the theory is not working well enough, surely one can't stick with it because it lacks a successor. Indeed, it could be said that presently, there isn't a theory.

Chapter 4

CORPORATE INVESTIGATIONS

David Carson[*] *and Barry Robinson*[**]

Introduction

Corporate investigations occur in business because corporate and white-collar crimes are a reality. Often-cited familiar cases from the 1990s and early 2000s such as Enron,[1] WorldCom[2] and Poly Peck,[3] are reminders that frauds do occur within organisations and can serve as useful case studies to learn the lessons of history from both a corporate governance and anti-fraud perspective. Companies today are not immune to being subject to investigation following allegations of wrongdoing. We have become familiar with headlines emanating from the motor industry in recent times, for example, in relation to Volkswagen's internal investigation into emissions tests.[4] Recent high profile corporate failures in the financial services sector in Ireland in the last ten years such as Anglo Irish Bank[5], Irish Nationwide Building Society,[6] and Quinn Insurance Limited,[7] have led to several corporate investigations by various bodies including liquidators, administrators and regulators. The last decade has seen advancements in the prevention and detection of fraud, including the use of data analytics and machine learning to detect fraud for example in the healthcare,[8] credit card,[9]

---

* David Carson is the Partner in charge of Deloitte Forensic in Ireland.

** Barry Robinson is a Director in Deloitte Forensic in Ireland.

1 Robert Wearing, *Cases in Corporate Governance* (Sage Publications 2005) 67-82.

2 ibid 83-94.

3 ibid 40-53.

4 Reuters, *Daimler hires Deloitte for internal emissions probe* (30 April 2016), available at: <https://www.reuters.com/article/us-daimler-emissions/daimler-hires-deloitte-for-internal-emissions-probe-idUSKCN0XR07R> (accessed 26 March 2018).

5 *DPP v FitzPatrick* (Circuit Criminal Court (Judge Aylmer) 23 July 2017), available at: <https://static.rasset.ie/documents/news/sean-fitzpatrick-full-ruling.pdf> (accessed 30 November 2018).

6 Central Bank of Ireland, 'Settlement Agreement between the Central Bank of Ireland (the 'Central Bank') and Irish Nationwide Building Society ('INBS'), 2017', available at: <https://www.centralbank.ie/docs/default-source/news-and-media/legal-notices/settlement-agreements/irish-nationwide-building-society.pdf?sfvrsn=6> (accessed 25 March 2018).

7 Central Bank of Ireland, 'Settlement Agreement between the Central Bank of Ireland and Quinn Insurance Limited (Under Administration), 2013', available at: <https://www.centralbank.ie/docs/default-source/news-and-media/legal-notices/settlement-agreements/quinn-insurance-ltd-(under-admintn).pdf?sfvrsn=6> (accessed 25 March 2018).

8 Guido van Capelleveen *et al*, 'Outlier detection in healthcare fraud: A case study in the Medicaid dental domain' (2016) 21 International Journal of Accounting Information Systems 18-31.

9 Siddhartha Bhattacharyya *et al*, 'Data mining for credit card fraud: A comparative study' (2011) 50 Decision Support Systems 602.

and insurance sectors.[10] During this period, there has been an increase in the use of technological solutions when undertaking corporate investigations, which have been endorsed by the Irish courts, most notably in the case of *Irish Bank Resolution Corporation Limited & Ors v Sean Quinn & Ors*.[11] Detection of fraud schemes has long involved searching for patterns in behaviour, actions, relationships and the movement of money. Today, forensic analytics can help companies identify, thwart and prevent attacks by integrating artificial intelligence (AI)-based data analysis with skilled forensic investigation of a fraudster's motives and methods.[12]

In this chapter, we provide an overview of the different types of fraud schemes that can give rise to corporate investigations, who investigates them, and how they occur through consideration of the fraud triangle and fraud diamond theories. We also provide an overview of an investigation methodology matrix of the steps to be considered when investigating such schemes based on Deloitte's Global Investigation Methodology and international best practice. This methodology matrix can be tailored to different types of investigations depending on the nature of the allegations, the purpose of the investigation and sources of documentation available. Corporate investigations may be in the form of the types set out below in Figure 1.

Figure 1: Types of Corporate Investigations

10 Thomas C. Ormerod *et al*, 'Informing the Development of a Fraud Prevention Toolset through a Situated Analysis of Fraud Investigation Expertise' (2012) 31(4) Behaviour & Information Technology 371.

11 *Irish Bank Resolution Corporation Limited & Ors v Sean Quinn & Ors* [2015] IEHC 175.

12 Deloitte, *Forensic Analytics in Fraud Investigations* (2018), available at: <https://www2.deloitte.com/us/en/pages/advisory/articles/forensic-analytics-in-fraud-investigations.html> (accessed 5 June 2018).

Who Conducts Corporate Investigations?

Increasingly, companies who are the victims of corporate and white-collar crime use the expertise of forensic accountants, lawyers and IT specialists to determine what happened, the quantum of any loss suffered and to obtain advice on what steps the company can take to recover funds and prevent such an event from happening again. Both Williams and Meerts discuss the advantages of using such expertise to undertake the investigation. Meerts identified that forensic accountants and IT specialists, working with lawyers, bring together a wide variety of skills and expertise which are applied to provide clients with swift results that can be used to prevent future incidents.[13] The skills of a forensic accountant are broad, and allow for the review of complex accounting transactions, identification of breaches of internal systems and controls and the interview of witnesses and suspects. Williams described 'forensic accounting' as a 'unique constellation of investigative, legal and advisory services'[14] and this is the case when forensic accountants, IT specialists and lawyers combine to investigate incidents of alleged fraud or wrongdoing. The legal framework in which the investigation is undertaken determines the reporting requirements and necessity to involve regulatory authorities or law enforcement.

A Victimless Crime?

Corporate and white-collar crime is not a victimless crime. Finnegan J reinforced this view in his judgment in the case of *DPP v Murray,* in which he noted that crimes involving the loss of public monies are not victimless.[15] This extends to all forms of corporate and white-collar crime. The cost of corporate and white-collar crime can often be difficult to quantify. The most recent study by the Association of Certified Fraud Examiners (ACFE) in their 2018 'Report to the Nations on occupational fraud and abuse' estimated that the typical organisation loses 5 percent of revenues in a given year as a result of fraud.[16] Figures published by the Centre for Counter Fraud Studies at the University of Portsmouth show that in 2017 fraud was costing UK organisations approximately £190 billion.[17] In order for organisations to identify how fraud occurred and potentially seek recovery of funds, it is necessary for them to undertake a thorough investigation to ascertain the facts and to take steps to improve the controls in place to prevent fraud from occurring in the future.

---

13 Clarissa Meerts, 'A World Apart: Private Investigations in the Corporate Sector' (2006) 9 Erasmus L Rev 162.

14 John Williams, 'Reflections on the private versus public policing of economic crime' (2005) 45(3) The British Journal of Criminology 316.

15 *DPP v Murray* [2012] IECCA 60.

16 *ACFE, Report to the Nations on occupational fraud and abuse* (2018), available at: <https://s3-us-west-2.amazonaws.com/acfepublic/2018-report-to-the-nations.pdf> (accessed 5 June 2018).

17 Jim Gee and Mark Button, *The Financial Cost of Fraud 2017*, available at: <https://www.croweclarkwhitehill.co.uk/wp-content/uploads/sites/2/2017/02/crowe-the-financial-cost-of-fraud-2017.pdf> (accessed 26 March 2018).

'Creative Accounting' or Fraud?

The complex nature of accounting can lead to manual manipulation and the concealment of a company's true financial position. Griffiths highlighted that companies had an extensive range of techniques available to them within the accounting regulations which could be used to massage figures when presenting them to the public.[18] Griffiths argued that the accounting rules gave companies flexibility and that there was nothing illegal in companies using these rules to their advantage.[19] Griffiths was one of the first to define this practice as 'creative accounting'. Jones considered companies who took this a step further to deliver a particular set of financial results and identified this as 'aggressive accounting'.[20] Giroux argued that companies were incentivised to what he termed 'game the system', which usually took the form of increasing earnings.[21] Giroux identified a link between a company's short term earnings performance and executive pay and the stock price, implying that if an executive wanted to achieve a certain level of pay or bonus, or achieve a certain stock price, then he or she could engage in creative accounting or aggressive accounting as long as the presentation of the financial statements were allowed by generally accepted accounting practices (GAAP). In contrast to permissible earnings management, Giroux considered the practices of managers who had a deliberate intention to misstate financial information for their own personal benefit and defined this as 'earnings magic'.[22] Understanding the difference between creative accounting and fraud in any corporate investigation is an important factor when having to consider how and when the pursuit of corporate profits crosses the line into criminal behaviour.

Types of Fraud Schemes

Fraud schemes can vary in nature and in order to prevent, detect or investigate fraud, it is necessary to understand these fraud schemes as much as possible.[23] The ACFE has designed a model for classifying different schemes of occupational fraud, which it has called the 'Fraud Tree', as reproduced in simplified form in Figure 2.[24] This provides a comprehensive overview of the different types of fraud schemes that can give rise to corporate investigations.

---

[18] Ian Griffiths, *New creative accounting : How to make your profits what you want them to be* (Macmillan 1995).

[19] ibid.

[20] Michael Jones, *Creative Accounting, Fraud and International Accounting Scandals : Fraud and International Accounting Scandals* (John Wiley & Sons 2011) 9.

[21] Gary Giroux, *Earnings magic and the unbalance sheet: The search for financial reality* (Wiley 2006).

[22] *ACFE, Report to the Nations on occupational fraud and abuse* (2018) 11, available at: <https://s3-us-west-2.amazonaws.com/acfepublic/2018-report-to-the-nations.pdf> (accessed 5 June 2018).

[23] Tommie Singleton and Aaron J Singleton, *Fraud Auditing and Forensic Accounting* (4th edn, Wiley 2010).

[24] ibid.

Figure 2: The Fraud Tree (Occupational Fraud and Abuse Classification System)

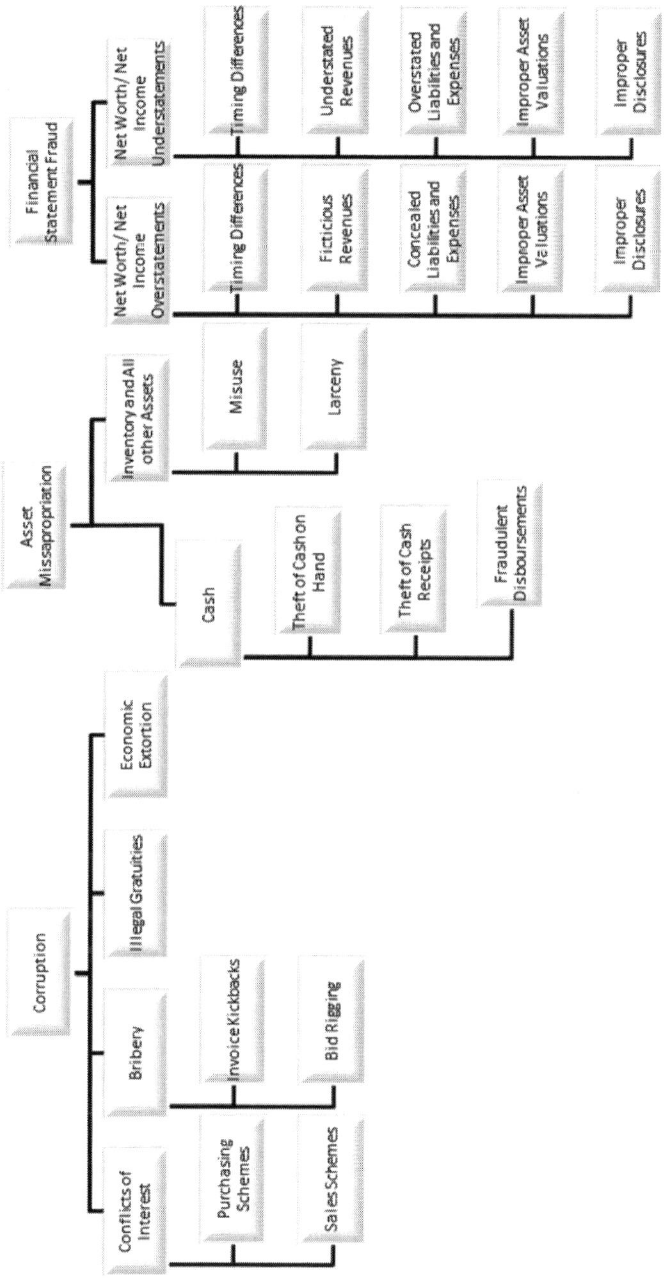

Source: ACFE, 2018 Report to the Nations on occupational fraud and abuse

Comer identified five main categories of fraud that can give rise to a corporate investigation.[25] These are also aligned to the Fraud Tree:

---

[25] Michael J Comer, *Investigating Corporate Fraud* (Routledge 2016) 4.

1. Corruption, which is defined by the Department of Justice as 'an abuse of a position of trust in order to gain an undue advantage'[26];
2. Conflicts of interest, which Comer defines as 'where employees may have private, undisclosed interests that could interfere with their work and fiduciary obligations to their principals'[27];
3. Misappropriation of assets, such as theft of cash or the misuse of company assets for personal gain;
4. False reporting or falsifying performance, including false accounting or manipulating financial records to conceal the misappropriation of assets; and
5. Technological abuse, which involves a person gaining unauthorised access to IT systems or data to which they are not entitled or other computer related frauds.

The Elements of Fraud

There are three elements to Cressey's Fraud Triangle: pressure, opportunity and rationalisation.[28] Fraud or white-collar crime can occur when these three elements are present. More recently Wolfe and Hermanson added a fourth element, capability, and advanced the theory that fraud cannot be committed unless the perpetrator has the capability to do so.[29] This has led to the Fraud Diamond Theory, as shown in Figure 3, which is a vital theory for organisations in understanding how fraud and white-collar crime occurs and how to prevent, detect or investigate it.

Figure 3: The Fraud Diamond

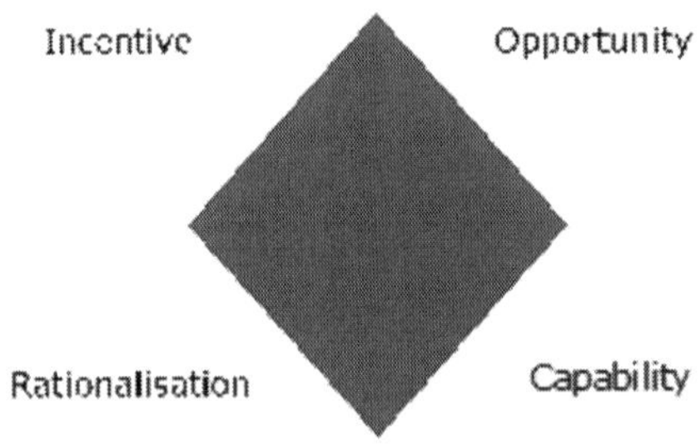

Source: Wolfe and Hermanson (2004)

Albrecht et al identified that fraud is comprised of three practical elements

[26] Department of Justice and Equality, *Tackling bribery and corruption,* available at: <http://www.anticorruption.ie/> (accessed 25 March 2018).

[27] Michael J Comer, *Investigating Corporate Fraud* (Routledge 2016) 5.

[28] Donald R Cressey, *Other people's money; a study* of the *social psychology of embezzlement* (Free Press 1953).

[29] David T Wolfe and Dana R Hermanson, 'The Fraud Diamond: Considering the Four Elements of Fraud' (2014) 74(12) CPA Journal 38.

carried out by a perpetrator: (1) the 'theft act', in which assets are taken, (2) 'concealment', which is the attempt to hide the fraud from others, and (3) 'conversion', in which the perpetrator spends the proceeds or converts the misappropriated assets to cash.[30] Frauds are often concealed within accounting systems using variations of 'earnings management' techniques. Albrecht et al advocate that in order to investigate fraud, an investigation methodology aligned with the three practical elements of fraud be followed, which they have defined as the 'Fraud Triangle Plus Inquiry Approach to Investigations', as shown in Figure 4.[31]

Figure 4: 'Fraud Triangle Plus Inquiry Approach to Investigations'

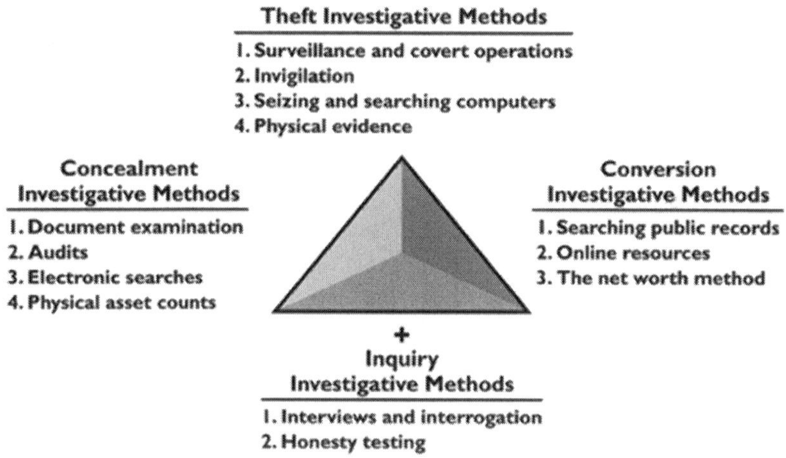

Source: Steve Albrecht et al (2016)

Examples of Corporate Investigations

Before setting out the detailed steps to undertake in a corporate investigation, a number of examples are discussed below where corporate fraud occurred in the form of misstatement of financial statements. These cases give an overview of the types of issues faced by forensic accountants and investigators when undertaking a corporate investigation. They can be used to understand which elements of the accounting practices resulted in management finding themselves across the line into criminal behaviour.

In 2003 Royal Ahold ('Ahold') was investigated for irregular accounting practices, including fraud in one of its divisions in the USA. The Securities Exchange Commission (SEC) commissioned an investigation which found that a number of divisions had reported incorrect volumes of goods sold and

[30] Steve Albrecht *et al*, *Fraud Examination* (Cengage Learning 2016).

[31] ibid 215.

had overbilled a number of vendors.[32] In 2014, Tesco Plc announced to the London Stock Exchange that the UK's Serious Fraud Office had commenced an investigation into accounting practices at the company.[33]

In 2004, three executives of Computer Associates pleaded guilty to securities fraud, which involved a practice of booking sales in the previous accounting period than the sale actually occurred, therefore deliberately overstating revenues and profits.[34] One of the executives who pleaded guilty was reported in the media as saying 'I knew my conduct was wrong at the time…I knew that what I was doing was wrong, and I accept full responsibility.'[35] The CEO who was in charge during the relevant period also pleaded guilty in 2006 to pleaded guilty to a conspiracy charges and interfering with the subsequent federal investigation. He was sentenced to 12 years' in prison.[36] According to the SEC, Computer Associates prematurely recognised $2.2 billion in revenue in FY2000 and FY2001 and more than $1.1 billion in premature revenue in prior quarters.[37] In addition a number of former executives 'obstructed the SEC's investigation into the company's accounting practices.'[38]

In 2018, the former Chief Executive of Anglo Irish Bank was convicted in the Irish Courts for conspiracy to defraud contrary to common law and false accounting contrary to s 10 of the Criminal Justice (Theft and Fraud Offences) Act 2001 relating to €7.2 billion worth of transactions.[39]

The Laws of Natural Justice and Corporate Investigation Procedures

Before undertaking any corporate investigation in Ireland, it is necessary for the investigation team to have regard to the laws of natural justice. Procedural

---

32 Security Exchanges Commission, *SEC Charges Royal Ahold and Three Former Top Executives with Fraud; Former Audit Committee Member Charged with Causing Violations of the Securities Laws* (2018), available at: <https://www.sec.gov/news/press/2004-144.htm> (accessed 25 March 2018).

33 Tesco Plc, *Regulatory update*, available at <https://www.tescoplc.com/news/news-releases/2014/regulatory-update> (accessed 25 March 2018).

34 Alex Bererson, '3 Plead Guilty in Computer Associates Case' *New York Times* (9 April 2004), available at: <https://www.nytimes.com/2004/04/09/business/3-plead-guilty-in-computer-associates-case.html> (accessed 25 March 2018).

35 ibid.

36 Michael J de la Merced, '*Ex-Leader of Computer Associates get 12 year sentence and fine*' *New York Times* (3 November 2006), available at: <https://www.nytimes.com/2006/11/03/technology/03computer.html> (accessed 25 March 2018).

37 Security Exchange Commission, 'SEC Files Securities Fraud Charges Against Computer Associates International, Inc., Former CEO Sanjay Kumar, and Two Other Former Company Executives' (22 February 2004), available at: <https://www.sec.gov/news/press/2004-134.htm> (accessed 25 March 2018).

38 ibid.

39 *Director of Public Prosecutions v David Drumm*, unreported, Dublin Circuit Criminal Court, 20 June 2018. See <https://www.irishtimes.com/news/crime-and-law/this-court-is-not-sentencing-mr-drumm-for-causing-the-financial-crisis-judge-s-remarks-in-full-1.3537672> (accessed 30 November 2018).

issues have been the subject of a number of critical comments from the Irish Judiciary in recent Irish cases, which give valuable insight into how a corporate investigation must be planned, managed and executed. In the case of *Minnock v Irish Casing*,[40] Clarke, J was clear in terms of what an individual the subject of an investigation is entitled to when he stated:

> '...The Plaintiff is not entitled to be able to prevent an inquiry going ahead without his agreement on the procedures. That is not to say that the defendants do not have an obligation to set out the process that they intend to embark on, and in particular, when asked to do so to set that out in advance...'

The investigation plan must therefore stand up to scrutiny from anyone who may be investigated.

The Five Phases of a Corporate Investigation

Having regard to the above, we set out below the 'Five Phases' of a corporate investigation. This methodology is based around Deloitte Forensic's Global Investigations Methodology used for investigating fraud and white-collar crime, as noted in Figure 5, and other relevant guidance. This methodology advocates five phases:

(a) Initiation;
(b) Planning;
(c) Gathering of Information;
(d) Analysis and interpretation; and
(e) Reporting and closure.

Other terminology may be used by different firms conducting investigations, but the phases are likely to be broadly the same. A number of other useful guides are available internationally, including the American Institute of Certified Public Accountants (AICPA) guide entitled 'How to Organize a Forensic Accounting Investigation'.[41] The Institute of Internal Auditors Practice Guides are entitled 'Engagement Planning: Assessing Fraud Risks'[42] and 'Internal Auditing and Fraud.'[43]

---

40 *Minnock v Irish Casing Co. Ltd. and Stewart* [2007] ELR 229.

41 Deloitte, 'Global Investigations Methodology–A Resource for Conducting Investigations' (Deloitte 2018).

42 The Institute of Internal Auditors, *Engagement Planning: Assessing Fraud Risks* (IIA 2017).

43 The Institute of Internal Auditors, *Internal Auditing and Fraud* (IIA 2009).

Figure 5: The Five Phases of an Investigation

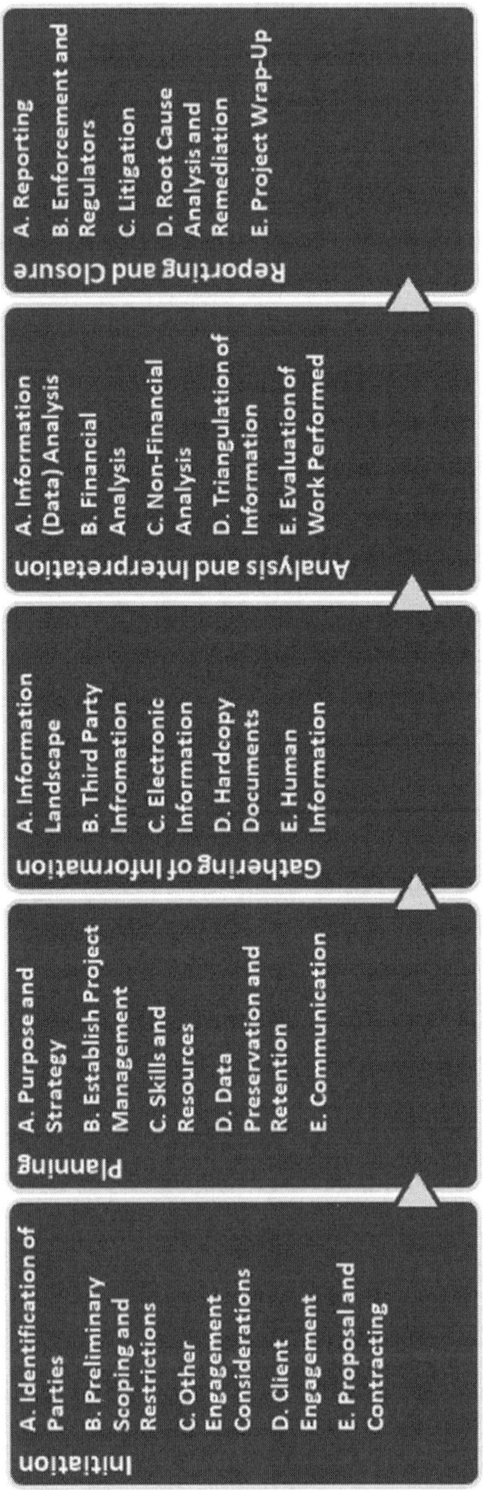

Phase 1: Initiation

The objective of this phase is to identify all of the relevant parties to the investigation, confirm the initial scope of the investigation and to initiate the engagement based on initial contact with the client if the investigation is being undertaken by an external party. At the initiation stage, it will be necessary to determine the legal privilege requirements of the engagement. Legal privilege is extremely important as it generally protects information that is discussed or uncovered during the course of the investigation. If the attorney/legal counsel on the case is consulted about privilege and how to maintain it throughout the course of the investigation, the benefit is that privilege will be maintained in the correct manner.

Phase 2: Planning

Planning is essential to help ensure that the investigation has clear objectives and that the engagement strategy aligns with the objectives. Investigations, by their nature, can evolve rapidly and lead an investigation team in many directions. Therefore, it is important that each step in the investigation process is properly considered in terms of what work is going to be completed and what will be achieved. Planning enables the investigation team to answer critical questions including:

- What are the engagement's objectives?
- What are the fraud hypotheses which are to be tested?
- What is the progress towards achieving our objectives during the engagement?
- What other parties may be working together on the investigation (e.g., Counsel, discovery service providers, etc.) and are the roles and responsibilities of each party defined.

The work plan needs to be cognisant of specific jurisdictional issues, as well as specific limitations or requirements that are unique to the practice area. When planning an engagement and preparing to formulate a work plan, the following issues are to be considered:

- Issues surrounding or inherent in the facts of an investigation;
- Nature of the evidence/information to be collected, e.g. hard copy documents, electronic documents;
- Professional standards and regulatory/legal standards.

The first step in the planning phase is to determine the purpose of the investigation, as well as the strategy to be used. Usually the purpose and approach are determined during the engagement initiation phase. The approach is further detailed in the investigation work plan. Project management is of utmost importance, especially when performing large and/or cross border investigations. Project management enables the investigation team to plan, perform, monitor and adapt the activities that need to be performed to achieve the engagement objectives. Furthermore, it helps investigation teams to detail and monitor progress. Project management of an investigation includes the following elements:

- Setting up project management roles and responsibilities;
- Establishing work protocols for the investigation ream, taking into consideration basic elements such as confidentiality of information, secured storage, project rooms, ethical walls, etc;
- Designing the work plan – What are the engagement objectives? What is the strategy to achieve the engagement objectives? What are the roles and responsibilities in the strategy?;
- Monitoring progress of the activities in the work plan – How is the investigation progressing towards achieving its objectives?;
- Revising the work plan based on the progress and new information (if needed);
- Communicating progress – Ongoing communication on the progress of the objectives towards relevant stakeholders;
- Managing production of deliverables – what report(s) and/or other deliverables will be required and by when?; and
- Concluding the work plan – Were all the engagement objectives achieved?

A work plan allows the investigation team to establish timing, priorities, dependencies and milestones. This will form a clear and documented framework that provides transparency to relevant stakeholders. The content of the work plan and the structure of the investigation team into work streams highly depends on the size and nature of the investigation. Data preservation and retention requires detailed planning and usually requires specific skills and resources. These skills and resources are engaged, where appropriate, during the planning stage to ensure the data preservation and retention are undertaken in compliance with the relevant legislation.

Identifying the Key Issues

It is important to identify the matters that are understood to be of relevance to the investigation at the planning stage. This will often include a description of what a company thinks may have happened, which will form a hypothesis. By way of example, in the well-known case of Poly Peck, it was alleged that the company's founder Asil Nadir had embezzled over £370 million and several theories were formed as to how this alleged fraud occurred.[44] Taking embezzlement as the hypothesis as a starting point in a corporate investigation, Howe and Malgwi propose understanding what embezzlement or theft looks like as a means of gaining an understanding in how to investigate such a fraud.[45] Bologna and

[44] James Gallagher *et al*, 'Polly Peck: The Breaking of an Entrepreneur' (1996) 3(1) Journal of Small Business and Enterprise Development 3.

[45] Martha A Howe and Charles A Malgwi, 'Playing the Ponies: A $5 Million Embezzlement Case' (2006) 82(1) Journal Of Education For Business 27.

Linquist suggest that embezzlers do not make 'one grand hit for a million dollars then run away', that the embezzlement is likely to occur over a much longer period of time.[46] They suggest that embezzlers have a pattern of theft that is unique to them, for example, through the use of an account category that gets an inordinate amount to cover up the loss.[47] The investigation plan will need therefore to include an element of pattern identification where irregularities or odd transactions are identified.

Howe and Malgwi identified that to be able to perpetrate an embezzlement fraud, a complete knowledge of the system in which the organisation operated would be required.[48] This supports our suggested approach that an investigator must gain a similar understanding of that organisation in order to identify if and how a fraud occurred. Bologna and Linquist advocate investigators looking for transactions that are odd or irregular with particular regard to[49]:

(a) the time they occurred (time of day, week, month, year or season);
(b) their frequency (too many or too few);
(c) the places to which they relate (too far, too near and too 'far out');
(d) their amount (too high, too low, too consistent, too alike, too different); and
(e) the parties to which they relate.

In an asset misappropriation or embezzlement case it will be important to ascertain, for each amount allegedly taken by the suspected perpetrator:

(a) The amount taken;
(b) The date the transaction occurred;
(c) How it occurred;
(d) Who instructed the transaction to occur;
(e) The destination of the funds taken;
(f) The bank statement or other record on which the transaction is recorded;
(g) Whether it was authorised by the company or not; and
(h) How it was recorded in the books and records of the company from whose bank account it was taken.

The physical evidence required to determine all of the above facts will need to be established and will likely include electronic evidence (see Collection Phase).

In devising the investigation plan, it is necessary to identify transactions that are unusual, suspicious or unauthorised. This can be done by way of using data

---

46 Jack Bologna and Robert J Lindquist *Fraud auditing and forensic accounting: new tools and techniques* (Wiley 1995) 137.

47 ibid 138.

48 Martha A Howe and Charles A Malgwi, 'Playing the Ponies: A $5 Million Embezzlement Case' (2006) 82(1) Journal of Education for Business 27.

49 Jack Bologna and Robert J Lindquist *Fraud auditing and forensic accounting: new tools and techniques* (Wiley 1995).

analytics, including the application of Benford's Law,[50] or by taking an iterative approach by identifying a transaction that can be proven to be fraudulent, and searching for similar transactions that occurred in the same way. In planning and preparing for a corporate investigation, an area to consider in any potential fraud scheme is the concealment of the fraud within the accounting system. Jones sets out the most common methods of the use of earnings management techniques,[51] which may often be used to conceal fraud, as shown in Table 1.

Table 1: Most common methods of earnings management

Strategy	Methods
Increase income	(a) boost sales through related parties (b) premature income recognition, include non-operating profits (c) treat loan as sales (d) transfer to reserves (e) long-term contracts (f) swaps (g) pyramid sales (h) gains and losses on sales (i) sales terminology
Decrease expenses	(a) capitalising expenses (b) provision accounting (c) deferring expenses (d) expenses to reserves (e) increase depreciation periods (f) stock options (g) generous with bad debts (h) reduce taxation charge (i) increase closing stock (j) goodwill
Increase assets	(a) stock (b) revalue fixed assets (c) inflate debtors (d) current assets (e) prepaid assets (f) investments (g) intangible assets
Decrease liabilities	(a) off balance sheet financing (b) understating liabilities (c) reclassifying debt as equity

50 Cindy Durtschi *et al*, 'The effective use of Benford's Law to assist in detecting fraud in accounting data' (2004) 5(1) Journal of Forensic Accounting 17.

51 Michael John Jones, *Creative accounting, fraud and international accounting scandals* (John Wiley & Sons 2011) 45-64.

Prior to commencing any corporate investigation, it would be beneficial to identify whether any allegations of fraud were previously raised within the company through whistleblowing and whether these have been documented. Consideration will need to be given to the Protected Disclosures Act 2014 in this regard for corporate investigations in Ireland.

Phase 3: Gathering of Information/Data Collection

The objective of this phase is to assemble relevant evidence in order to focus the investigation. In any corporate investigation, there are generally four sources of information: Hard copy documents, Electronically Stored Information ('ESI'), Third party information and an individual's information which is collected by way of interviewing (see interviews). Hardcopy documents and ESI may be obtained, created, copied, stored, or transmitted by the investigation team, and produced to third parties during the course of an investigation. It is therefore vital to consider local and country specific regulations and laws during this stage.

Collection of Hardcopy Documents

Investigations might require collection of hardcopy documentation. The chain of custody of the collection is imperative to any investigation as the evidence might be used in court. The collection of (large volumes) of hard copy documentation is controlled by, for example, keeping a chain of custody register of the person and/or location from which the hard copy documentation/data is obtained. If hard copy documentation is obtained as part of search procedures it is advised to take photos of how and where the documents are found. These photos are included in the hard copy documentation register.

Collection of ESI

ESI includes, but may not be limited to: emails (including web based emails such as Gmail or Hotmail), text messages, instant and other electronic correspondence; financial records; internet history; deleted files and other temporary or auto recovery files. It will include data stored on PCs, laptops or servers including emails, spreadsheets, PDF documents, word processed documents, accounting databases or systems. ESI may extend to data stored on external drives, USB drives, and mobile phones or on a cloud-based service, back-up servers or back-up storage tapes which can often be located off-site from the primary location of the investigation or even in another jurisdiction. The Electronic Discovery Reference Model (known as 'EDRM'), reproduced in a simplified form in Figure 6, is an internationally recognised model for best practice in the stages of electronic discovery, and is suitable for any investigation involving ESI, including those that may end up in legal proceedings.[52]

---

[52] Duke Law EDRM website, available at: <https://www.edrm.net/frameworks-and-standards/edrm-model/> (accessed 30 November 2018).

Figure 6: The Electronic Discovery Reference Model

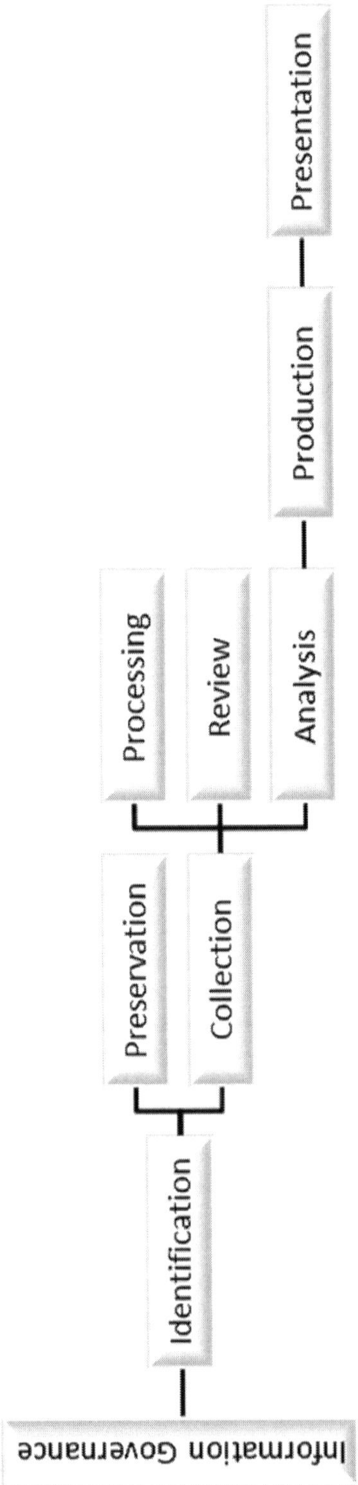

The investigation team will often use E-Discovery specialists to aid in the collection of data, as their expertise in discovery will be able to provide the preservation, collection, processing, hosting, review, and production expertise for data subject to the investigation. It is highly recommended that the team engages E-Discovery specialists and Data Analytics specialists when gathering ESI. Following the introduction of SI No 93 of 2009: Rules of the Superior Courts (Discovery) 2009,[53] the Commercial Litigation Association of Ireland produced the 'Good Practice Discovery Guide'[54] which provides useful guidance on electronic discovery and is relevant to the issues faced by an investigation team at the collection stage. The guide recommends, in respect of collection, that 'appropriately skilled personnel be engaged to complete this process. Such personnel will be adept in verifying the accuracy and completeness of documents which have been collected.'[55]

Collection of Third Party Information

Collection of third-party information can help investigation teams uncover and assess data obtained from external databases, local public records and a network of contacts. Specifically, in investigations, this information can assist in obtaining a more comprehensive understanding of the background of the entity, individual or group as well as locating assets or persons. Albrecht identifies four main sources of public records that can be used in obtaining information that can be used to determine the assets and liabilities of an individual, including government sources, private sources, online databases, and internet searches.[56] Crumbley, Heitger and Smith highlight that due diligence techniques using public sources can identify property assets and political donations.[57] The Centre for the Advancement of Public Integrity identifies three primary sources of information: open source, i.e. publicly available; restricted, i.e. only available to law enforcement, and protected, i.e. that which is protected by law and may require a Court Order to obtain.[58]

Interviews

The decision of when to interview witnesses or suspects depends on the ultimate goal of the client as well as the availability of other information/evidence and the availability of the people to be interviewed. Document and data collection interviews support existing information by providing investigators with an understanding of the interviewee and his/her objectives. Interviews are prepared for by defining the purpose of the interview and determining whether it is process

---

[53] Rules of the Superior Courts (Discovery) 2009, SI No 93 of 2009.

[54] Commercial Litigation Association of Ireland, Good Practice Discovery Guide (2015) 32, available at: <http://www.clai.ie/userfiles/file/Discovery/CLAI%20-%20Good%20Practice%20Discovery%20Guide%20v2_0.pdf> (accessed 26 March 2018).

[55] ibid 32.

[56] W Steve Albrecht *et al*, *Fraud Examination* (5th edn, Cengage 2016) 261.

[57] D Larry Crumbley *et al*, *Forensic and Investigative Accounting* (6th edn, Wolters Kluwer 2013).

[58] Center for the Advancement of Public Integrity, *What is Asset Tracing? A Primer on 'Following the Money' for Integrity Practitioners and Policymakers* (2016) 2.

or purpose driven, as well as identifying interviewers and interviewees. It is important that the interviewer understands the desired outcome of the interview and the assumptions that need to be confirmed or dispelled by the interviewee. Therefore, it is important that the interviewer gathers relevant information ahead of any interviews.

It is helpful to identify themes / areas to address during the interview. These are to be listed in chronological order if appropriate. In doing this, may even be possible to draft interview questions and prepare reference documents to accompany them. However, interviewers must be flexible to allow the interviewee to expand on specific topics. Being prepared for an interview can often be the difference between a good or bad interview. Interview outlines are often prepared to ensure that the interview outline is well thought out and considers all available information. This will allow the interviewer to reference between any supporting documentation and the interview outline. Data is retained and safeguarded for an agreed timeframe taking into account legal requirements. Where the engagement involves a regulatory authority, any specific documentation requirements of the regulator need to be considered.

In 2014, the Institute of Internal Auditors published useful guidelines entitled 'Conducting an Interview – Top Tips' as to how interviews are to be conducted in the context of an internal audit, and these are relevant when considering interviewing as an evidence gathering technique in a corporate investigation.[59] These 'Top Tips' include:

(a) 'Send meeting invitations well in advance.
(b) Make sure adequate time has been allocated for the meeting.
(c) Be clear about the purpose of the interview; write down the aims and objectives — do your research.
(d) Draw up a list of questions; be clear about what you want to say and ensure they are structured in a series of linked and progressive points.
(e) Have information printed/copied if you want to discuss or refer to specific documents during the meeting.'

When asking questions, it is important to use a mix of open and closed questions and to document the interview which will form the basis of the evidence collected. Regardless of whether new information is provided in an interview, an interviewee is able to reference, support, deny, or acknowledge the evidence at hand. Interviews provide an experienced interviewer with the opportunity to identify deceptive behaviours or subject matters that require further inquiry. Research into whether deceit can be detected through non-verbal behaviour is inconclusive, with Vrij concluding that there is no 'Pinocchio's growing nose', i.e. there is no common sign of deceit that everyone displays during the act of deception.[60] Notwithstanding this, it has been proven that certain individuals can

[59] Chartered Institute of Internal Auditors, *Conducting an Interview – Top Tips* (IIA 2014) 1.

[60] Albert Vrij. *Detecting lies and deceit: pitfalls and opportunities* (John Wiley & Sons Ltd 2008) 55.

often present non-verbal physical indicators of deceit. For example, Hirsch and Wolf studied the testimony of former President of the United States of America, Bill Clinton about his relations with a former employee and concluded that the former President often touched his nose when he was giving false testimony, compared to not touching his nose at all when he was telling the truth.[61] In the context of an interview of a suspect by a forensic accountant, Crumbley et al identified that as much as 60 percent of communication is non-verbal and suggests that the interviewer looks for physical signs of lying including but not limited to the interviewee covering their mouth with their hand, avoiding eye contact, touching their nose, playing with their collar or even sweating.[62]

Phase 4: Analysis and Interpretation

The objective of the analysis and interpretation phase is to analyse the information that was collected during the gathering information stage to assist in proving or disproving the fraud hypotheses and to ultimately arrive at a factual conclusion. Early in the investigation, the investigations team will have gained an understanding of the issues important to the client and set expectations with respect to procedures and deliverables. Prior to commencing an analysis of the information gathered, it is important to revisit the key characteristics of the investigation. This will help to ensure that the analysis is completed according to the client's expectations and will give the investigation team the opportunity to determine whether any characteristics have changed which would require a revised analytical approach.

Prior to undertaking any analysis, the investigation team assesses the credibility, completeness, and accuracy of the source documentation collected. Electronic and even non-electronic information can be incomplete or inaccurate due to intentional or unintentional reasons. Performing an analysis on incorrect data can be time consuming and costly. Data verification techniques include: summing totals, verifying date ranges, and tying information from source documentation to audit work papers or financial documents (and vice versa). Whilst completing the analysis it is important to remember two important concepts: professional scepticism and information bias. An investigation team always thinks critically and questions the data appropriately. It is important that the investigator approach the analysis with an open mind and not let their assumptions of what occurred get in the way of their analysis and fact finding. As a result, it is important that the investigation team considers every piece of information whether it proves or disproves the hypotheses.

The key activities of the analysis phase are set out below.

---

61 Alan R Hirsch and Charles J Wolf, 'Practical methods for detecting mendacity: a case study' (2001) 29(4) The Journal of the American Academy of Psychiatry and the Law 438.

62 D Larry Crumbley *et al*, *Forensic and Investigative Accounting* (6th edn, Wolters Kluwer 2013) 4-39.

Information (Data) Analysis

Prior to any information being analysed, it is necessary to define what analyses will be completed on the different data sets (depending on the matter being investigated). In the planning stage, the general tests that were to be performed were discussed and agreed upon (e.g. testing of transactions within a specific general ledger account e.g. suspense account). Once the investigation team has gathered and performed a preliminary review of the documentation provided they will:

(a) Develop and document rules, tests and sets. During this step. the tests and attributes of certain transactions being analysed are defined. Consider involving the client and/or legal counsel when designing the rules, tests and procedures;
(b) Perform transaction selection. There are a number of different ways to identify the population of transactions that need to be analysed as part of an investigation. In general, the investigation team first considers the allegations, which may detail a few particular transactions of interest or may be more general and include larger subsets of data. The investigation team needs to consider information learned from interviews and other work steps to define their sample population;
(c) Link the data to hypotheses and lines of enquiry. Ensure that the hypotheses defined as part of the planning phase are the basis for the analyses. The investigation ream always needs to ensure that they are working within the scope of the investigation and that the analyses being performed will allow the investigation team to conclude on the hypotheses.

Though the data to be analysed during an investigation comes from a variety of sources, at its core it can be broadly broken down into two categories: financial and non-financial. Both types of data (and the relationships between them) are analysed carefully to determine whether there is evidence that proves or disproves the hypotheses.

The High Court in Ireland has endorsed the use of technology assisted reviews (TAR), or predictive coding, most recently in the case of *Irish Bank Resolution Corporation Limited & Ors v Sean Quinn & Ors.*[63] E-Discovery tools such as Relativity, Brainspace and others allow investigators to review and analyse hundreds of thousands, or even millions of documents and undertake early case assessments using algorithms and machine learning to identify key documents that are central to the issues under investigation. An example of data visualisation of clusters of similar type documents by theme, which is taken from the Enron data, is shown below in Figure 7:

63 [2015] IEHC 175.

Figure 7: Data Visualisation of the Enron Data using Brainspace[64]

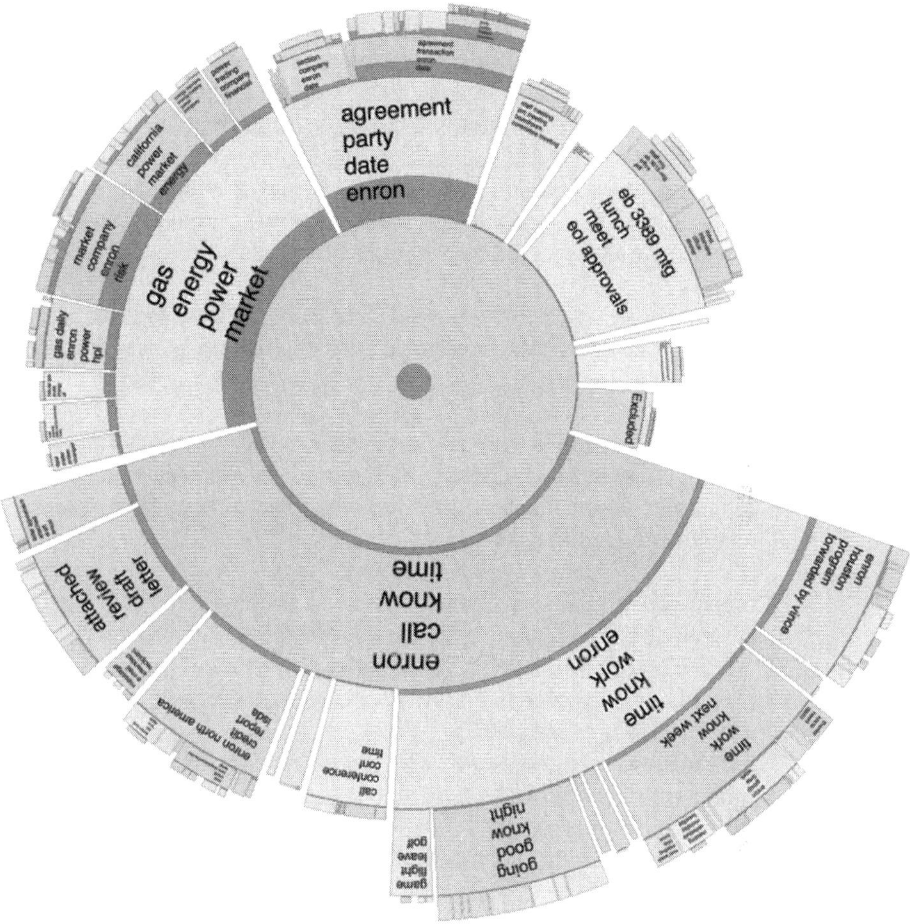

Financial Analysis

Depending on the type of investigation, financial data may help the investigation team to support or disprove their hypotheses. Because every investigation is different, the type of financial data that is needed to be analysed and the nature of the analysis performed may differ. In order to appropriately design financial analysis procedures, it is important for the investigation team to understand the business and its financial processes. It would be difficult to make sense of financial accounting data without first having an understanding of the systems and how the transactions are recorded in the books and records. Though their applicability will depend on the allegations, some procedures that may be performed on financial data include:

64 Images via Brainspace Discovery 5 using a publicly available data set from <http://www.edrm.net/resources/data-sets/edrm-enron-email-data-set> (accessed 30 November 2018).

(a) Relationship Testing. This involves looking for relationships between subsets of financial data and analysing whether the relationships make sense (e.g., if sales increase or decrease, testing to see whether there are other accounts showing a direct correlation);
(b) Journal Entry Analysis. This involves gaining an understanding of the flow of funds through a company's books and records. This may entail understanding which accounts were involved and where transactions were booked;
(c) Account/Accounts Payable Analysis. This may involve calculating how much money was deposited or withdrawn from a specific account or how much money was paid to a specific vendor/individual/third party;
(d) Accounting/Finance Procedures. This may involve performing accounting/finance procedures, such as calculating gross/net income, tax obligations, etc.

The AICPA guide, entitled 'How to Organize a Forensic Investigation – A resource for conducting investigations',[65] includes useful guidance on some of the most common analytical procedures. This guide notes that the common analytical procedures include:[66]

- Comparison of company financial data versus operational data, such as production levels, number of employees and square footage;
- Comparison of current company data versus historical periods;
- Comparison of actual financial results versus company budgets, forecasts or projections;
- Comparison of company data versus industry and competitor data;
- Comparison of financial statement information with income tax returns;
- Comparison of financial statements submitted to different parties or regulators;
- Comparison of subsets of company data versus other subsets of company data (i.e., comparison of data on a disaggregated basis such as by division, product, location or employee);
- Analyses of financial data in context of external events (i.e., economic, political, etc.) or circumstances; and
- Vertical, horizontal, financial statement and financial ratio analyses.

Non-Financial Analysis

Whilst the analysis of financial information is generally important in the course of an investigation, it is important to analyse non-financial information. Non-financial data can simply be defined as all information that is not of a financial nature. This includes but is not limited to emails, company memos, policies/

---

65 Gary Kleinrichert and Annette M. Stalker, *How to Organize a Forensic Accounting Investigation–A Resource for Conducting Investigations* (AICPA 2018).
66 ibid.

procedures, etc. The following list contains some indicative steps that may be conducted when reviewing non-financial evidence:

(a) Analysis of statements/information obtained from witnesses. Verify the accuracy of the information provided against other supporting documentation and information provided by other interviewees. Identify inconsistencies in information provided by witnesses;
(b) Test transactions against the company's policies and procedures. Review transactions in the context of a company's policies and procedures to determine whether transactions were in compliance with said policies and procedures;
(c) Review of email correspondence. Use search terms to analyse email correspondence.

Triangulation of Information

Once the various types of data have been analysed, the next step in the investigation process is to triangulate all of the information which will assist you in identifying all of the facts based on your analysis. This may assist the investigation team to come to a conclusion on any hypotheses. There are many different ways to present information so that it is easier to digest and easier to triangulate. Two of the most popular ways are chronological and visual analyses. Chronological analysis involves creating a timeline of key dates/events and visual analysis involves creating visual depictions of the data analysed and relationships between pieces of data. Ultimately, all of the information that is triangulated needs to support the conclusion of whether the hypotheses were proved or disproved. The analysis process is to be clearly documented, so that anyone with or without knowledge of the engagement, is able to clearly determine how the investigation team derived their results.

Evaluate Work Performed

Once the conclusions have been reached and before the report is written, it is important to evaluate the work performed to determine whether all hypotheses have been tested/investigated properly and thoroughly and to ensure that the evidence corroborates the findings. This last point is extremely important, as the factual evidence must support the findings.

Phase 5 – Reporting and Closure

The objective of this phase of the investigation is to report findings from the investigation that are analysed into meaningful and actionable recommendations, and can withstand scrutiny if required to give evidence in court. Prior to determining the format of the report, consider the audience (e.g. board of directors, management, counsel). This will help ensure that the report includes information relevant to the stakeholders. For example, a Board of Directors may be keen to have an executive summary, whilst management may be more focused on operational implications. Legal counsel may be interested to identify any potential findings that may or may not lead to criminal or civil proceedings. The intended use of the report needs to be considered at all times during the course of the investigation. For example, could it be used for litigation purposes or is it only for internal use? Discussions early on in the investigation will facilitate planning for the reporting phase of the engagement.

The structure of the report should be agreed early on. Typically, it includes an investigation background, summary of procedures, detailed procedures followed, findings, restrictions related to the use and distribution of the report, and recommendations for remedial actions as appropriate. In some investigations and depending on the nature of the work, the report may result in being used as evidence in legal proceedings. Thus, any documentation produced (including internal drafts of reports, correspondence, e-mails, and working papers, whether in hard copy or electronic format) may be subject to disclosure. Therefore, it is recommended that the quality of all documentation must remain consistent and be adequate to withstand scrutiny. Specific considerations are made to but not limited to: the process in which the information was obtained, laws and regulations governing 'chains of custody', restrictions of transfer or access across borders.

In the event personnel are required to provide testimony, they will be required to assist the court by providing the facts verbally. There are generally two types of testimony: (i) Factual testimony where facts are presented in court leaving aside any personal opinions and interpretations and (ii) Expert evidence where the expert is engaged by a party to provide an opinion, usually this would be in the case of a complex technical matter (i.e. expert opinion, assessing or interpreting evidence).

It is common to provide recommendations in the report which can vary depending on the investigation. The types of recommendations may include: (i) Remedial recommendations that may assist the company to recover from financial or other loss; (ii) Operational recommendations and (iii) Additional investigative procedures on specific issues identified. An investigation requires closure which may be coordinated by setting up a structure for project decommissioning (e.g., return of documentation, assets, access passes). It is important that engagement files are complete and conclusive for internal quality review purposes as well as third party reviews. Files and work papers are logged and archived in a systematic manner so that documents / issues are easily identified. Finally, the investigation team debriefs to identify lessons learned and evaluate any client surveys and engagement performance reviews.

Conclusion

The landscape in which investigations are conducted is evolving. The volume of data, and how a company stores and processes data in the future, will have a significant impact on how an investigation is conducted. This will undoubtedly involve an increase in the use of data analytics and machine learning tools and techniques. The process followed, regardless of the tools and techniques employed, will remain the most important component of any investigation. Investigators must be cognisant of the importance of adhering to the laws of natural justice and due process, reinforced by Aylmer J in his judgment in the matter of *DPP v Fitzpatrick* in which he stated: 'the investigation fell far short of the standard impartial, unbiased and thorough investigation in which the paramount duty was to seek out and preserve all evidence which was or might potentially be relevant to innocence as well as guilt, which is guaranteed under the constitution in this jurisdiction.'[67] As public policy in Ireland moves towards a new era in relation to fraud and white-collar crime,[68] it is expected that the Government's 2017 published suite of measures aimed at enhancing corporate governance, increasing transparency and strengthening Ireland's response to white-collar crime will assist companies to prepare for the possibility of initiating or undergoing a corporate investigation.[69]

---

67 *DPP v FitzPatrick* (Circuit Criminal Court, 23 July 2017), available at: <https://static.rasset.ie/documents/news/sean-fitzpatrick-full-ruling.pdf> (accessed 30 November 2018).

68 Joe McGrath, *Corporate and White-collar Crime in Ireland, A New Architecture of Regulatory Enforcement* (Manchester University Press 2015).

69 'Measures to Enhance Ireland's Corporate, Economic and Regulatory Framework', available at: <https://merrionstreet.ie/MerrionStreet/en/ImageLibrary/20171101_Measures_to_Enhance_Regulatory_Framework.pdf> (accessed 26 March 2018).

Chapter 5

IRELAND'S LONG AND WINDING ROAD TO ADEQUATE WHISTLE-BLOWER PROTECTION

Cathal Grennan[*] and Kenan Furlong[**]

Introduction – A Significant Step in the Right Direction

The Irish philosopher Edmund Burke is often misquoted has having said 'the only thing necessary for evil to triumph is for good men to do nothing'.[1] While clearly an admirable sentiment, it perhaps fails to take account of how difficult it can be to be a whistle-blower. In the past, Irish whistle-blowers responsible for uncovering serious wrongdoing have found themselves entirely at the mercy of their employer's retribution with little or no form of protection. In his report regarding the Garda response to the whistle-blowing allegations of Sergeant Maurice McCabe, Sean Guerin SC, recognises that 'the paradigm of the whistle-blower is an unattractive one. The whistle-blower, like the referee from whom he gets his name, is seen as someone who is not on the team.'[2]

That said, legal protection for whistle-blowers in Ireland has improved significantly in recent years. The Protected Disclosures Act 2014 (the 'Act') aims to provide a comprehensive suite of protections for a broad category of people who would seek to 'blow the whistle' on wrongdoing discovered at work. Alongside other legislative reforms regarding the regulation of lobbying and bribery and corruption, the Act represents a credible attempt by the Irish legislature to address a culture wherein Ireland has been perceived as a 'cold house' for whistle-blowers. The Act is not a panacea for all ills and there are areas where clarification and improvement is warranted. However, the authors submit that it represents a significant step in the right direction on Ireland's long and winding road to adequate whistle-blower protection.

This chapter aims to trace the evolution of whistle-blower protection under Irish-law, examine the measures introduced by the Act and analyse the effectiveness

---

* Cathal Grennan is a Senior Associate at A&L Goodbody.

** Kenan Furlong is a Partner at A&L Goodbody

1 The misquote, while an expression of some of Burke's ideas, likely arose from confusion with Thomas Jefferson's quote 'All tyranny needs to gain a foothold is for people of good conscience to remain silent'.

2 Sean Guerin, *Report to An Taoiseach, Enda Kenny TD on a Review of the Action Taken by An Garda Síochána pertaining to Certain Allegations made by Sergeant Maurice McCabe* (6 May 2014).

and, where appropriate, shortfalls inherent in some of those measures. In order to achieve this aim, the authors will cover the following areas:

- the evolution of Ireland's treatment of whistle-blowers beginning with the historical sectoral approach to whistle-blower protection;
- the genesis and adoption of the pan-sectoral approach culminating in the passage of the Act;
- key concepts and definitions contained in the Act such as 'worker', 'relevant wrongdoing', motive and the tiered disclosure regime;
- the panoply of protections provided by the Act; and
- the areas where the provisions of the Act require clarification or where protections might be improved.

'The Past is a Foreign Country; they do Things Differently There': The Sector by Sector Approach

Ireland had no significant whistle-blower protection laws until the late nineties. The 1993 report by Catherine McGuinness SC on systematic failures by the Irish health authorities, which had facilitated a long-running case of incest and child abuse, represented the first important public recommendation for both mandatory reporting and protection for those making disclosures of certain types of information.[3] One of the Report's key recommendations was that 'there should be immunity from legal proceedings' for designated persons upon whom a mandatory reporting obligation was imposed in respect of child abuse. The Report also recommended that 'persons other than those designated should also be entitled to report abuse and receive the same immunity provided they do so in good faith'.[4] When 15-year-old Kelly Fitzgerald died in 1993 and her parents were subsequently prosecuted for wilful neglect, the ensuing controversy over failures by the Irish health authorities generated another parliamentary report. Barnardos' Director, Owen Keenan's Report recommended immunity but only for designated persons upon whom a mandatory obligation was imposed, failing to go as far as Ms Justice McGuinness had three years earlier.[5]

The legislative reaction to these child abuse scandals was to pass the Protections for Persons Reporting Child Abuse Act 1998 (the '1998 Act'). Section 3 of the 1998 Act provides civil immunity to a person in respect of a communication to the relevant civil authorities of his or her opinion that a child is at risk unless it is proved that he or she has not acted reasonably and in good faith in forming

3 Catherine McGuinness, *Kilkenny Incest Investigation: Report presented to Mr Brendan Howlin T.D., Minister for Health by the South Eastern Health Board* (Stationery Office 1993).

4 This is technically an example of 'bell-ringing' as opposed to 'whistle-blowing'; the distinguishing factor being whether the disclosure of information relates to wrongdoing within an organisation of which the discloser is a member. This distinction is further examined later in this chapter.

5 Owen Keenan, 'Kelly: A child is dead Report of the Committee of Enquiry' (Stationery Office 1996).

and communicating that opinion. In the context of that legislation, there is a presumption of reasonableness and good faith. It would be for the person bringing the action (for example for defamation or breach of confidentiality) to prove that the reporter did not act reasonably and in good faith. Section 4 of the 1998 Act prohibits an employer from penalising an employee for making any such report. The 1998 Act also criminalised the making of a knowingly false report. Unlike some later whistle-blower protection legislation, the 1998 Act did not criminalise an employer who breached the prohibition on penalisation.

The 1998 Act was the template for a range of sectoral legislation enacted in Ireland, each act dealing with whistle-blower protection in a different industry sector. Ireland's first pan-sectoral whistle-blower protection bill was introduced as a Private Member's Bill to the Oireachtas in March 1999. It lingered on the government's legislative programme for seven years before disappearing in 2006 when the sectoral approach was formally embraced. In its 2007 Annual Report, the Company Law Review Group supported the sectoral approach pointing out that there was no 'evidence of endemic failure in relation to corporate governance or its enforcement in Ireland that negatively affects the investment climate and which requires enhanced whistle-blowing provisions.'[6] The Review went on to highlight some of the risks of introducing whistle-blower protection for those reporting breaches of company law, namely, that Ireland's reputation as a lightly regulated economy could suffer.

The sectors attracting whistle-blower protection ranged from financial services to health to public office and could be described as reactionary in terms of when and where they were enacted. Notably, there were no protections whatsoever for would-be whistle-blowers seeking to report breaches of company law generally. There are far too many examples of sectoral legislative provisions granting whistle-blower protection enacted prior to the passing of the Act to analyse each in detail here. However, there are common characteristics which are worth a mention. As a general rule, many of the earlier Acts:

- Prohibit disciplinary action and penalisation of the whistle-blower;
- Allow a whistle-blower to claim up to two-years compensation from their employer if they feel they have been penalised for whistle-blowing;
- Criminalise persons who knowingly make false disclosures and employers who breach prohibitions on penalising persons who make valid disclosures. In one of the more draconian examples, the Health Act 2007 provides for up to three years imprisonment for making a disclosure that a person ought to reasonably have known to be false; and
- Provide limited civil and criminal immunity to the whistle-blower.

Unlike in certain other jurisdictions, blanket immunity from prosecution in

6 Company Law Review Group, Report of the Company Law Review Group 2007 (CLRG 2008) para 6.4.6.2.

respect of any underlying criminal activity which the whistle-blower may have been engaged in was not and is not currently a feature of Irish whistle-blower protection law. The one exception to this is the Cartel Immunity Programme (CIP) operated by the Competition and Consumer Protection Commission. The scope of the CIP was broadened in January 2015 to lift a previous restriction on eligibility for those applicants who might have instigated the cartel or played a lead role in the illegal activity.[7] Under the CIP, the Director of Public Prosecution retains discretion not to prosecute a complicit whistle-blower where that whistle-blower complies with certain stringent criteria, including being the first member of the cartel to blow the whistle.[8]

Other features of some jurisdictions (most notably the United States of America) that we are unlikely to see embraced in Ireland any time soon are incentives for whistle-blowers (as opposed to protections). On 19 March 2018, the Securities and Exchange Commission announced its highest ever Dodd-Frank whistle-blower awards with two whistle-blowers sharing a nearly $50 million award and a third whistle-blower receiving more than $33 million. The SEC has awarded more than $262 million to 53 whistle-blowers since 2012.[9] While this approach has garnered some academic interest in Ireland,[10] the fact that uncapped compensatory awards for dismissal and/or penalisation in connection with whistle-blowing were considered by the legislature in the context of the Act and rejected in favour of a five-year salary cap make the adoption of incentives unlikely in the foreseeable future.

This piecemeal approach to whistle-blowing protections was not without criticism. Transparency International Ireland cited a number of high profile cases demonstrative of the lacunae in whistle-blower protection existing under the sectoral approach describing it as leaving 'thousands of people with little or no guidance or protection against legal action and retaliation for speaking out against wrongdoing.'[11]

'The Winds of Change': The Pan-Sectoral Approach

In the first general election following the Irish banking crisis and resulting economic downturn, the Fine Gael/Labour coalition swept into government on

7 Conor Talbot, 'The Protected Disclosures Act 2014 and the Cartel Immunity Programme 2015' (2015) 22(7) CLP 178.

8 See James Hamilton, 'Prosecuting Corruption in Ireland' (Burren Law School, May 2010) in which the DPP reminded the audience of this power and its utilisation in the Guinness plc fraud trial.

9 SEC, 'SEC Announces Its Largest-Ever Whistleblower Awards' (19 March 2018), available at: <https://www.sec.gov/news/press-release/2018-44> (accessed 30 November 2018).

10 Patrick Longworth, 'Using a Carrot to Catch a Crook: Part 2–The Case for a Whistle-blower Incentive Programme to Combat White-Collar Crime in Ireland' (2016) 23(5) CLP 135.

11 Transparency International Ireland, *An Alternative to Silence: Whistleblower Protection in Ireland* (January 2010), available at: <https://www.transparency.ie/sites/default/files/2010_Alternative_to_Silence_Ireland_v1.pdf> (accessed 30 November 2018).

a wave of public appetite for change and reform. The coalition published its Programme for Government 2011 – 2016 which contained a vague commitment to 'introduce whistle-blower legislation'.[12] The original 1999 pan-sectoral whistle-blower protection bill had been introduced by Deputy Pat Rabbite; whistle-blower protection remained a core issue for the Labour party over the years.

Two reports added impetus to the creation of a robust and comprehensive pan-sectoral framework for whistle-blower protection in Ireland:

a) On 19 April 2011, the Minister for Finance Mr. Michael Noonan T.D. published the Commission of Investigation's (Banking Sector) Report.[13] The Irish Government had established a Statutory Commission of Investigation in 2010 asking a Finnish banking expert, Dr. Peter Nyberg, to investigate and prepare a report into the Irish banking crisis. Amongst his many findings, Dr. Nyberg found that some banking insiders who might otherwise have attempted to alert market participants about escalating property values stayed silent, in part, to avoid possible sanctions. He reported that there was a strong belief in Ireland that whistle-blowers would be 'informally (though sometimes even publicly) sanctioned or ignored, regardless of the quality of their analysis or their place in organisations.'[14];
b) The Final Report of the Tribunal of Inquiry into Certain Planning Matters and Payments (the 'Mahon Report'), published on 22 March 2012, added significantly to the pressure on the government to act on whistle-blower protection. The Tribunal had spent 15 years investigating allegations of corruption in the planning and development process in Ireland.[15] It maintained that whistle-blower protection played an important role in the detection of corruption offences and that the protection offered to prospective whistle-blowers should be as robust as possible. The Report pointed out that corruption is an offence committed by the wealthy and powerful in society and that would-be whistle-blowers sensibly feared the consequences for their careers and employment prospects of speaking up. Whistle-blower protection could help to alleviate those fears, thus facilitating the detection and prosecution of corruption offences. The Report criticised the sectoral approach to whistle-blowing protection and doubted its ability to deliver effective whistle-blower protection.

---

12 'Statement of Common Purpose', available at: <https://www.taoiseach.gov.ie/eng/Work_Of_The_Department/Programme_for_Government/Programme_for_Government_2011-2016.pdf> (accessed 30 November 2018).

13 Peter Nyberg, *Misjudging Risk: Causes of the Systemic Banking Crisis in Ireland: Report of the Commission of Investigation into the Banking Sector in Ireland* (March 2011), available at: <http://www.bankinginquiry.gov.ie/Documents/Misjuding%20Risk%20-%20Causes%20of%20the%20Systemic%20Banking%20Crisis%20in%20Ireland.pdf> (accessed 30 November 2018).

14 ibid para 5.5.6.

15 *The Final Report of the Tribunal of Inquiry into Certain Planning Matters and Payments* (Stationery Office 2012).

> The Report stated that the sectoral approach 'lead to a very complex and opaque system for protecting whistle-blowers which is likely to deter at least some from reporting corruption offences'.[16] The Tribunal specifically recommended that pan-sectoral whistle-blower protection legislation be introduced at the earliest opportunity protecting all those reporting suspected offences and/or breaches of regulatory measures from any form of liability or penalisation arising from that report.

The General Scheme of the Protected Disclosures in Public Interest Bill 2012 was published a month before the Mahon Report. The General Scheme was subjected to intense pre-legislative scrutiny by the Joint Committee on Finance, Public Expenditure and Reform (the 'Committee'). The Committee held hearings over six days during which a number of interested parties and stakeholders, including one of the authors of this paper, made submissions. On foot of a submission by the Irish Business and Employers' Confederation (IBEC), the Committee recommended that the Bill should undergo a regulatory impact analysis (RIA). The RIA carried out by the Reform Unit of the Department of Public Expenditure and Reform suggested that the legislation would mean all significant employers in both the public and private sectors would need to put in place arrangements that would allow their workers to report matters of concern on a no fault basis.

Upon its commencement in July 2014, the Act was widely hailed as representing a new standard of international best practice for whistle-blower protection. Before assessing whether the Act has lived up to these expectations in the four years since its enactment, we shall briefly outline its key provisions.

'Workers of the World Unite': Who is Covered?

One of the most commonly used definitions of whistle-blowing is that of Near and Miceli, who define it as 'the disclosure by organisation members of illegal, immoral or illegitimate practices under the control of their employers, to persons or organizations that may be able to effect action'.[17] A key factor in this definition is that the individuals making the disclosure be part of the organisation. More recently it has been suggested that the term whistle-blower should be reserved only for those who face some element of reprisal as a result of their disclosure.[18] This suggests that 'outsiders'–those who report wrongdoing but are not within an organisation — should not be considered whistle-blowers because they are not subject to the level of risk that those who speak up about wrongdoing within their organisations are. The starting point for considering which class of person would be entitled to protection under the Act appears to have been the Near and Miceli definition i.e. organisation members as opposed to 'outsiders'. However, the question of which 'members' would fall within the scope of the Act

16 ibid Chapter 18, para 7.48.

17 Maria P Miceli and Janet P Near, 'Characteristics of organizational climate and perceived wrongdoing associated with whistle-blowing decisions' (1985) 38(3) Personnel Psychology 525.

18 C Fred Alford, *Whistleblowers: Broken Lives and Organisational Power* (Cornell University Press 2001).

generated considerable debate during the legislative process. The Act applies to all 'workers', including employees (both public and private sector), contractors, trainees, agency staff, former employees and individuals on work experience (the latter category is subject to one exception dealt with below).

The concept of 'worker' is necessarily broader than the definition of 'employee' under employment legislation. The inclusion of trainees and contract staff within the definition of workers sensibly recognises that those without long service records can often be the most likely to blow the whistle on corporate wrongdoing, having not yet become part of an organisation's culture.[19] While the broader application of the Act is to be welcomed, the definition of workers would appear to exclude volunteers from its scope. This exclusion fails to take account of the realities of how a number of sectors heavily reliant on volunteer support operate; the charity sector is a classic example and it is difficult to understand why at least of some of the protections in the Act were not extended to volunteers. The Department of Public Expenditure and Reform, in its recently published Statutory Review of the Protected Disclosures Act 2014 (the 'Review'), suggests that to include volunteers would '*open up the provisions of the Act to the general public which would dilute its purpose and focus*' and as such the definition should not be extended to those who do not have an employment relationship. However, the Department then references the guidance issued by the Minister which echoes the authors' view that the protections should be available to volunteers in so far as possible. This apparent lack of clarity is unfortunate and is likely to create inconsistencies in the extent to which the protections under the Act are made available to volunteers across different organisations.

Furthermore, while all workers are afforded some protections, the strongest protections remain available solely to employees creating a two-tier system of protection under the Act. In its submission on the Review, Transparency International Ireland highlighted the fact that only employees were entitled to seek remedies through the employment law framework (such as the Workplace Relation Commission) whereas other workers were required to issue proceedings through the courts systems; a significantly costlier and lengthier process.[20] By contrast, the UK provides redress for all workers through the employment law framework.

There is one other aspect of the definition of 'worker' worth briefly mentioning and that is the exclusion of those on work experience pursuant to a training course or programme 'by an educational establishment on a course provided by the establishment'.[21] The Department of Public Expenditure and Reform is of the view that this clause excludes university students on work placements from protection under the Act. It is difficult to rationalise this exclusion by reference

---

19 Joanne Hyde, 'The Protected Disclosures Act 2014: An Overview' (2014) 11(4) IELJ 114.

20 Public Consultation on the Protected Disclosures, *Submission of Transparency International Ireland to the Department of Public Expenditure and Reform 2017*, available at: <https://www.transparency.ie/resources/submissions/tii-submission-department-public-expenditure-and-reform-2012-consultation-regulation-lob> (accessed 30 November 2018).

21 s 3(1)(d)(ii).

to the modern economy where an increasing number of university courses utilise lengthy work placements as part of the learning experience. Indeed, the Protected Disclosures (Extension of the Meaning of Worker) Order 2015 amended the equivalent UK legislation, the Public Interest Disclosure Act (PIDA), to include student nurses and midwives in recognition of the fact that such individuals were well-placed to identify and report wrongdoing in the National Health System and no good reason existed for their exclusion from the ambit of the legislation.

What is a Protected Disclosure?

In general terms, a protected disclosure is a disclosure of relevant information which, in the reasonable belief of the worker, tends to show one or more relevant wrongdoings and which came to the worker's attention in connection with his/her employment. The requirement that the information must have come to the worker's attention in connection with his/her employment is an important one. A similar concept can be found in s 42 of the Criminal Justice (Money Laundering and Terrorist Financing) Act 2010 which requires designated persons to report knowledge, suspicion or reasonable grounds for suspicion that another person has been or is engaged in money laundering or terrorist financing). The knowledge or suspicion must be based on information obtained in the course of carrying on business as a designated person. Reid and Ashe contend that while the phrase 'in the course of carrying on business' is not defined in the legislation, its meaning will normally be a matter of common sense. They submit that information obtained through conversations over a client dinner or on a corporate golf outing would appear to clearly fall within the course of business whereas information acquired while on a private holiday would not.[22] Similar rules are likely to apply to information obtained in connection with one's employment and it is important to note that the concept is likely to capture more than solely information obtained 'at work'.

'Relevant wrongdoings' are defined exhaustively in the 2014 Act as follows:

- The commission of an offence;
- Failure to comply with a legal obligation other than one arising from the worker's contract of employment or another contract for personal work and/or services;
- Occurrence of a miscarriage of justice;
- Endangerment of the health and/or safety of an individual[23];
- Damage to the environment;
- Unlawful or improper use of public funds or resources;

---

22 Michael Ashe and Paul Reid, *Anti-Money Laundering: Risks, Compliance and Governance* (Round Hall 2013) 182-183.

23 Interestingly, the Irish SME Association in its submission on the Public Consultation on the review of the operation of the Act, sought to exclude disclosures where the whistle-blower has failed to exhaust the procedures already provided for under the Safety, Health and Welfare at Work Act on the basis that this particular ground was being abused by would-be complainants.

- An act or omission of a public body which is oppressive, discriminatory, grossly negligent or constitutes gross mismanagement; or
- The destruction of information tending to show any of the above.

It is no surprise that the definition of 'relevant wrongdoing' encompasses a breach of a legal obligation or the commission of a criminal offence. However, the inclusion of concepts like environmental and health and safety issues would appear to grant whistle-blowers broad scope to report issues free from fear of reprisal. There is no guidance as to what might comprise a 'miscarriage of justice'. The courts have not yet had an opportunity to interpret the language and the Review gives no view on what might constitute a miscarriage of justice. It is worth noting that the definition includes events that have occurred in the past, are occurring presently or are likely to occur in the future.

There are no geographical limits placed on where a relevant wrongdoing occurs; a worker who makes a disclosure regarding a relevant wrongdoing outside the state will be protected. Furthermore, in proceedings involving an issue as to whether a disclosure is protected or not, the burden of proof will be on the employer; it will be presumed, until the contrary is proved, that the disclosure is protected.

It is also important to note that the 2014 Act has retrospective effect; disclosures made prior to July 2014 can attract protection where the employer seeks to penalise the worker after the Act came into effect. The retrospective operation of the Act can be seen by the first successful claim for penalisation under the Act which was determined by the Labour Court on 5 September 2016, 26 months after the enactment of the legislation. In *Monaghan v Aidan and Henrietta McGrath Partnership,*[24] the complainant was a care assistant at a nursing home in Galway who alleged that she had made a number of protected disclosures to both HIQA and her employer and was subsequently penalised as a result. The question of whether or not the complainant had in fact made a protected disclosure turned on the status of the information disclosed at various times. Notwithstanding a direct conflict of evidence between the complainant and the respondent, the court found that during an appraisal meeting held on 29 April 2014 — before the 2014 Act commenced — the complainant disclosed to the respondent information concerning alleged wrongdoings regarding patient care which she reasonably believed was occurring within the nursing home and which had come to her attention in connection with her employment. The concerns related to alleged health and safety risks to residents thus falling within the definition of relevant wrongdoing under s 5(3)(d) of the Act. The fact that the information was disclosed prior to the enactment of the Act did not deprive Ms Monaghan of legislative protection.

[24] *Monaghan v Aidan and Henrietta McGrath Partnership* Labour Court Determination no. PDD162, 5 September 2016 [2017] 28 ELR 8.

When is a Protected Disclosure not a Protected Disclosure?

There is an interesting exclusion contained in s 5(5) of the Act which states that

> 'a matter is not a relevant wrongdoing if it is a matter which it is the function of the worker or the worker's employer to detect, investigate or prosecute and does not consist of an act or omission on the part of the employer.'

It would appear that the reason for this exclusion is that certain workers should not be afforded legislative protection merely for performing their job.

In *Donegal County Council v Liam Carr* the appellant, a fire station officer, contended that he had been penalised for making six protected disclosures to his line managers in the Retained Fire Service, four of which related to the behaviour of firefighters in the station, one of which related to a payment claim and one of which related to the physical capacity of two firefighters to carry out their duties.[25] The court held that the matters the subject of the disclosures could not reasonably be argued to be outside the function of a station officer in the fire service to detect and did not relate to an alleged omission by his employer. Having concluded that no protected disclosures were made, the court was not required to (and did not) consider the question of penalisation.

It is difficult to rationalise the usefulness of this provision and there are a number of instances in which it could operate to deprive a genuine whistle-blower of protections: for example, an individual working in an internal audit or compliance function who uncovers and discloses to his or her superiors a relevant wrongdoing within a company and is penalised before having the opportunity to make a protected disclosure in the stricter sense. It remains to be seen how the court will identify an 'act or omission' on the part of the employer; the issues with trying to attribute liability to a company in the context of corporate criminal liability are well documented. Another area where this could have had a significant impact was amongst An Garda Síochána where 'employer' is defined as the Garda Commissioner. This exclusion appeared to deprive a member of An Garda Síochána of protection for disclosing information to GSOC unless that information related to an act or omission of the Commissioner. However, the Review, on foot of advices obtained from the Office of the Attorney General, explicitly states that s 5(5) of the Act will not exclude members of the Gardaí or the Defence Forces from the protections of the Act.[26]

'Tell me Why you did it': Motive

The motivation for making a disclosure is irrelevant to whether or not it will

---

[25] Labour Court Determination no. PDD161, 7 June 2016 [2017] 28 ELR 259.

[26] Submission from the Department of Justice and Equality, 'Review of the Protected Disclosures Act' (20 October 2017), available at: <https://www.per.gov.ie/en/public-consultation-on-the-review-of-the-protected-disclosures-act-2014/> (accessed 30 November 2018).

be protected under the 2014 Act. The employee who makes a whistle-blowing report against a fellow worker in retaliation for that worker ending their romantic relationship is therefore ostensibly entitled to the same protection as the whistle-blower who is purely motivated by a sense of duty, providing he/she meets the other immunity criteria.

However, notwithstanding the apparently clear wording of s 5(7) of the Act which states that 'the motivation for making a disclosure is irrelevant to whether or not it is a protected disclosure', a whistle-blowers motive can be interrogated in a number of respects and can prove material in determining the level of protection afforded to them.

In accordance with the tiered disclosure regime analysed further below, a whistle-blower who makes an otherwise protected disclosure to the media will lose all protection available under the Act if it is proved that the disclosure was made for personal gain. Personal gain in this scenario is unlikely to be limited to monetary payment and could conceivably apply to a worker who makes a disclosure to the media in the hope that it might result in a promotion.

Furthermore, in determining the amount of compensation that is just and equitable to be paid to a worker who has been dismissed or penalised for whistle-blowing, the court can take into account that the investigation of the relevant wrongdoing was not the sole or main motivation for making the protected disclosure. In doing so, the court has the discretion to reduce the compensation payable by a maximum of 25%.

Finally, one of the protections afforded to whistle-blowers under the Act is the automatic defence of qualified privilege available where a whistle-blower is sued for defamation on foot of a protected disclosure. A successful plea of qualified privilege by a defendant will provide a full defence against a plaintiff's defamation claim. However, the defence of qualified privilege can be defeated by malice. Cox and McCullough state that malice arises wherever a person uses the occasion of privilege for some indirect or wrong motive unconnected to the public policy justification for the privilege.[27] The recent case of *Ryanair Ltd v Van Zwol* demonstrates how the Irish courts are likely to interpret the concept of malice in the context of a defamation trial.[28] Mr Justice Barrett noted the distinction between every-day and legal malice; the latter is the malice which a plaintiff will need to prove in order to defeat a would-be whistle-blower's defence of qualified privilege. Mr Justice Barrett stated that

> "These people bear us ill-will'. That is not malice in the context of qualified privilege. Malice in the context of qualified privilege involves mis-using an occasion for some purpose that is irrelevant to the privilege.'

[27] Neville Cox and Eoin McCullough, *Defamation Law and Practice* (Clarus Press 2014) 288.

[28] *Ryanair Ltd v Van Zwol* [2016] IEHC 616.

How the courts will determine this in the context of defamation proceedings arising on foot of a protected disclosure remains to be seen. In order to attract protection in the first place, the disclosure will need to qualify as a 'protected disclosure' under the Act which would appear to, at first principles, preclude any analysis of the whistle-blower's motive. However, a plaintiff in a defamation action seeking to prove malice will need to interrogate that motivation if they are to defeat the qualified privilege defence. It is difficult to envisage how a court could find that a statement of information protected under the Act was not sufficiently connected to the Act's public policy goals so as to meet the threshold of malice required to defeat a qualified privilege defence without doing a certain degree of violence to the wording of s 5(7).

'One, Two, Three': The Key Levels of Disclosure

The Act introduced a tiered disclosure regime and we analyse the three key disclosure channels below.

Disclosure to an Employer

The whistle-blower must meet certain criteria in order for his/her disclosure to be 'protected' under the Act. The Act encourages disclosures to be made to the employer in the first instance by providing that the least demanding criteria apply where a disclosure is made to an employer.

A worker may make a protected disclosure to his or her employer where he or she reasonably believes that the 'relevant wrongdoing' that the disclosure tends to show relates mainly to his employer. Where he or she reasonably believes that the relevant wrongdoing relates to someone else or someone else has legal responsibility for that wrongdoing, he or she can make the disclosure to that person. This envisages a situation whereby a contractor who might be employed by an agency is working with a company and relevant information comes to the contractor's attention regarding a relevant wrongdoing being committed by an employee of that company. In such circumstances, a disclosure by the contractor to the relevant individual within the company to which he or she is contracted shall be treated as a disclosure to their employer.

Where a worker makes a disclosure to a third person in accordance with a procedure authorised by his or her employer, any such disclosure will be treated as a disclosure to his or her employer. For example, where a company has a whistle-blowing policy allowing for disclosure to a confidential hotline operated by an external company, this will be treated as a disclosure to the employer and, the worker will be afforded protection under the 2014 Act without having to surmount the higher thresholds imposed where disclosure to third parties are concerned.

Disclosure to a Prescribed Person

Section 7 of the Act allows for a disclosure to be made to persons prescribed by the Minister for Public Expenditure and Reform who he deems to be appropriate recipients of relevant information by virtue of their responsibilities and functions. Seventy-two such persons who, for the most part, are chief executives of various regulatory authorities have been so prescribed. Further persons are likely to be prescribed in the future and the relevant Statutory Instrument will be updated accordingly. Where a worker elects to make a protected disclosure to a prescribed person, there is a higher threshold to overcome.

The worker must reasonably believe that the relevant wrongdoing falls within the description of matters in respect of which the person is prescribed (i.e. where the protected disclosure is made to the Director of the Office of Corporate Enforcement, the relevant wrongdoing must relate to a breach of company law). More importantly however, the worker must reasonably believe that the information disclosed and any allegation contained therein is substantially true. Hence, unlike in the employer channel, the worker is not entitled to simply pass on information without first assessing if it is likely to be true.

The rationale for the increased threshold in respect of the second tier of disclosure was to encourage most disclosures to be made to the employer in the first instance. In reality, it is submitted that most workers making a protected disclosure to their employer believe the relevant information to be substantially true thereby giving such workers, in practice, a right of election between making a disclosure to their employer or a prescribed person.

Disclosures to the Media

Section 10 provides for disclosures that fall outside all of the above and encompasses all other types of disclosure, including those to the media. There is a substantially higher threshold to be met for reports to the media if a worker wants to avail of the protections under the Act. As with a disclosure to a prescribed person, the worker must reasonably believe that information disclosed and any allegation therein is substantially true. Furthermore, as outlined above, the disclosure must not be made for personal gain and it must be, in all the circumstances of the case, reasonable for the worker to have made the disclosure.

In ascertaining whether it was reasonable to do so, regard will be had to the following:

- The identity of the person to whom the disclosure was made;
- The seriousness of the relevant wrongdoing;
- Whether the relevant wrongdoing is continuing or likely to continue in the future;
- If the disclosure has already been made to an employer, a prescribed person or the relevant Minister, any actions taken (or not taken as the case may be) on foot thereof; and

- If the disclosure has already been made to an employer, the extent to which the employer's whistle-blowing policy was adhered to by the worker.

In addition to the above, one of the following conditions must also be met:

- The worker believes that if the disclosure was made to an employer, a prescribed person or the Minister, he or she will be penalised by his or her employer;
- If there is no relevant prescribed person, the worker believes that it is likely that evidence relating to the relevant wrongdoing will be concealed or destroyed if the worker makes a disclosure to his or her employer;
- The worker has already made a disclosure of substantially the same information to an employer, a prescribed person or the relevant Minister; or
- The relevant wrongdoing is of an exceptionally serious nature.

Whistle-blowing reports to the media can obviously be hugely damaging for businesses, even if they ultimately prove to be unfounded. It is therefore entirely appropriate that the immunity criteria for those who whistle-blow to the media should be significantly more strict than those which apply for reports to employers or regulators. Furthermore, it is also appropriate that a court should take into account the extent to which an employee complied with an employer's whistle-blowing policy in determining whether it was reasonable to report the matter to the media. It is not unreasonable to expect employees to exhaust these internal procedures where employers have in good faith established sophisticated and practical whistle-blowing policies and procedures, unless there is a good reason for not doing so.

One of the issues currently under consideration by the Department of Public Expenditure and Reform is whether it should be mandatory for businesses with employees over a certain number to have in place either a code of practice or internal procedures for the handling of protected disclosures. It is mandatory for public sector bodies to have in place such procedures. An 'Integrity at Work' survey conducted by Transparency International Ireland in September 2016 revealed that while 94% of public sector employers had such procedures in place, the corresponding number in the private sector was only 34%.[29] By contrast, the Sapin II Act enacted by the French Parliament in December 2016 requires all businesses employing over 50 employees to have in place whistle-blowing policies and procedures while the Sarbanes Oxley Act has required all publicly listed US companies to have such procedures in place since 2002. It is submitted that a mandatory requirement to have in place whistle-blowing policies and procedures for all private sector companies employing more than

[29] TI Ireland, 'First national survey on whistleblowing points to positive attitudes but need for action by employers' (22 September 2016), available at: <https://transparency.ie/news_events/first-national-survey-whistleblowing-points-positive-attitudes-need-action-employers> (accessed 30 November 2018).

50 workers would be a welcome development in the Irish whistle-blower protection framework. The Department of Public Expenditure and Reform has accepted that such a requirement would be beneficial (albeit difficult to enforce in the private sector). This issue will likely be further clarified in the context of the EU Commission Directive for the protection of whistle-blowers, once it has been agreed.

There are other disclosure channels outside of the tiered disclosure regime. The 2014 Act also prescribes that a disclosure made by the worker in the course of obtaining legal advice from a barrister, solicitor or a trade union official will be protected. Furthermore, where a disclosure is made by a worker employed by a public body, a disclosure made to the Minister on whom any function relating to that body is conferred, will be protected.

Protection from Unfair Dismissal

An employee is protected under the Act from dismissal for making a protected disclosure in that they have recourse to the remedies under the Unfair Dismissals Acts 1977–2007 without being subject to the requirements therein e.g., a person is not required to have one year of continuous service before they can do so. Normally the maximum compensation available to a person under the Unfair Dismissals Acts who had been unfairly dismissed is two years' remuneration. However, an employee who has been unfairly dismissed for making a protected disclosure can recoup up to five years' remuneration in compensation. This is a significant protection for whistle-blowers and is likely to be a significant deterrent to employers contemplating dismissing an employee who has made a protected disclosure.

While the deterrent value in increasing the maximum compensation cannot be denied, it is also worth noting that historically many whistle-blowers ultimately find themselves effectively blacklisted in their industries.[30] This may result in their earning potential being reduced over the course of their career meaning that the level of compensation, even at five years may be inadequate.

Interim Relief

Crucial for those contemplating making a protected disclosure is the availability of interim relief. The Circuit Court can restrain an employer from dismissing an employee where it appears likely to the court that there are substantial grounds for contending that the dismissal results mainly from the employee making a

[30] A 1999 survey of 761 whistle-blowers in the United Stated found that 64% were blacklisted from getting another job in their field. See: Joyce Rothschild and Terance D Miethe 'Whistle-Blower Disclosures and Management Retaliation: The Battle to Control Information about Organization Corruption' (1999) 26(1) Work and Occupations 107, cited by Kim R Sawyer, Jackie Johnson and Mark Holub 'The Necessary Illegitimacy of the Whistleblower' (2010) 29(1) Business & Professional Ethics Journal 85.

protected disclosure. If the court so finds, it will ask the employer to reinstate the employee or to re-engage them in another position on terms and conditions not less favourable to the employee's prior position pending the outcome of the employee's substantive unfair dismissal claim. If either the employer or the employee is unwilling to agree to the above, or, where the employee refuses such an offer from his or her employer (and the court deems such refusal to be reasonable), then the court may make an order that the contract of employment continues for the purposes of accruing benefits and continuous service for the employee and regarding the payment of salary.

In the four years since the Act was commenced, Schedule 1 relating to interim relief has been invoked on a number of occasions. The first reported application for interim relief under the Act was determined by the Cork Circuit Court on 12 June 2015.[31] The applicant had accrued seven months of a planned five-year fixed term contract before being dismissed for what the respondent described as significant interpersonal difficulties with the Executive Team. The applicant sought an order of reinstatement from the Employment Appeals Tribunal on the basis that he was dismissed for making a protected disclosure (which would have also resulted in the disapplication of the one-year length of service requirement required under the Unfair Dismissals Acts 1977 – 2007). Within the context of his unfair dismissal proceedings, the applicant also sought interim relief under Schedule 1 of the Act. The applicant made a number of claims of financial mismanagement and wrongdoing against the respondent. The court noted, however, that no financial or other information was disclosed to support the claims. Judge O'Donoghue considered the application for interim relief as 'akin to injunctive relief'. The Judge found that 'the Court has only to satisfy itself that the beliefs and disclosures were reasonable' and while the court accepted that the applicant was 'sincere without reservation', the beliefs and disclosures were held not to have been reasonable in the circumstances rendering the disclosures unprotected by the Act. Accordingly, the application for interim relief was rejected.

In *Dougan and Clark v Lifeline Ambulances Limited*, three employees made a disclosure to the Revenue Commissioners in January 2016 after which two of whom (being the applicants) were made redundant.[32] In this case, the respondent took no issue with the characterisation of the disclosure as protected under the Act; it merely rejected the proposition that the redundancies were connected to the disclosure. Judge Comerford in the Naas Circuit Court outlined the relevant test was not whether the protected disclosure caused the dismissal but rather whether there were substantial grounds for contending that the dismissal was wholly or mainly a result of the disclosure.

Notwithstanding the statement by Judge O'Donoghue that the application was akin to injunctive relief, the test applied in this case was clearly a much lower threshold than that applied to determine whether an applicant is entitled to an

---

31 *Philpott v Marymount University Hospital and Hospice* [2015] IECC 1.

32 *Dougan and Clark v Lifeline Ambulances Limited* (Circuit Court, 29 July 2016).

injunction.[33] The court found that the test had been satisfied and, in light of the respondent's refusal to reinstate the applicants and the applicants' refusal to accept the reengagement offered (deemed reasonable by the court), the court made an order continuing the applicants' salary payment until such time as their substantive claims had been determined.

One question which remains to be settled is the status of payments made during the interim relief period vis a vis the ultimate award for unfair dismissal should one materialise. It will be interesting to see whether the court sees fit to offset continuance payments against an award for unfair dismissal. It is unclear whether this is permissible under the legislation but it is difficult to imagine an employer failing to seek an order to that effect.

Protection Against Penalisation

An employer is prohibited from penalising, threatening to penalise, or causing or permitting another to penalise, an employee for having made a protected disclosure. Penalisation is widely defined as being any act or omission that affects a worker to his or her detriment including the following:

- Suspension, lay-off or dismissal;
- Demotion or loss of opportunity for promotion;
- Transfer of duties, change of location of place of work, reduction in wages or change in working hours;
- The imposition of or administering of any discipline, reprimand or other penalty (including a financial penalty);
- Unfair treatment;
- Coercion, intimidation or harassment;
- Discrimination, disadvantage or unfair treatment;
- Injury, damage or loss; and
- Threat of reprisal.

The case of *Monaghan v Aidan and Henrietta McGrath Partnership* (considered above) represented the first award for penalisation under the Act and outlined the test to be applied when determining the causal link between a protected disclosure and alleged penalisation.[34] Ms. Monaghan appealed the finding of an Adjudication Officer that the issues under consideration did not relate to protected disclosures under the Act; therefore no penalisation had occurred. The court recognised that the Act was a new piece of legislation with limited cases available to guide its hand. The court also recognised, however, that the provisions regarding penalisation were broadly similar to those contained in the

[33] As outlined in *Campus Oil v Minister for Industry and Energy (no 2)* [1983] IR 88. In Ireland, an applicant seeking an interlocutory injunction must show that: (1) There is a serious question to be tried; (2) That by virtue of the harm that he or she faces as a result of the wrong damages would be an insufficient remedy; and (3) The balance of convenience favours the granting of the injunction.

[34] See fn 24.

Safety, Health and Welfare at Work Act 2005 and followed its own determination of those provisions in *O'Neill v Toni and Guy Blackrock Limited*.[35] The court stated that:

> 'where there is more than one causal factor in the chain of events leading to the detriment complained of, the commission of a protected act must be an operative cause in the sense that 'but for' the complainant having committed the protected act, he or she would not have suffered the detriment. This involves a consideration of the motive or reasons which influenced the decision-maker in imposing the impugned treatment.'

Applying the 'but for' test to Ms Monaghan's suspension, the court found that it would not have occurred but for the protected disclosure and awarded Ms Monaghan €17,500 in damages.

This test was applied by an Adjudication Officer in *A Senior Official v A Local Authority*.[36] The complainant in this case was a long-serving senior civil servant who had been the local authority representative on the board of directors of a limited company operating a sports project. The limited company operating the sporting project went into liquidation in 2011 and the project ended. The complainant made disclosures of information in relation to the respondent's financial exposure to the sports project and the veracity of statements made by or on behalf of the respondent. The matter was investigated and, in January 2015, a report concluded that there was nothing substantive to investigate. The complainant alleged that he was transferred from the head of a local department to a role in a reduced section of a central function. Notwithstanding that his remuneration was not reduced, the complainant saw this transfer as an effective demotion and alleged penalisation. The WRC Adjudication Officer, Kevin Baneham, found that, having regard to the lengthy passage of time between the events the subject of the disclosures (which occurred between 2006 and 2011) and the complainant's transfer, the alleged causal connection between the alleged penalisation and the disclosure was too remote to meet the 'but for' test.

Protection of Whistle-Blower's Identity

In the first instance, a person to whom a protected disclosure is made 'shall not disclose to another person any information that might identify the person making the disclosure.'[37] However, there are a number of important exceptions to this obligation as follows:

- Where the person to whom the disclosure was made took all reasonable steps to avoid disclosing any such information;
- Where the person to whom the disclosure was made reasonably

---

35 *O'Neill v Toni and Guy Blackrock Limited* [2010] ELR 21.
36 Workplace Relations Commission Adjudication Reference ADJ-00001721, 11 May 2017.
37 s 16(1), Protected Disclosures Act 2014.

believes that the person making the disclosure doesn't object to the disclosure of any such information;

- Where the person to whom the disclosure was made reasonably believes that disclosing such information is necessary for the effective investigation of the wrongdoing concerned, the prevention of serious risk to the security of the State, public health, public safety or the environment, or the prevention of a crime or prosecution of a criminal offence; or
- Where the disclosure of any such information is necessary in the public interest or is required by law.

A whistle-blower whose identity is disclosed in breach of s 16 will have an actionable claim where the disclosure has caused him or her loss. The practical difficulties with effectively investigating the subject matter of an anonymous protected disclosure, particularly in circumstances where an investigation evolves into a disciplinary matter involving the subject of a protected disclosure, are obvious. It will be interesting to see how the courts balance the right to natural justice (including the right to know one's accuser) against the whistle-blower's right to anonymity in the future.

Protection from Victimisation by Fellow Workers

Anyone who suffers detriment because they or a third person has made a protected disclosure will have an action in tort against the person responsible for causing the detriment. Detriment, in this respect, is defined as including the following:

- Coercion, intimidation or harassment;
- Discrimination, disadvantage or adverse treatment in relation to employment (or prospective employment);
- Injury, damage or loss, and
- Threat of reprisal.

It is noteworthy that a person may not take such a tort case against the same person about whom they have made a complaint to a Rights Commissioner or against whom they have taken an unfair dismissal claim. This restriction, as well as the types of detriment listed, clearly envisages an action for victimisation being taken against a co-worker or other third party as opposed to an employer. It is relatively rare for a statute to create a new right of action in tort and the breadth of the applicability of a s 13 claim for detriment has been widely noted since the Act has come into force. Firstly, the claim is not limited to a worker who has made a disclosure and subsequently suffered detriment. O'Riordain is of the view that family members of a whistle-blower who suffer detriment as a result of a protected disclosure could issue proceedings under this section. Furthermore, prospective employees who do not get a job due to having made a protected disclosure in a previous position may also have a stateable claim.[38] One reported unforeseen consequence of this provision has been the vulnerability felt by employees who feel personally exposed to an action by a person making a disclosure in the civil courts for actions taken by them in the course of their duties.[39]

Civil and Criminal Immunity

Where a person is being prosecuted for any offence prohibiting or restricting the disclosure of information, for example, under the Data Protection Acts, it will be a defence for a person to show that they reasonably believed the disclosure to be protected under the Act. Due to the nature of prosecutorial discretion in Ireland, it is unlikely that this section will be utilised much, if at all. However, its inclusion is likely to give further comfort to those contemplating making a protected disclosure where they fear criminal prosecution in doing so. The Act also bestows limited civil immunity upon whistle-blowers. Section 14 of the Act states that no cause of action shall lie in civil proceedings against a person in respect of making a protected disclosure. This will mainly apply to actions for breach of confidence.

Defamation proceedings are excluded from the civil immunity granted by the Act. However, the Act grants a protected disclosure the status of attracting qualified privilege in defamation proceedings. Qualified privilege arises where a publisher of defamatory information is deemed to have a legal, moral or social duty to publish the offending material and the recipient has a reciprocal interest in receiving it.[40] Where publication of material occurs on an occasion of qualified privilege, this will afford a defendant in a defamation action a full defence provided that the plaintiff cannot prove that the defendant was acting with malice.[41] It is submitted that this particular protection is somewhat illusory as it is likely that most statements meeting the threshold for being a protected disclosure would also satisfy existing criteria for attracting qualified privilege. Indeed, it is difficult to imagine a statement that would qualify as a protected disclosure that would not attract qualified privilege in its own right were the defence not automatically extended under the provisions of the Act.

---

38 Donal O'Riordain 'The Protected Disclosures Act 2014 – Practicalities and Recent Developments' (2017) 14(1) IELJ 10.

39 Houses of the Oireachtas Service, 'Public Consultation on the review of the operation of the Act' (12 October 2017), available at: <https://www.per.gov.ie/en/public-consultation-on-the-review-of-the-protected-disclosures-act-2014/> (accessed 30 November 2018).

40 Neville Cox and Eoin McCullough, *Defamation Law and Practice* (Clarus Press 2014) 243.

41 The implications of the fact that malice can defeat a defence of qualified privilege are examined earlier in this chapter.

Room to Improve

On 17 August 2017, the Department of Public Expenditure and Reform, as required by s 2 of the Act, opened a public consultation for reviewing its effectiveness three years on. The consultation identified 13 specific issues and both it and the submissions generated provided significant food for thought.[42] In July 2018, the Department published its Review (referred to throughout this chapter). The authors discuss below some of the issues raised during the consultation and how these have been addressed in the Review. It is important to note that any proposed changes to the legislation will have to be considered by the Department in the context of the upcoming European Commission's Directive for the protection of whistle-blowers.

One of the issues identified by the consultation is the manner in which the Act interacts with the other protections for whistle-blowers contained in sectoral legislation. For example, s 38 of the Central Bank (Supervision and Enforcement) Act 2013 (the '2013 Act') provides protections for persons who report certain matters regarding regulated financial service providers to the Central Bank of Ireland (CBI). However, unlike the Act, s 38 of the 2013 Act requires disclosures to be made in good faith. Furthermore, s 38(3) of the 2013 Act states that 'a disclosure made anonymously shall not be a protected disclosure'.

At first glance, it would appear that any matter in respect of which a disclosure can be made under the 2013 Act will also qualify as a protected disclosure under the Act entitling the would-be financial services whistle-blower to all of the protections outlined above. However, the Act amends s 38 of the 2013 Act inserting s 38(1)A which states that the 2013 Act will not apply to a protected disclosure under the Act. Crucially, the Act does not repeal the whistle-blower protection provisions in the 2013 Act. This strongly implies that there is a sub-set of information which will only be protected under the 2013 Act and not under the Act. Imagine the financial services whistle-blower who discloses such information under the impression that he or she will be entitled to five years' remuneration and/or interim relief in the event of a dismissal only to find that no such protection is available under the 2013 Act. Worse still, imagine the anonymous or bad faith financial services whistle-blower who could conceivably find themselves with no protection whatsoever. Both the Department of Health and the HSE raised this issue in their respective submissions regarding the lack of clarity surrounding the interaction between the provisions of the Act and the Health Act 2004 (as amended). Interestingly, the CBI itself elected not to raise the issue choosing instead to focus on why it should not be required to investigate a protected disclosure nor to communicate with a whistle-blower on foot of a protected disclosure.

The Department's response merely states that 'any disclosure falling within the

---

42 Public Consultation on the Review of the Protected Disclosures Act 2014, available at: <http://www.per.gov.ie/en/public-consultation-on-the-review-of-the-protected-disclosures-act-2014/> (accessed 30 November 2018).

meaning of the Protected Disclosures Act is dealt with under that Act.' Therefore, the discloser can avail of the protections of the Act but sectoral protections will remain available in the event that a disclosure falls outside the Act's ambit. It is submitted that this response fails to substantively address the concerns raised during the consultation.

Another matter which generated significant commentary amongst the 25 bodies that made submissions were data protection considerations, particularly against the backdrop of Ireland's transposition of the General Data Protection Regulation. The Data Protection Commissioner sought an express reference in any amending legislation dispelling any notion that the Commissioner might be excluded from conducting an investigation into an alleged data protection breach on the basis that said breach might have occurred in the context of a protected disclosure. The Department of Defence, the Department of Education and Skills, GSOC and the Houses of the Oireachtas expressed similar concerns. The Review states that it would be prepared to introduce regulations under data protection legislation to provide some restriction to data subject access rights to protect the discloser's confidentiality. In the authors' view this would be a welcome development, providing further clarity on the relationship between the Act and data protection law.

Another widely held concern regarding the Act appears to be the frequency with which would-be whistle-blowers attempt to utilise its provisions in the context of 'personal employment complaints'. A frequently made suggestion was to amend the provisions of the Act to clarify its non-applicability to personal employment complaints.[43] Some consideration was given to the inclusion of a public interest requirement to counter this. It is submitted, however, that the provision of the Act excluding from the definition of a 'relevant matter', a breach of a legal obligation that arises under a worker's contract of employment, will in time have the desired effect i.e. the exclusion of personal employment disputes from the scope of the Act. This view is shared by the Department of Public Expenditure and Reform. However, the Department is planning to give further consideration to the matter.

The proliferation of the same disclosures through multiple channels to multiple recipients and the duplication of investigative resources caused by this practice also generated significant concern. According to the Department of Justice, the confusion caused by multiple disclosures is compounded by the confidentiality provisions which prevent the Department from identifying where a single whistle-blower has made multiple disclosures to, for example, the Minister for Justice, the Garda Commissioner and GSOC.[44] It is submitted that a provision requiring a would-be whistle-blower to identify where he or she has made the

[43] See further the submissions by the Department of Defence; the Department of Health; the Department of Housing, Planning and Local Government; and the Health Service Executive, 'Public Consultation on the Review of the operation of the Act' available at: <https://www.per.gov.ie/en/public-consultation-on-the-review-of-the-protected-disclosures-act-2014/> (accessed 30 November 2018).

[44] Department of Justice and Equality, 'Submission from the Department of Justice and

same disclosure of information through another channel would not prove too much of a burden on the whistle-blower. The Department of Public Expenditure and Reform appears to have rejected this suggestion in its Review. Instead, it considers that having multiple channels is in fact a benefit in that it helps to illuminate limitations specific to individual channels. However, the Department is prepared to consider issuing further guidance to public bodies on how they should deal with disclosures that have been made using multiple channels.

Conclusion: A Lot Done, More To Do

Whistle-blowers have taken centre-stage in Ireland in recent years. In the four short years since the passage of the Act, two Garda Commissioners and one Minister for Justice have resigned in connection with their handling of whistle-blower reports within An Garda Síochána. A significant number of workers and/or employees have received awards for penalisation and/or dismissal in connection with protected disclosures. At the time of writing, investigations arising out of protected disclosures made by former Independent News and Media executive, Robert Pitt, were ongoing.

The Act was a welcome and, in the authors' view, overdue development in the legislative framework for whistle-blower protection in Ireland. The current regime is not perfect and will continue to evolve. The Act has already been amended on foot of a European Directive on trade secrets; disclosures that reveal trade secrets will now only be protected if the discloser was motivated by the protection of the public interest. This amendment has generated some controversy, drawing criticism from bodies such as Transparency International. As outlined above, there are a number of gaps in the legislation, some of which the Department intends to address. The authors are encouraged by the Review and await the Department's proposed changes to the Act following implementation of the European Directive on the protection of whistle-blowers. Notwithstanding the issues identified in this chapter, the authors are firmly of the view that the Act represents, at the very least, a significant step forward on Ireland's long and winding road to adequate whistle-blower protection.

Equality' (20 October 2017), available at: <https://www.per.gov.ie/en/public-consultation-on-the-review-of-the-protected-disclosures-act-2014/> (accessed 30 November 2018).

Chapter 6

THE ROLE OF THE REGULATOR IN SUPERVISING CULTURE IN FINANCIAL SERVICES FIRMS

Ciaran Walker[*]

Introduction

In recent years, a wide range of misconduct scandals has come to light in the financial services industry around the world. Financial services regulators have increasingly recognised that a core underlying issue, giving rise to these problems, is the culture of financial services firms. Regulators internationally are, accordingly increasingly focusing their attention on supervising the underlying cultures and behaviours that are the drivers of unethical/illegal conduct within firms. This chapter looks at the efforts of financial services regulators internationally, including in Ireland, to address issues of culture within financial services firms and considers the role of the regulator in effecting improvements in culture in firms.

The Nature of the Problem of Misconduct in Financial Services

In recent years, a significant number of financial services industry 'scandals', causing significant harm to customers, have come to light in jurisdictions across the globe. In Ireland, for example, the on-going tracker mortgage issue has garnered enormous press attention. [1] Some estimates have indicated that resolving this issue will cost the Irish banks in the order of €1 billion.[2] Also, the Central Bank of Ireland (CBI) has stated that 'all the main banks will be subject to Central Bank enforcement investigations'[3]. The Minister for Finance and Public Expenditure and Reform, Paschal Donohoe, noted that the CBI's

---

* Consultant, Eversheds Sutherland, and former Deputy Head of Enforcement at the Central Bank of Ireland.

1 Tracker Mortgage Examination, available at: <https://www.centralbank.ie/consumer-hub/tracker-mortgage-examination> (accessed 30 November 2018).

2 'Latest: Tracker mortgage scandal to cost close to €1bn' *Irish Examiner* (18 January 2018), available at:<https://www.irishexaminer.com/breakingnews/ireland/latest-tracker-mortgage-scandal-to-cost-close-to-1bn-victims-to-be-compensated-by-end-of-june-823441.html> (accessed 30 November 2018).

3 Ed Sibley, 'Is it legal? A Question of Culture' (Eversheds Sutherland conference: Leadership and Culture Change in Financial Services, November 2017), available at: <https://www.centralbank.ie/news/article/is-it-legal-a-question-of-culture—-deputy-governor-ed-sibley> (accessed 1 March 2018).

tracker mortgage examination 'has laid bare the fact that very poor cultural and governance issues still exist within lending institutions in Ireland post the banking crash and that if banks are to regain the trust of customers than they must be prepared to change their attitudes significantly.'[4]

On 25 October 2017, the Minister announced that, in light of the tracker mortgage issue, he had ordered the CBI to prepare a report for him on 'the current cultures and behaviours and the associated risks in the retail banks today and the actions that may be taken to ensure that banks prioritise customer interests in the future'.[5] The CBI's report,[6] discussed further below, was published in July 2018. It covers the five main Irish retail banks: AIB Group, Bank of Ireland Group, Permanent TSB, Ulster Bank Ireland and KBC Bank Ireland. The report found, *inter alia*, that 'it is clear that customer-focused cultures in the banks remain under-developed, and that the banks need to overcome obstructive patterns of behaviour in order to transition to maturity.'[7]

More generally, the Deputy Governor of the CBI, Ed Sibley, noted in a February 2018 speech:

> 'If we look at the causes of the financial crisis, we can see clear linkages to behaviour, culture and diversity. It is clear that there were multiple failures and multiple individual and collective decisions leading up to the financial crisis. For example, collective groupthink, business model and strategy failures, governance and control issues, financial misconduct, excessive optimism, regulatory failures, political interference and so on. There are behavioural and cultural linkages across all of these failures. The behaviours and underlying cultures within financial services firms were wholly inappropriate. Short termism was incentivised, particularly with respect to shareholder returns. Effective internal challenge of the prevailing views was not. While many improvements have been made, not enough progress has been made with respect to underlying behaviours, cultures and incentives.'[8]

In other words, in order to address misconduct issues effectively in the financial services industry in Ireland, culture issues need to be addressed. A similar

---

4 Pascal Donohoe, 'Statement to the Joint Oireachtas Committee on Finance, Public Expenditure & Reform and Taoiseach – Tracker Mortgages & Our Public Service 2020' (16 January 2018), available at: <http://paschaldonohoe.ie/statement-to-the-joint-oireachtas-committee-on-finance-public-expenditure-reform-and-taoiseach-tracker-mortgages-our-public-service-2020/> (accessed 30 November 2018).

5 Pascal Donoghue, 'Statement on the tracker mortgage examination', (25 October 2017), available at: <http://paschaldonohoe.ie/statement-on-the-tracker-mortgage-examination/>.

6 Central Bank of Ireland, '*Behaviour and culture of the Irish retail banks*', July 2018, available at: <https://www.centralbank.ie/docs/default-source/publications/corporate-reports/behaviour-and-culture-of-the-irish-retail-banks.pdf?sfvrsn=2> (accessed 30 November 2018).

7 ibid 18.

8 Ed Sibley, 'The Importance of Diversity in Financial Services' (FuSIoN Network, 13 February 2018), available at: <https://www.centralbank.ie/news/article/the-importance-of-diversity-in-fs-sibley-13-Feb-2018> (accessed 30 November 2018).

conclusion has been reached by financial services regulators in many other jurisdictions. In the words of the Bank of England's then Deputy Director, Minouche Shafik, who describes the issue as one of 'ethical drift' in the financial services industry:

> 'the wave of misconduct which has emerged in the aftermath of the financial crisis suggests that 'this time is different'. ..... Never before has misconduct occurred so systematically, in such a scale and across multiple jurisdictions. *Clearly it was not the case of a few bad apples, but something was rotten in the entire barrel.*'[9]

With regard to personal misconduct, in a detailed review of professional standards and culture in the banking industry in the UK, the UK Parliamentary Commission on Banking Standards reported in 2013 that 'Bankers prioritised short term gain over their customers and shareholders and recklessly failed to prevent wrongdoing. It was a culture, in places, suffused with corruption.'[10] Similarly, the US Financial Crisis Inquiry Report stated: 'We witnessed an erosion of standards of responsibility and ethics that exacerbated the financial crisis'[11]. The Wells Fargo 'scandal' in the US, together with the Libor and FX cases in the UK, indicate the scale of the issue of misconduct internationally in the financial services industry. Also, Mark Carney, Governor of the Bank of England, recently stated that 'the incidence of financial sector misconduct has risen to a level that has the potential to create systemic risks by undermining trust in both financial institutions and markets.'[12]

The Limited Effectiveness of Standard Enforcement Tools as Deterrents?

Deterring Firms

In addressing the problems of unethical behaviours and excessive risk-taking, regulators have significantly increased their enforcement activity and levels of fines imposed on financial services firms. Indeed, it has been estimated

---

[9] Minouche Shafik, 'From 'ethical drift' to 'ethical lift': Reversing the tide of misconduct in global financial markets' (Reforming Culture and Behaviour in the Financial Services Industry conference, Federal Reserve Bank of New York, 20 October 2016) [emphasis added], available at: <http://www.bankofengland.co.uk/publications/Pages/news/2016/078.aspx> (accessed 1 March 2018).

[10] UK Parliamentary Commission on Banking Standards (June 2013), *Changing banking for good*, vol. II, para. 48, available at: <http://www.parliament.uk/business/committees/committees-a-z/joint-select/professional-standards-in-the-banking-industry/news/changing-banking-for-good-report/> (accessed 30 November 2018).

[11] US Financial Crisis Inquiry Commission, The Financial Crisis Inquiry Report (U.S. Government Printing Office, 2011), xxii, available at: <https://www.gpo.gov/fdsys/pkg/GPO-FCIC/pdf/GPO-FCIC.pdf> (accessed 30 November 2018).

[12] Mark Carney, 'Building a Resilient and Open Global Financial System to Support Sustainable Cross-Border Investment' *Financial Stability Board* (30 August 2016) 7, available at: <http://www.fsb.org/wp-content/uploads/FSB-Chair's-letter-to-G20-Leaders-in-advance-of-their-meeting-in-Hangzhou-on-4-5-September..pdf> (accessed 30 November 2018).

that, since the financial crisis in 2007, large financial firms have paid fines in excess of $320 billion worldwide in connection with employee misconduct.[13] Nevertheless, despite the significant recent increase in the level of fines, some regulators are sceptical that this has led to a sufficient improvement in behaviours in the industry.

Whilst enforcement activity may address issues of accountability for past behaviours, it is less clear that this also leads to improved industry behaviours (the deterrent effect). As noted in a recent UK Financial Conduct Authority (FCA) paper entitled 'Behaviour and compliance in organisations':

> 'The evidence that we have suggests that there are limitations on the extent to which greater compliance can be achieved by increasing fines and the probability of detection. For example, there is a tendency of certain firms to carry on breaking rules in spite of continuing to accrue large fines.'[14]

This FCA paper provides some useful behavioural economics insights on this issue, noting that individuals may be influenced by behavioural biases (such as confidence bias, confirmation bias) in assessing the likelihood of being 'caught' or assessing the unethical nature of their conduct so that they may not be sufficiently deterred by the risk of sanctions from engaging in unethical behaviour. Also, 'people behave differently when they are in groups, meaning that rule breaking depends on the culture and social norms within firms'.[15] Also, as noted in a December 2017 paper from the New York Fed, whilst imposing fines 'can be a useful mechanism to provide incentives to invest in compliance and controls', they may be 'insufficient' due to the cultural nature of the problem.[16]

Deterring Individuals

Regulators internationally are also increasingly focusing on issues of individual accountability. The UK, for example, has introduced a new Senior Managers and Certification Regime (SMCR), following the publication of the 2013 final report of the UK Parliamentary Commission on Banking Standards and subsequent Banking Reform Act 2013. This UK regime is intended to address one of the significant cultural weaknesses identified in many financial services firms, that of wilful blindness. As noted in 2013 final report of the UK Parliamentary Commission on Banking Standards:

---

13 Gavin Finch, 'World's Biggest Banks Fined $321 Billion Since Financial Crisis', Bloomberg (2 March 2017), available at: <https://www.bloomberg.com/news/articles/2017-03-02/world-s-biggest-banks-fined-321-billion-since-financial-crisis> (accessed 30 November 2018).

14 Financial Conduct Authority, *Behaviour and Compliance in Organisations*, (FCA Occasional Paper No 24, December 2016) 16, available at: <https://www.fca.org.uk/publications/occasional-papers/no-24-behaviour-compliance-organisations> (accessed 30 November 2018).

15 ibid 3.

16 Federal Reserve Bank of New York 'Misconduct risk, culture and supervision' (White Paper, December 2017) 12, available at: <https://www.newyorkfed.org/medialibrary/media/governance-and-culture-reform/2017-whitepaper.pdf> (accessed 30 November 2018).

> 'Too many bankers, especially at the most senior levels, have operated in an environment with insufficient personal responsibility. Top bankers dodged accountability for failings on their watch by claiming ignorance or hiding behind collective decision-making.'[17]

International research on the psychological aspects of accountability suggests that a focus on individual accountability (which does not necessarily equate to individual sanctions) is likely to improve behaviours. As noted by the Dutch financial services regulator, De Nederlandsche Bank (DNB):

> 'Why does accountability make people adjust their behaviour or decision-making process? Accountability fuels the basic human need for approval from others (Baumeister & Leary, 1995) and makes people want to perform well in the eyes of their supervisors (Baumeister & Hutton, 1987). Particularly in situations where people have to justify their actions, they try to communicate positively about their abilities and performance to make a good impression on the supervisor (Frink & Ferris, 1998). After all, those who are held accountable by a supervisor expect to be evaluated and expect this evaluation to have consequences.'[18]

The UK regime for 'Senior Managers' commenced in March 2016. It focuses in particular on the most senior individuals in firms who hold key roles or have overall responsibility for whole areas of relevant firms. Under this regime, firms need to ensure, in particular, that each Senior Manager has a Statement of Responsibilities setting out the areas for which they are personally accountable; that the firm produces a Firm Responsibilities Map that knits these together; that all Senior Managers are pre-approved by the regulator before carrying out their roles.

Also, under the Bank of England and Financial Services Act 2016, a 'duty of responsibility' is imposed (from May 2016) on 'Senior Managers', under which the Financial Conduct Authority and the Prudential Regulation Authority can take action against Senior Managers if they are responsible for the management of any activities in their firm in relation to which their firm contravenes a regulatory requirement, and they do not take such steps as a person in their position could reasonably be expected to take to avoid the contravention occurring (or continuing).

As discussed further below, it is intended that a UK-style Senior Managers regime

---

17 UK Parliamentary Commission on Banking Standards (June 2013), *Changing banking for good*, vol. I, 8, available at: <http://www.parliament.uk/business/committees/committees-a-z/joint-select/professional-standards-in-the-banking-industry/news/changing-banking-for-good-report/> (accessed 30 November 2018).

18 DNB, *Supervision of behaviour and culture: foundations, practice & future developments*; (DNB, 2015) 309-310, available at <https://www.google.ie/url?sa=t&rct=j&q=&esrc=s&source=web&cd=1&ved=0ahUKEwjF8u7GyfrPAhUqDsAKHZTYDKgQFgggMAA&url=https%3A%2F%2Fwww.dnb.nl%2Fbinaries%2FSupervision%2520of%2520Behaviour%2520and%2520Culture_tcm46-334417.pdf&usg=AFQjCNFFrjy79m7BrKZ380NArue5nREXxg&bvm=bv.136811127,d.ZGg> (accessed 30 November 2018).

be introduced in Ireland, to be known as a 'Senior Executive Accountability Regime'.

Any such regime in Ireland would be a significant extension to the current law, under which individuals may be held accountable (under the Administrative Sanctions Regime and Fitness and Probity regime)–the current law does not deal effectively with certain issues such as 'wilful blindness' by senior management.

It should be noted, however, that whilst the UK regime for Senior Managers has important attractions (in particular in terms of focusing minds within organisations on the question of who exactly is responsible for what and on reducing the temptation for 'wilful blindness' by senior management), it may have some limitations in terms of shifting behaviours in financial services organisations. Firstly, in large complex organisations involving multiple levels of decision-making on an enormous range of issues, there may continue to be difficulties in determining individual accountability and levels of responsibility for particular actions taken within the organisation. Secondly, given the complexities of the legal and factual issues (not least of which relate to the procedural rights of the individual), the CBI could realistically conclude only relatively few cases each year. Thirdly, it is unclear what impact the existence of such a system would have on individual behaviours, in light of the behavioural biases referred to above.[19]

Culture: Tackling Underlying Causes Rather than Symptoms

To address the underlying regulatory concerns, regulators internationally are increasingly turning their supervisory focus to firms' governance and culture, in an effort to address underlying causes of potential issues before they arise. As stated in a December 2017 paper from the New York Fed:

> 'Root cause analyses of many recent cases of misconduct in the financial sector, however, suggest that misconduct is not just the product of a few individuals or bad processes, but is the result of wider organizational breakdowns. Often, large numbers of employees and managers were either complicit in improper conduct, encouraged it, or turned a blind eye to troubling behavior….
>
> Though there are undoubtedly many contributing factors that give rise to this type of widespread breakdown, there is a growing academic literature that focuses on a firm's *organizational culture* as a key driver of behaviour and resultant misconduct risk. In this framing, culture is the

[19] See: Chris Hodges and Ruth Steinholtz, Ethical business practice and regulation: A behavioural and values-based approach to compliance and enforcement (Hart Publishing 2017) 184, where they criticised the UK Senior Managers and Certification Regime in the following terms: 'This approach is simply not going to work. It is not credible and scandals will continue. The deterrence policy can only go in the direction of increasing penalties, whether on firms or individuals, which will ultimately be seen as unfair and ineffective in achieving behavioural change'.

> set of attitudes, beliefs, practices, and values that mitigate or enhance misconduct risk. These cultural elements can be hard to define ex ante, but the impact ex post can be easily seen in the resulting behaviours and outcomes.'[20]

In Europe, the importance to regulators of a firms' culture is well explained in the following terms in a speech by Danièle Nouy, Chair of the Supervisory Board of the European Central Bank's Single Supervisory Mechanism:

> 'Culture and ethics are at the heart of banks' decisions in terms of risk-taking and safe and sound management practices. This means that understanding culture – what one does 'when nobody is watching' .... can help us to recognise, and even predict, some behaviours.'[21]

The CBI is also increasing its focus on the culture of regulated financial services firms. In an important recent speech, the Deputy Governor of the CBI noted that 'culture is a critically important topic' and that:

> 'Culture ... drives the values and beliefs that govern how individuals treat others, perform their tasks, take decisions, assess risk, and perhaps most importantly, do the right thing to ensure they operate in a safe and sound manner. It is the foundation upon which effective governance is built and is critical to firms' long-term prosperity. Importantly, experience shows that behaviour has a predictive value with respect to firms' future stability. It is clear, therefore, that regulated firms' behaviours and cultures are within the purview of regulators, both from a prudential and a conduct perspective.'[22]

What do we Mean by a Firm's 'Culture'?

The concept of a firm's 'culture' has usefully been described by the UK Financial Conduct Authority's Director of Supervision, Jonathan Davidson, in a recent speech as:

> 'the typical, habitual behaviours and mindsets that characterise a particular organisation. The behaviours are the 'way things get done around here';

---

20 Federal Reserve Bank of New York 'Misconduct risk, culture and supervision' (White Paper, December 2017) 4, available at: <https://www.newyorkfed.org/medialibrary/media/governance-and-culture-reform/2017-whitepaper.pdf> (accessed 30 November 2018).

21 'Towards a New Age of Responsibility in Banking and Finance: Getting the Culture and the Ethics Right', speech by Danièle Nouy, Chair of the Supervisory Board of the SSM, 23 November 2015; available at: <https://www.bankingsupervision.europa.eu/press/speeches/date/2015/html/se151123.en.html> (accessed 30 November 2018).

22 Ed Sibley, 'Is it legal? A Question of Culture' (Eversheds Sutherland conference: Leadership and Culture Change in Financial Services, November 2017), available at: <https://www.centralbank.ie/news/article/is-it-legal-a-question-of-culture—-deputy-governor-ed-sibley> (accessed 1 March 2018). See also FCA, Transforming culture in financial services (DP18/2 2018), available at: <https://www.fca.org.uk/publications/discussion-papers/dp18-2-transforming-culture-financial-services> (accessed 30 November 2018).

they are the way that we act, speak and make decisions without thinking consciously about it. And sitting underneath these behaviours or habits are mindsets inside people's heads; the beliefs or values that people feel are important. We can't see these mindsets but they are a main determinant of behaviour from the trading floor to the Board. The mindsets themselves are influenced by the incentives inherent within each firm.'[23]

Also, as stated by the Dutch regulator, the DNB, in its ground-breaking book 'Supervision of behaviour and culture; foundations, practice and future developments':

> 'For employees, organisational culture is the social glue that holds the organisation together by providing appropriate standards for the ways employees should behave. As a consequence, culture reduces employees' uncertainty and anxiety about appropriate and expected behaviours'.[24]

Identifying and supervising a firm's culture, however, is not at all straightforward. As noted by Andrew Bailey, then CEO of the UK Prudential Regulation Authority, 'As supervisors, we cannot go into a firm and say 'show us your culture''.[25] Furthermore, as stated by the CBI, 'effective culture in the first instance is a matter for each individual organisation to define and embed'[26] – it would not be appropriate or realistic for the regulator to determine the appropriate culture for a firm, still less a one-size-fits all culture for all firms.

Overview of Regulatory Approaches to Supervising Financial Services Firms' Culture

The Netherlands

The DNB has set out in considerable detail in a recent book its approach to supervision of behaviour and culture.[27] As the DNB acknowledges in its book, its

23 Jonathan Davidson, 'Getting culture and conduct right – the role of the regulator' (2nd Annual Culture and Conduct Forum for the Financial Services Industry, London, July 2016), available at: <https://www.fca.org.uk/news/speeches/getting-culture-and-conduct-right-role-regulator> (accessed 30 November 2018).

24 DNB, *Supervision of behaviour and culture: foundations, practice & future developments*; (DNB, 2015) 45, available at <https://www.google.ie/url?sa=t&rct=j&q=&esrc=s&source=web&cd=1&ved=0ahUKEwjF8u7GyfrPAhUqDsAKHZTYDKgQFgggMAA&url=https%3A%2F%2Fwww.dnb.nl%2Fbinaries%2FSupervision%2520of%2520Behaviour%2520and%2520Culture_tcm46-334417.pdf&usg=AFQjCNFFrjy79m7BrKZ380NArue5nREXxg&bvm=bv.136811127,d.ZGg> (accessed 30 November 2018).

25 Andrew Bailey, 'Culture in financial services – a regulator's perspective', (City Week Conference, London, July 2016), available at: <https://www.bankofengland.co.uk/speech/2016/culture-in-financial-services-a-regulators-perspective> (accessed 30 November 2018).

26 Central Bank of Ireland, *Behaviour and culture of the Irish retail banks* (CBI, 2018) 5, available at: <https://www.centralbank.ie/docs/default-source/publications/corporate-reports/behaviour-and-culture-of-the-irish-retail-banks.pdf?sfvrsn=2> (accessed 30 November 2018).

27 DNB, *Supervision of behaviour and culture: foundations, practice & future*

supervisory model on behaviour and culture is strongly based on the conceptual work of the organisational psychologist Edgar Schein.[28] According to Schein, culture exists simultaneously on three levels: on the surface are artefacts, under which are values and at the core are basic assumptions. Based on Schein's work, the DNB uses the metaphor of an iceberg to describe its approach to assessing a firm's culture. There are three layers to the iceberg. The top of the iceberg is the visible part above water. This encompasses behaviours, in particular around decision-making, leadership and communication, which are readily observable. Under these behaviours are a firm's group dynamics (interaction within a group or between groups, e.g. is there an atmosphere where people can address 'bad' behaviour?) and, below that, is the mindset, i.e. deeply held beliefs and values that often guide group dynamics and individual behaviour. Both the group dynamics and mindset are beneath the metaphorical water-line and only indirectly observable.

The work of the DNB is particularly helpful in setting out in considerable detail views on a role for regulators in supervising firms' culture. The focus of the DNB's supervisory work on behaviour and culture in firms relates to the role of the top leaders, as these are considered by the DNB to be the primary 'levers' for achieving culture change. Also, the DNB pays particular supervisory attention to behaviours related to decision-making, leadership and communication at this level 'because these behaviours are considered important for groups that work together and depend on each other to achieve goals and results', [29] together with the drivers of these behaviours, in particular, group dynamics; 'group composition, group climate and status differences are important touchstones in assessing group dynamics'.[30]

The DNB employs a number of expert organisational psychologists in its supervisory work. Its supervisory work on behaviour and culture include, for example, attending as observers at board meetings (to assess board dynamics relating to decision-making, leadership and communication). Where the DNB identifies risks or other issues in the context of its supervision of behaviour and culture in a firm, the outcome is likely to be a 'challenging dialogue' between the regulator and the firm. Other than in exceptional circumstances, the DNB is not likely to formally require a firm to make specified changes, as changes to behaviours and culture are unlikely to be achieved successfully through regulatory requirements rather than through constructive dialogue, involving 'reflection, involvement and willingness'[31] on the part of the firm. Given the expertise that the DNB has developed in this area, since it set up a separate

developments; (DNB, 2015) 309-310, available at: <https://www.google.ie/url?sa=t&rct=j&q=&esrc=s&source=web&cd=1&ved=0ahUKEwjF8u7GyfrPAhUqDsAKHZTYDKgQFgggMAA&url=https%3A%2F%2Fwww.dnb.nl%2Fbinaries%2FSupervision%2520of%2520Behaviour%2520and%2520Culture_tcm46-334417.pdf&usg=AFQjCNFFrjy79m7BrKZ380NArue5nREXxg&bvm=bv.136811127,d.ZGg> (accessed 1 March 2018).

28 ibid 46.

29 ibid 48, 201, 223.

30 ibid 201, 223.

31 ibid 91.

internal team in 2011 to address behaviour and culture in firms, its approach has been particularly influential internationally, including in the context of prudential supervision by the European Central Bank and national regulators under the Single Supervisory Mechanism. The CBI has worked closely with the DNB in developing the CBI approach to supervision of culture and, indeed, the DNB is supporting the CBI in its inspections in the context of its culture review of the five retail banks.[32]

UK

In its 2016/17 Business Plan, the UK Financial Conduct Authority (FCA) stated:

> 'Our focus on the culture in financial services firms and its impact on conduct has been, and remains, a priority, and we will continue this work with firms and other bodies. As regulators, our focus is on the most significant drivers of good or poor mindsets and behaviours, such as incentives and remuneration, and the steps firms take which address associated risks. We are interested in the direction of travel of firms' cultures and if indicators show progress.'[33]

In this regard, the FCA has developed a conduct risk framework called the '5 Conduct Questions',[34] which it uses in its supervisory engagements with firms to assess potential conduct risk issues. The five questions are:

1. What proactive steps do you take as a firm to identify the conduct risks inherent within your business?
2. How do you encourage the individuals who work in front, middle, back office, control and support functions to feel and be responsible for managing the conduct of their business?
3. What support (broadly defined) does the firm put in place to enable those who work for it to improve the conduct of their business or function?
4. How does the Board and ExCo (or appropriate senior management) gain oversight of the conduct of business within their organisation and, equally importantly, how does the Board or ExCo consider the conduct implications of the strategic decisions that they make?
5. Has the firm assessed whether there are any other activities that it undertakes that could undermine strategies put in place to improve conduct?

FCA supervisors use these lines of inquiry to probe directors and senior

32 Derville Rowland, 'We continue to challenge the effectiveness of the underlying culture in banks' (7 February 2018), available at: <https://www.centralbank.ie/news/article/challenge-underlying-culture-in-banks-derville-rowland-7-February-2018> (accessed 30 November 2018).

33 FCA, *Business Plan 2016/17*, 34, available at: <https://www.fca.org.uk/publication/corporate/business-plan-2016-17.pdf> (accessed 30 November 2018).

34 FCA, 5 Conduct Questions Programme (02 May 2018), available at: <https://www.fca.org.uk/firms/5-conduct-questions-feedback> (accessed 30 November 2018).

managers' efforts to identify potential cultural weaknesses in their firm and reduce misconduct risk. The '5 Conduct Questions' framework also allows the FCA to compare and contrast firms' efforts to combat misconduct, and to share the range of practices across the industry. More generally, in recent speeches, the FCA has set out the four key 'levers' for managing culture that it reviews to assess how the management of a firm is managing the culture of the firm:

- 'The first lever is a clearly communicated sense of purpose and approach. Clearly communicating the 'what' and the 'how' are very important to getting a firm to work effectively and efficiently. But they pale into the background when contemplating the power and effect of a well communicated and resonant 'why'. It is the tacit understanding, shared by employees, of a company's true purpose. This is not necessarily what is articulated formally in a company's mission statement and values. I often learn more about a firm's sense of meaning by reading the strategic plans. And I suspect that employees do too.
- The second lever available to senior managers is 'tone from the top' – what staff hear and see from senior management. What are the behaviours that senior managers role model to their employees?
- The third lever is the formal governance processes and structures, the policies and systems that specify expected behaviours and decisions. From a conduct culture point of view, we look for a well thought through conduct risk framework: is there a clear exposition of conduct risks, the systems and controls for mitigating them and risk indicators for monitoring them?
- Finally, there are people related practices, including incentives and capabilities. Remuneration, promotion and recognition criteria all matter. Does a firm's pay structure reward misconduct? Is the pressure to turn a profit driving employees to act against consumers' interests?
- People capabilities are becoming more and more important to having the right culture. It's not enough to be motivated to behave in a new way; people also need to understand how to be successful with the new behaviours.'[35]

Ireland

In recent speeches, the CBI has indicated that the culture of firms is 'critically important'.[36] The CBI carries out supervisory reviews of the culture of financial institutions. It is also, as required by the Minister for Finance and Public Expenditure and Reform, preparing a report for the Minister on 'the current

---

35 Jonathan Davidson, Culture and conduct–extending the accountability regime', (City and Financial Summit, London, September 2017), available at: <https://www.fca.org.uk/news/speeches/culture-conduct-extending-accountability-regime> (accessed 30 November 2018).

36 Ed Sibley, 'Is it legal? A Question of Culture' (Eversheds Sutherland conference: Leadership and Culture Change in Financial Services, November 2017), available at: <https://www.centralbank.ie/news/article/is-it-legal-a-question-of-culture---deputy-governor-ed-sibley> (accessed 1 March 2018).

cultures and behaviours and the associated risks in the retail banks today and the actions that may be taken to ensure that banks prioritise customer interests in the future.'[37] The CBI's review of firms' culture includes a review of firms' diversity and inclusion culture, given that, in the view of the CBI,

> 'a lack of diversity at senior management and board level in organisations is a leading indicator of elevated behaviour and culture risks, and consequently prudential and conduct risks' and 'there remains a serious deficit in diversity of background, experience, and, critically, thinking at senior levels in financial services in Ireland'.[38]

The CBI has also stated,

> 'diversity is supervisable. We can legitimately expect regulated firms to meaningfully address diversity and inclusion in the boardroom, at the executive level and the pipeline of talent needed to run the organisation in the long-term'.[39]

In March 2017, the CBI introduced a new Consumer Protection Risk Assessment Framework (CPRA).[40] The purpose of the CPRA model is to provide the CBI with a framework to assist supervisors in carrying out an assessment of how consumer protection risk is managed within regulated firms. The CBI's expectation is that, over time, all firms engaged in the provision of financial services will have risk management structures that are aligned to this framework, proportionate to the nature, scale and complexity of the firm. Underpinning the CPRA is 'people and culture'. As part of this, the CBI has listed aspects of a firm's behaviours and culture that the CBI will review as part of its supervisory activities[41]:

- 'Clear documentation of the vision and values in the firm, specifically in relation to treatment of consumers and this is evidenced by, for example consideration of the impact of the firm's decisions on its customers;
- The firm can demonstrate, with clear examples, how leadership actions and communications are encouraging a culture of consumer protection throughout the firm, from top to first line;

---

37 Pascal Donoghue, 'Statement on the tracker mortgage examination' (25 October 2017); available at: <http://paschaldonohoe.ie/statement-on-the-tracker-mortgage-examination/> (accessed 30 November 2018).

38 Ed Sibley, 'The Importance of Diversity in Financial Services' (FuSIoN Network, 13 February 2018), available at: <https://www.centralbank.ie/news/article/the-importance-of-diversity-in-fs-sibley-13-Feb-2018> (accessed 30 November 2018).

39 ibid.

40 CBI, 'Central Bank introduces new Consumer Protection Risk Assessment Model (28 March 2017), available at: <https://www.centralbank.ie/news/article/central-bank-introduces-new-consumer-protection-risk-assessment-model> (accessed 30 November 2018).

41 CBI, A Guide to Consumer Protection Risk Assessment, (March 2018), available at: <https://www.centralbank.ie/docs/default-source/regulation/consumer-protection/170328-cpra-guide-28-march-2017.pdf?sfvrsn=0> (accessed 30 November 2018).

- Clear oversight, responsibility and accountability for culture and behaviours related to consumer protection;
- Remuneration structures reward consumer protection behaviours over sales volumes;
- Performance management and remuneration processes include assessment of and reinforces employee behaviours relating to Consumer Protection Risk;
- Promotion process takes account of employees' behaviour, including where employees have/ have not consistently exhibited commitment to the firm's values and desired behaviours in relation to consumer protection;
- Employees are aware of escalation channels with respect to consumer protection matters, and feel they are encouraged to 'raise their hand' without fear of reprisal and can provide examples of where they have done this; and
- Consumer Protection Risk is tracked and monitored.'

On-site assessments by the CBI of firms, based on this CPRA model, results in the firm being provided with a risk rating. Where the CBI has identified risk concerns, it may impose a risk mitigation programme on the firm. More generally, in a recent speech, the Deputy Governor of the Central Bank, Ed Sibley, identified a number of 'clear actions' that firms can take to seek to ensure that their culture is improved and is in line with the culture espoused by the Board of the firm. These 'clear actions' include:

> 'The board taking responsibility for the culture of the firm and understanding the behaviours that culture drives — for example through the … measurement or monitoring by the board of the firm's culture ...'; … 'The board actively promoting diversity and inclusion at all levels of the firm to improve decision-making'; 'Requiring Internal Audit to include a culture audit in the annual audit plan'; 'Ensuring all three lines of defence have a responsibility for driving culture at a business line level rather than enterprise level so that culture is truly embedded in the institution's risk management framework'; 'Ensuring incentivisation (in its broadest sense, i.e. not just financial) is fundamentally linked to appropriate behaviours, for example, ensuring promotion, recognition, and the variable compensation element of remuneration is consistent with the behaviours expected of employees to ensure the culture of the firm is reinforced'; 'actively celebrating, incentivising (e.g. recognising and promoting), those who come forward to identify issues and behaviours that are not in line with or are at least risk factors regarding the espoused values and desired culture of the firm.'[42]

In July 2018, the CBI published its report on 'Behaviour and culture of the

[42] Ed Sibley, 'Is it legal? A Question of Culture' (Eversheds Sutherland conference: Leadership and Culture Change in Financial Services, November 2017), available at: <https://www.centralbank.ie/news/article/is-it-legal-a-question-of-culture---deputy-governor-ed-sibley> (accessed 1 March 2018).

Irish retail banks'.[43] The report notes that consumer-focused culture in the Irish retail banks remained under-developed and that all of these banks 'have a distance to travel'[44] in their transformation towards a more consumer-focused organisational culture. It states that several of the banks' executive committees displayed 'firefighting behaviour', focusing on urgent and short-term issues, which was reminiscent of a crisis-era mindset – this limited the time available to senior executives to undertake the kind of proactive engagement with staff that is necessary to promote new behaviours. The report also concludes that the CBI had concerns regarding 'command and control' leadership styles and a lack of empowerment and decision-making ability of senior staff. Also, 'the banks have much more work to do in terms of ensuring their organisations are sufficiently diverse and inclusive, particularly at senior level, to prevent group-think, guard against over-confidence and promote internal challenge.'[45]

The July 2018 CBI report stated that each of the five retail banks covered by the report would be provided with an individual Risk Mitigation Programme, requiring each bank to devise and implement an action plan to address each of the CBI's findings in respect of them. Also, the CBI recommended that it be given power under legislation to introduce an enhanced Individual Accountability Framework, that would include:

- Conduct Standards, setting out the standard of behaviour the CBI expects of firms and individuals working within them, a breach of which would be subject to possible enforcement action;
- A Senior Executive Accountability Regime, along the lines of the UK Senior Managers and Certification Regime;
- Enhancements to the current Fitness & Probity regime, in particular to strengthen the onus on firms to proactively assess the fitness and probity of persons in the firm who fall within the scope of the Fitness & Probity regime;
- A unified enforcement process, applying to all contraventions by firms or individuals of financial services legislation (including to remove the hurdle of 'participation' by an individual in a breach by the firm in order to progress a case against an individual under the Administrative Sanctions Process).

On 25 October 2018, the Minister for Finance and Public Expenditure and Reform, Paschal Donohoe, announced that, on the back of the CBI's July 2018 report, he plans to introduce a new Central Bank Amendment Bill in early 2019 that 'addresses the recognised failings set out by the Culture Report'.

---

43 Central Bank of Ireland, *Behaviour and culture of the Irish retail banks*, (CBI 2018), available at: <https://www.centralbank.ie/docs/default-source/publications/corporate-reports/behaviour-and-culture-of-the-irish-retail-banks.pdf?sfvrsn=2> (accessed 30 November 2018).

44 ibid 4.

45 ibid 5.

Irish Banking Culture Board

On 31 December 2017, the Minister for Finance and Public Expenditure and Reform, Paschal Donohoe, announced that the chief executives of the five main retail banks in Ireland (Allied Irish Banks, Bank of Ireland, KBC, Permanent TSB and Ulster Bank) had informed the Department of Finance of their intention to establish an Irish Banking Standards Board (since renamed the Irish Banking Culture Board, IBCB), to be modelled on the UK Banking Standards Board. It is anticipated that the new IBCB will be operational in early 2019. As set out in the Minister's announcement, it is envisaged that the core functions of the new IBCB will include:

- 'Promoting the highest ethical business standards by leading and overseeing the collective effort to raise banking industry standards;
- Driving a continuous improvement culture across the Irish banking industry for incumbents and new entrants by requiring participating banks to commit to a programme of improvement under the headings of competence, culture and customer outcomes;
- Setting standards of best practice by identifying activities where voluntary standards serve the customer and public interest and work with practitioners, regulators, government and other stakeholders to develop any required procedures;
- Developing a single banking industry code;
- Providing a best practice advisory role to assist banks in implementing and embedding new codes of conduct.'[46]

The IBCB, which will be funded by the retail banks and, according to the Minister's statement, is to be made up of expert people from across civil society 'all of whom are committed to and focused on enhancing competence, culture, reputation and trust across the Irish banking industry.'[47] Also, according to the statement issued by the Minister, the Board will not act as a lobbying or representative organisation for the retail banks.

The main activities of the UK Banking Standards Board have included an annual culture survey of its members (in March 2018, an overview of the results of its second annual comprehensive survey of 25 member banks and building societies, including survey responses from over 36,000 was published[48]), issuing Statements of good practice (its first, in relation to assessing fitness and propriety, was issued in February 2017[49]), and hosting thought-leadership events.[50] Also,

---

46 Pascal Donohoe, 'Minister Donohoe welcomes banking initiative that aims to rebuild trust in the industry' (31 December 2017), available at: <http://paschaldonohoe.ie/minister-donohoe-welcomes-banking-initiative-that-aims-to-rebuild-trust-in-the-industry/> (accessed 30 November 2018).

47 ibid.

48 UK Banking Standards Board, Annual Review 2017/18, available at: <https://www.bankingstandardsboard.org.uk/annual-review-2017-2018/> (accessed 30 November 2018).

49 BSB, 'Statement of Good Practice 1: Certification regime: assessing fitness and propriety', available at: <https://www.bankingstandardsboard.org.uk/bsb-fp-guidance/> (accessed 30 November 2018).

50 In March 2017, the UK BSB hosted an event at which eminent speakers provided insights.

in November 2017, the UK BSB published a Consultation Paper entitled 'What do good banking outcomes look like to consumers?'.[51] This Consultation Paper invites comments on the UK BSB's proposed approach and framework for assessing what a good banking culture and outcomes look like for consumers. The criteria it identifies in this paper for good consumer outcomes are: access; choice; clarity and transparency; safety and security; redress and being listened to; value for money; and fairness.

It will be interesting to see how the Irish BSB evolves in due course, in particular in light of the work of the UK equivalent body, and what impact it may have on the culture of financial services firms in Ireland. In this regard, a December 2017 paper from the New York Fed, entitled 'Misconduct risk, culture and supervision',[52] notes that firms tend to under-invest in addressing potential misconduct risk issues in their organization for various reasons including reasons related to 'market failure', such as the 'co-ordination failure' problem i.e. 'firms seeking to reduce misconduct risk face a coordination challenge, where short-term competitive pressures make it difficult to make long-term investments in cultural capital'. The New York Fed paper noted that the UK BSB 'should help solve coordination failures and drive industry solutions.' It will be interesting to see how effective the UK and Irish banking culture organisations will be at addressing this 'co-ordination failure' problem.

Some Thoughts on Key Relevant Factors Affecting Behaviours and Culture in Firms and the Role of the Regulator

Market Structure Issues

In broad terms, markets which are competitive and in which consumers can readily switch supplier and tend to do so are more likely to operate to the benefit of consumers and the firms in these markets are more likely to be customer-focused. Conversely, markets which are less competitive and in which consumers are unlikely to switch supplier readily are more likely to give rise to consumer detriment issues as firms have relatively less incentive to be customer-focused. As stated in a recent UK Competition and Markets Authority (CMA) retail banking market investigation report:

> 'The behaviour of customers can play a central role in providing competitive constraints on providers. This happens if customers are

In the lead-up to the event, the UK BSB commissioned a number of leading bankers, academics, law professionals and UK Board members to write short blog pieces on the issue of trustworthiness and banking See: UK BSB, 'Worthy of trust? Law, ethics and culture in banking', available at: <https://www.bankingstandardsboard.org.uk/worthy-of-trust-law-ethics-and-culture-in-banking/> (accessed 30 November 2018).

51 UK BSB, 'BSB Consultation: What do good banking outcomes look like to consumers?; available at:<https://www.bankingstandardsboard.org.uk/bsb-consultation-what-do-good-banking-outcomes-look-like-to-consumers/> (accessed 30 November 2018).

52 Federal Reserve Bank of New York 'Misconduct risk, culture and supervision' '(White Paper, December 2017) 12, available at: <https://www.newyorkfed.org/medialibrary/media/governance-and-culture-reform/2017-whitepaper.pdf> (accessed 30 November 2018).

> engaged and willing to search for and implicitly threaten to switch to another provider, which offers them a better deal. Conversely, a lack of customer engagement in the market reduces banks' incentives to compete.'[53]

Questions that therefore arise include: how competitive are financial services markets in Ireland? How readily can and do retail consumers switch supplier of financial services in Ireland? A June 2017 study by the Competition and Consumer Protection Commission, for example, found that the Irish mortgage market is 'distorted. It is characterised by a high concentration of a small number of lenders, limited competition between these lenders and low levels of entry by new players.'[54] Interestingly, in the UK, the Financial Conduct Authority is currently carrying out a market study of the UK mortgage market.[55] The study is exploring two questions in particular. Firstly, at each stage of the consumer journey, do the available tools (including advice) help mortgage consumers make effective decisions? Secondly, do commercial arrangements between lenders, brokers and other players lead to conflicts of interest or misaligned incentives to the detriment of consumers? The final report of this market study is expected to be published in Winter 2018.

As for the switching by customers of their supplier of financial services, a November 2017 bulletin from the CBI noted that the number of current accounts held by personal consumers in Ireland in H1 2017 was just over 5.28 million and that during this period the number of switches of current accounts was 2,715 i.e. a switching rate of 0.05%.[56] This rate of switching is considerably lower than the 3% annual rate noted by the UK CMA for personal consumer accounts in its study of the UK market, which rate the CMA considered to be 'very low' and was a factor resulting in the imposition of regulatory remedies on the banks.[57]

---

53 CMA, *Retail Banking Market Investigation, Final Report* (9 August 2016) para 74, available at: <https://assets.publishing.service.gov.uk/media/57ac9667e5274a0f6c00007a/retail-banking-market-investigation-full-final-report.pdf> (accessed 30 November 2018).

54 CCPC, *Options for Ireland's mortgage market* (15 June 2017) para 1.7, available at: <https://www.ccpc.ie/business/ccpc-publishes-mortgages-options-paper/> (accessed 30 November 2018).

55 Information on the FCA Mortgages market study available at: <https://www.fca.org.uk/publications/market-studies/mortgages-market-study> (accessed 30 November 2018).

56 CBI, 'Consumer Protection Bulletin – Current Accounts and Switching' (November 2017), available at: <https://www.centralbank.ie/docs/default-source/regulation/consumer-protection/compliance-monitoring/reviews-and-research/consumer-protection-bulletin---current-accounts-and-switching---november-2017.pdf?sfvrsn=5> (accessed 1 March 2018). The Irish government has also launched a 'Switch Your Bank Campaign'. See, Pascal Donoghue, 'Minister Donohoe Launches Phase Two of Switch Your Bank Campaign' (22 January 2018), available at: <http://paschaldonohoe.ie/minister-donohoe-launches-phase-two-of-switch-your-bank-campaign/> (accessed 30 November 2018). It noted, 'The Department of Finance is running this campaign as part of a range of competition measures agreed with the European Commission to raise awareness and promote customer switching in the retail financial product area. This was agreed in the context of the restructuring plans for AIB and PTSB. The campaign is being funded entirely by the two banks.'

57 CMA, *Retail Banking Market Investigation, Final Report* (9 August 2016) para 11.3, available at: <https://assets.publishing.service.gov.uk/media/57ac9667e5274a0f6c00007a/retail-banking-market-investigation-full-final-report.pdf> (accessed 30 November 2018).

With regard to the UK CMA's recent major competition investigation into the retail banking sector in the UK, under s 134 of the Enterprise Act 2002, the CMA may carry out an investigation of a market, to assess whether 'any feature, or combination of features, of each relevant market prevents, restricts or distorts competition in connection with the supply or acquisition of any goods or services in the United Kingdom or a part of the United Kingdom'. Where such anti-competitive effects are identified, the CMA is required to take such action as it considers reasonable and practicable to remedy, mitigate or prevent the adverse effects on competition.

The CMA found that, with regard to the supply of personal current accounts, a number of features of the market gave rise to anti-competitive outcomes. In particular: it was difficult for customers to compare different banks' products and services and there were few effective tools available to help them choose the best account; customers perceived that switching personal current accounts was burdensome and there was a fear that something would go wrong; few customers searched for better offers; and the number of customers switching PCAs, in part or in full, remained very low.[58] The CMA found that this combination of features:

> 'Leads to banks having unilateral market power over their existing market base. As a result, the incentives on banks to compete on prices, service quality and/or innovation are reduced.'[59]

As a result of these findings, in February 2017 the CBA announced a final order, requiring a range of changes in the banking industry, including measures to make switching bank accounts easier; 'Open Banking' under which 'for the first time innovative and secure apps will provide personalised services and information to cover all financial needs in one place, and make it easy for people to find out what bank account is best for them'; and requirements on banks to publish service quality statistics.[60] 'Open Banking' launched in the UK on 13 January 2018.[61]

In Ireland, whilst competition legislation is in place to address anti-competitive behaviours, such as anti-competitive agreements (e.g. cartels) and abuses of market dominance, no equivalent legislation to the UK Enterprise Act 2002 provisions dealing with reviews of market structure issues and imposing remedies exists.

Nevertheless, legislative changes (in particular the Second Payment Services Directive, known as PSD2) that facilitate market entry by technology and market innovators will likely have a material impact on future competition in financial services. Over time, PSD2 will facilitate greater competition and more choice for consumers. Also, as noted in a December 2017 New York Fed paper, 'We might also expect to see new entrants such as financial technology firms increase

---

58 ibid.

59 ibid para 11.5.

60 CMA, 'Open Banking revolution moves closer' (2 February 2017), available at: <https://www.gov.uk/government/news/open-banking-revolution-moves-closer> (accessed 30 November 2018).

61 Open banking website, available at: <https://www.openbanking.org.uk/> (accessed 30 November 2018).

market share over time if they are able to establish a stronger reputation and greater public confidence.'[62]

Financial Literacy Issues

It cannot simply be assumed that if the regulator requires firms to provide more information to consumers and makes it easier for consumers to switch supplier of financial services, this will impose a sufficiently material constraint on firms who may otherwise be inclined to engage in behaviours that are damaging to consumers' interests. There is still the problem that many consumers do not have a sufficiently high level of financial literacy to be in a position to make well-informed decisions about the financial services they wish to obtain. As noted by CBI Governor Philip Lane in a February 2017 speech:

> 'A vast empirical literature shows that consumers tend to make poor financial choices, taking on too much debt, misunderstanding investment risk and choosing financial products that do not match their needs.'[63]

Low levels of financial literacy is a problem that can enable poor behaviours and poor culture in financial services firms. This is clearly an issue in many jurisdictions; as noted in a recent European Banking Authority (EBA) report:

> 'Most NSAs [EU National Supervisory Authorities for banking] agree on the need to improve financial education. NSAs support this idea because of the increasingly complex financial choices that citizens must make, and some incidents of consumer detriment that they observed leading up to, during and after the financial crisis of 2008/9.'[64]

A cross-country comparison report on financial literacy, carried out by researchers from University College London and Cambridge University, which was published in March 2018, evidences the extent of the problem in various countries, including Ireland. The authors of the report concluded, with regard to England (and the data in the report relating to Ireland indicates that these conclusions are equally relevant for Ireland):

> 'This new research highlights how England is facing a crisis in terms of adults' financial literacy skills. We all need to be able to conduct basic financial calculations in order to make rational well-informed decisions. This includes how much we should save into our pensions, understanding the financial implications of borrowing money from payday loan sites,

---

62 Federal Reserve Bank of New York 'Misconduct risk, culture and supervision' (White Paper, December 2017) 11, available at: <https://www.newyorkfed.org/medialibrary/media/governance-and-culture-reform/2017-whitepaper.pdf> (accessed 30 November 2018).

63 Speech by Governor Lane, 23 February 2017; available at: <https://www.centralbank.ie/news/article/financial-regulation-protecting-consumers-governor-lane> (accessed 30 November 2018).

64 EBA, *EBA Financial Education Report 2017/18*, para 37, available at: <http://www.eba.europa.eu/-/eba-takes-stock-of-lessons-learned-on-financial-education-across-the-eu> (accessed 30 November 2018). One of the mandates conferred on the EBA is to review and co-ordinate financial literacy and education initiatives by the competent authorities.

through to whether we can really afford to buy a particular house. Our results bring into question how many adults in England really have the skills to make such complex financial decisions. The reality is that many adults struggle to complete even quite basic financial tasks.'[65]

Regulators, including the Competition and Consumer Protection Commission (CCPC), can assist consumers by encouraging and facilitating financial literacy e.g. through making relevant financial comparison information available to consumers in user-friendly formats (some such information is currently available on the website of the CCPC)[66] and ensuring consumers are more aware of their biases which can negatively influence their financial decisions; regulators can also further support the development of behavioural economics research into consumer decision-making in relation to financial products.[67] Regulators can also assist consumers through supervisory efforts to ensure that firms develop a more customer-focused culture. As noted by Governor Lane:

> 'We see a positive consumer-focused culture as one in which financial services firms communicate clearly with their customers, help customers to understand the financial products and options available to them and to make the financial decisions that best meet their needs. It is a culture in which consumers can be confident that firms are acting in their best interests. It is a culture in which boards and senior management set the tone through their commitment to achieving good outcomes for their customers. It is a culture where a firm engages constructively with customers who have queries or complaints and which rectifies its errors or mistakes. It is a culture where staff are incentivised to build good customer relationships and to aim to sell appropriate products rather than large numbers of products.'[68]

An Evidence-Based Approach to Assessing Culture

The UK Banking Standards Board has stated that 'to keep heading in the right direction, we need an understanding of the culture of banking that is based on evidence.'[69] Also, as noted by Bill Dudley, President and CEO of the New York

---

65 Aditi Bhutoria, John Jerrim, and Anna Vignoles, 'The financial skills of adults across the world. New Estimates from PIAAC' (March 2018 report), available at: <https://www.ucl.ac.uk/news/news-articles/0318/140318_financial_literacy> (accessed 30 November 2018).

66 CCPC, 'Financial Comparisons', available at: <https://www.ccpc.ie/consumers/financial-comparisons/> (accessed 30 November 2018).

67 See, for example, the work of the ESRI: Pete Lunn , Marek Bohacek, and Alicia Rybicki, 'An experimental investigation of personal loan choices' (July 2016); available at:<https://www.esri.ie/pubs/BKMNEXT314.pdf> (accessed 30 November 2018). See also, the recognition by the CBI of the importance of behavioural economics on devising regulatory requirements: Derville Rowland, 'Our culture assessments will analyse the leadership behaviour of management in banks', available at: <https://www.centralbank.ie/news/article/derville-rowland-speech-prague> (accessed 30 November 2018).

68 Philip Lane, 'The Role of Financial Regulation in Protecting Consumers' (University College Cork, February 2017), available at: <https://www.centralbank.ie/news/article/financial-regulation-protecting-consumers-governor-lane> (accessed 30 November 2018).

69 UK Banking Standards Board, *Annual Review 2016/17*, Chairman's Foreword, available at: <https://www.bankingstandardsboard.org.uk/annual-review-2016-2017/>.

Fed, 'Since the beginning of our work on culture, my colleagues and I have recognized that measurement is indispensable to improving bank culture.'[70] Indeed, in a recent speech, the Director of Insurance Supervision of the CBI stated that firms:

> 'need to find a way of measuring your culture and tracking cultural change as *'To measure is to know and what gets measured gets done.'* We would expect a company to have KPIs for financial performance and KRIs for risk appetite, likewise time and effort should be put into considering how you could develop measures for your culture.'[71]

As to the role of the regulator in ensuring that firms meet this expectation, it is noted, for example, that the CBI's Consumer Protection Risk Assessment framework, firms are expected to have in place 'a comprehensive risk management process, which is underpinned by the culture and behaviours within the firm'.[72] Appendix 1 of this CBI Guide on this issue lists a number of measurable factors, including those relating to culture (e.g. re training attending by Board/senior management; analyses of consumer complaints; root cause analyses), in respect of which firms could gather data in order to have a comprehensive overview of risk factors. Also, this approach is not necessarily specific to the management of consumer protection risks:

> 'There is no requirement to develop a separate and discrete framework for Consumer Protection Risk management, rather it is preferable that it is embedded throughout the firm's risk management and internal control framework.'[73]

Where the CBI considers that a firm does not have appropriate mechanisms in place to monitor its culture, the CBI could choose to impose relevant requirements on the firm, through e.g. a risk mitigation programme to address any risk issues.

More generally, the CBI carries out culture audits of credit institutions. As noted above, it recently carried out a culture review of the five main Irish retail banks. Whilst the detail of any actions the CBI requires of the banks arising from this review has not been published by the CBI (this is set out in individual Risk Mitigation Programmes provided by the CBI separately to each of the banks), such reviews may provide opportunities for the CBI to impose requirements

---

70 William Dudley, 'Reforming Culture for the Long Term' (21 March 2017), available at: <https://www.newyorkfed.org/newsevents/speeches/2017/dud170321> (accessed 30 November 2018).

71 Sylvia Cronin, 'The role of Culture in Insurance Supervision' (Association of Compliance Officers in Ireland, January 2017), available at: <https://www.centralbank.ie/news/article/remarks-by-director-insurance-supervision-sylvia-cronin-at-the-association-of-compliance-officers-in-ireland> (accessed 30 November 2018).

72 CBI, A Guide to Consumer Protection Risk Assessment (March 2017), 13, available at: <https://www.centralbank.ie/docs/default-source/regulation/consumer-protection/170328-cpra-guide-28-march-2017.pdf?sfvrsn=0> (accessed 30 November 2018).

73 ibid.

where it considers that the Board/senior management of a firm does not have adequate mechanisms in place to gather data and review such data relating to its culture that may impact on its approach to risk-taking and ethical behaviours. Also, as stated by Derville Rowland, Director General of the CBI, in a recent speech:

> 'This review [of the five retail banks] will shape our future supervisory and engagement strategy. Depending on what we uncover, we may require certain mitigating actions at our lending institutions. These could include, for example, requiring the lenders to conduct an annual internal audit of culture; requiring the boards of the lenders to set up ethics sub-committees; and linking incentivisation to appropriate behaviours'.[74]

In addition, under the Corporate Governance Requirements for Credit Institutions 2015, the Board of a credit institution is required to formally review its overall performance and that of individual directors, relative to the Board's objectives, at least annually and to document such review. The outcome of such reviews will provide further information to the CBI on how a firm's Board is monitoring the firm's culture and enable the CBI to intervene where it is not satisfied that the Board is doing enough to monitor the firm's culture in an effective way. Accordingly, it is important for firms to identify and monitor on a continuous basis relevant data relating to factors that influence culture, in order to be in a position to identify, supervise and influence their firm's culture effectively.

It seems that, in order for Boards to understand and influence the culture of their firm, they should have available to them trend data around the four key risk culture indicators identified by the G20 Financial Stability Board.[75] The first factor is the tone from the top. How, for example, is the Board satisfying itself that the espoused core values and expectations of the firm in relation to ethical and compliant conduct is known and understood across the firm? Reviews/360 degree review processes to assess the 'tone' of the Board and senior management in relation to the espoused values and expectations of the firm). The second factor is accountability. Is there evidence of consequences for individuals who fail to comply with the firm's espoused values and expectations in relation to conduct? The third factor is effective communication and challenge. Is there, for example, evidence of individuals 'speaking up' in relation to potential breaches of the firm's espoused values or expectations in relation to conduct and how this has been addressed? The fourth factor relates to incentives. Is there evidence, for example, of how the firm's staff incentives structures encourage ethical and compliant behaviours and how effective this is in practice?

---

74 Derville Rowland, 'Our culture assessments will analyse the leadership behaviour of management in banks' (The European Consumer Protection Conference in Prague, March 2018), available at: <https://centralbank.ie/news/article/derville-rowland-speech-prague> (accessed 30 November 2018).

75 FSB, 'Guidance on supervisory interaction with financial institutions on risk culture: A framework for assessing risk culture', available at: <http://www.fsb.org/2014/04/pr_140407/> (accessed 30 November 2018).

Also, it is considered important for firms to carry out some form of firm-wide culture survey, on a reasonably regular basis, as a form of diagnostic tool to identify any potential issues and assess progress. There is a wide variety of commercially available culture review consultancy services available to firms to assist them in assessing their internal culture, most of which would include the carrying out of internal staff surveys as part of the culture review process, to gauge staff perceptions of 'how things get done around here' and, for example, the extent to which the firm actually operates in accordance with its espoused values. As noted above, in March 2018, the UK Banking Standards Board published the high-level results of its second comprehensive annual culture survey of its members. There are a number of benefits from this survey. It provides benchmarked results to the firms involved so they can assess where they stand in relation to an industry norm. Also, as the survey is intended to be carried out annually, they will be in a position to assess their progress over time.

Aligning the 'Accountability' and 'Behavioural Change' Regulatory Objectives

Accountability is clearly a very important regulatory objective for the financial services regulator. Where regulatory issues arise, the regulator has a range of enforcement tools to hold firms and individuals to account for regulatory failings. Whilst 'accountability' is a particularly important regulatory objective for the purposes of identifying and resolving regulatory issues that have arisen, regulators need to be wary of assuming that increased 'accountability', in the form of more and higher sanctions, will result in improved industry behaviours (the deterrent effect of sanctions). The views of regulators internationally on this issue, outlined above, suggests that the deterrent effect of sanctions is, at best, limited. Overly-focusing on sanctions as a tool of deterrence may actually be counter-productive. It may result in a 'blame' culture in which firms and individuals in the firms are unlikely to engage constructively with the regulator about regulatory issues (other than in accordance with minimum legal requirements) and may be consciously or unconsciously disinclined to 'speak up' or carry out investigations of potential issues as to do so may result in evidence being produced which may be used by the regulator to sanction the firm and/or individual. This would simply result in many unethical behaviours/ breaches not being effectively addressed.

In an important recent study of the issue of the deterrent effect of enforcement action across various industries, Professor Chris Hodges and Ruth Steinholtz concluded that:

> 'Too many regulatory systems are built around the idea that anyone who breaks a rule is bad and that breaking rules needs to be deterred by strong punishment, This approach, however, is preventing ethical behaviour rather than increasing it. … Focusing solely on rules and responding to breaches of rules by deterrence and punishment simply does not work. … In fact,

> sometimes [regulators'] behaviour may act as a barrier to businesses acting ethically, albeit unintentionally.'[76]

Hodges' and Steinholtz's book develops their concept of a different approach to achieving the regulatory goal of behavioural change in regulated industries, based on their concept of Ethical Business Regulation: 'A relationship between public bodies and businesses based on a relationship of trust, built on suitable evidence that businesses (and public bodies) place ethical values at the core of their activities.'[77] Under their approach, the aim is to encourage firms and individuals to act ethically and adopt a 'learning' culture in which mistakes and breaches are investigated and remedied pro-actively by the firm in order to continually improve. Also, under this approach, firms would be encouraged and facilitated by their regulator (rather than sanctioned on the basis of a focus on the regulatory objective of 'accountability'), where there is clear evidence from the firm that it has acted and continues to act ethically. Clearly, however, firms and individuals acting unethically would not avoid sanctions. Also, such an approach only works where the regulated firms can be sufficiently trusted by the regulator (on the basis of a sufficient history of evidence from the regulated firm that it acts ethically) to address any ethical issues or breaches in an effective manner (including e.g. providing comprehensive redress to all customers who may have been financially disadvantaged as a result of breaches of requirements).

Firms may be more inclined to adopt this ethical and 'learning' culture if they conclude that acting ethically is good for their business. Hodges and Steinholtz find that 'there is ample and growing evidence that values-driven businesses are more successful and sustainable than others.'[78] This may lead to a more constructive relationship with their regulator which may lead to lower regulatory costs for them (e.g. general compliance costs; costs of sanctions, etc). The approach advocated by Hodges and Steinholtz places the onus on firms to decide for themselves as to whether they wish to develop such an ethical and 'learning' culture. In that respect, the approach fits with the views of a number of regulators that 'firms' behaviour will only transform for the better if change is chosen rather than imposed.'[79] This approach does, however, contrast somewhat with the supervisory approach of the DNB.

Whilst the DNB also considers that 'behaviour and culture are ultimately the responsibility of financial institutions',[80] the DNB's supervisory approach

---

76 Chris Hodges and Ruth Steinholtz, *Ethical business practice and regulation: A behavioural and values-based approach to compliance and enforcement* (Hart Publishing 2017) xxiv.

77 ibid xxxv.

78 ibid 110.

79 FCA, Transforming culture in financial services (DP18/2 2018), 4, available at: <https://www.fca.org.uk/publications/discussion-papers/dp18-2-transforming-culture-financial-services> (accessed 30 November 2018).

80 DNB, *Supervision of behaviour and culture: foundations, practice & future developments*; (DNB, 2015) 53, available at: <https://www.google.ie/url?sa=t&rct=j&q=&esrc=s&source=web&cd=1&ved=0ahUKEwjF8u7GyfrPAhUqDsAKHZTYDKgQFgggMAA&url=https%3A%2F%2Fwww.dnb.nl%2Fbinaries%2FSupervision%2520of%2520Behaviour%2520and%2520Culture_

involves in-depth assessments by the regulator of behaviour and culture in firms and making recommendations for change. This level of regulatory engagement has the considerable benefit of enabling both firms and their regulator gain a good understanding of behaviour and culture issues that may give rise to regulatory risk and how they can be addressed. There is, however, always the concern that if a firm is not genuinely committed to culture change, any requirements or recommendations from the regulator to the firm (e.g. to carry out a culture audit; to set up an ethics sub-committee of the Board) may result in the firm treating these requirements or recommendations as a 'box-ticking' exercise to satisfy minimum standards set by the regulator rather than trying to achieve meaningful culture change. In light of the particular history of financial services in Ireland, it might take some considerable time for an approach along the lines of that suggested by Hodges and Steinholtz to be accepted in Ireland. Nevertheless, there is merit for both the regulator and regulated firms in such an approach being pursued over time.

Conclusion

It is clear that, as noted by various financial services regulators globally, culture and ethics are at the heart of banks' decisions in terms of risk-taking and safe and sound management practices and are, therefore, key concerns for regulators. The increased focus by the CBI on supervision of culture in financial institutions is part of an international trend amongst regulators that can be expected to develop. The outcome of the CBI's on-going review of the culture of the five retail banks in Ireland will likely give further impetus to this. It is therefore incumbent on financial services firms to address their culture, as a key driver of behaviours relating in particular to risk-taking and to customer-focus. In order for this to be done effectively, the regulator has an important role not simply to 'enforce' minimum standards but also to provide guidance in order to assist in raising standards generally, through raising the level of expectations within industry as to what is acceptable behaviour and to work constructively with firms and industry generally (e.g. through the forthcoming Irish Banking Culture Board) to support their efforts at improving their cultures.

---

tcm46-334417.pdf&usg=AFQjCNFFrjy79m7BrKZ380NArue5nREXxg&bvm=bv.136811127,d.ZGg> (accessed 1 March 2018).

Chapter 7

CORPORATE WRONGDOING: THE CIVIL ENFORCEMENT TOOLKIT

*Mary Catherine Lucey**

Introduction

A reorientation of corporate enforcement in Ireland towards a regulatory enforcement architecture which, in contrast to conventional criminal law, is more concerned with efficiency, pragmatism, prevention and the management of risk has been identified.[1] The civil enforcement arsenal of a regulator and an enforcement agency are explored in this chapter.[2] By focussing specifically on the Central Bank of Ireland and the Competition and Consumer Protection Commission (CCPC),[3] this chapter hopes to crisply illustrate the polar extremes of a spectrum of civil enforcement tools. Shining a light on the measures available to the banking regulator is worthwhile not least because it accentuates the shortcomings of the toolkit available to the competition law enforcement agency.

This chapter pays attention to two types of instruments which allow the regulator and the agency to tailor civil pragmatic measures to tackle perceived corporate wrongdoing. These are, firstly, specific responses to particular instances of corporate wrongdoing and, secondly, advocacy and transparency initiatives broadly defined. By highlighting how these measures function in practice at the hands of a regulator and an agency it is hoped to demonstrate their contrasting sway or clout *vis-a-vis* corporate wrongdoers.

The contentious question of what constitutes 'white-collar crime' is examined thoroughly elsewhere in this collection. The approach of this chapter is to adopt a

* Associate Professor, Sutherland School of Law, University College Dublin. Non Governmental Advisor, Competition and Consumer Protection Commission (CCPC).
The author expresses her gratitude for the helpful comments of anonymous reviewer.

1 Joe McGrath, *Corporate and White-collar Crime in Ireland: A New Architecture of Corporate Enforcement* (Manchester University Press 2015) 124.

2 On criminal enforcement, see Joe McGrath, 'The Prosecution of White-Collar Crime in a Developing Economy: A Case Study of Ireland in the 20th Century' in Judith van Erp *et al* (eds), *Handbook on White-Collar Crime in Europe* (Routledge 2015); Joe McGrath 'Sentencing White-collar Criminals: Making the Punishment Fit the White-collar Crime' (2012) 22(3) ICLJ 72; Ursula Kilkelly and Shane Kilcommins (eds), *Regulatory Crime in Ireland* (First Law 2010).

3 In order to contain the analysis, the operation of the CCPC under Consumer Protection legislation is not examined.

broad attitude to what could be connoted 'corporate wrongdoing'.[4] Responsibility for enforcement within the broad territory of corporate wrongdoing is placed, unevenly, by various Irish legislative enactments, across a range of organisations basically comprising regulators and agencies.[5]

There are, of course, significant legal and functional distinctions as between regulators and agencies. The classic conception of regulation is framed in terms of 'control and command' where conduct is shaped through standard-setting, monitoring, compliance and enforcement.[6] Competition law, at first glance, appears very different in that it largely comprises prohibitions in order to deter anti-competitive conduct.[7] Yet, it has been argued that drawing a clear-cut distinction obscures the extent to which regulation and competition overlap[8] and that some hybridization[9] is evident. Maher suggests a continuum where command and control regulation occupies one end of the spectrum while the ordinary workings of a market based on contract law and property rights are at the other end, and that competition law is located somewhere in between because it constrains freedom of contract to the extent necessary to ensure competition.[10]

Constitutional Context

At the outset, it is essential to, at least briefly, touch on the defining influence of *Bunreacht na hEireann* on the general design of enforcement in Ireland. Article 34 provides that:

> '[J]ustice shall be administered in courts established by law by judges appointed in the manner prescribed by this Constitution and, save in such special and limited cases as may be prescribed by law, be administered in public.'

This has been construed so that, in general, judicial power can be exercised by

4 For a discussion of individual liability, see Remy Farrell, 'Prosecuting Companies and Directors' in this collection.

5 These include, for example, the Office of Director of Corporate Enforcement, Irish Auditing and Accounting Supervisory Authority, Irish Financial Services Regulatory Authority, Commission for Communications Regulation, Commission for Energy Regulation and the Broadcasting Authority.

6 Christopher Hood, Harry Rothstein and Robert Baldwin, *The Government of Risk: Understanding Risk Regulation Regimes* (Oxford University Press 2001) 23.

7 Typically competition law prohibits anti-competitive collusion and anti-competitive unilateral conduct. For EU Competition Law, see Arts 101-102 TFEU. Many competition regimes also control mergers.

8 Imelda Maher 'Regulating Competition' in Christine Parker, John Braithwaite, Colin Scott and Nicola Lacey (eds), *Regulating Law* (Oxford University Press 2004) 187.

9 Niamh Dunne, 'Between Competition Law and Regulation: Hybridized Approaches to Market Control' (2014) 2(2) Journal of Antitrust Enforcement 225.

10 Imelda Maher 'The Networked (Agency) Regulation of Competition' in Peter Drahos (ed), *Regulatory Theory: Foundations and Applications* (Australia National University Press 2017) 693.

courts alone.[11] This interpretation has exerted a chilling effect on the legislature's preparedness to confer on administrative bodies any powers which risk being regarded as judicial. It may be argued that the legislature has been unduly cautious in light of Art 37 of the Constitution which expressly permits the exercise of 'limited' judicial powers by non-judicial entities in civil cases.[12] Moreover, the Constitutional articles dealing with criminal cases cannot be ignored because sometimes it is not certain in advance whether a particular fine may be characterised as criminal. This is because courts may examine the quantum of a fine and/or its intent (in particular to ascertain if it is punitive) and conclude that its effect renders it a criminal sanction.[13] Thus, Art 38.1[14] and Art 38.5[15] may come into play because they confer procedural and substantive rights on persons accused of a crime which, in general, are not vindicated in administrative proceedings.[16] The combined effect of these aforementioned Constitutional articles is to create a peculiar constellation of civil regulatory/ administrative enforcement models in Ireland which has evolved incrementally and discretely in a number of sectors.[17]

Civil Toolkit

This chapter intentionally does not consider core instruments of the 'command and control'[18] type (such as, for example, withdrawal of licences[19]) because they are, by their nature, confined to regulators. Instead, its interest lies in those more generic measures which might be of use to a range of organisations

---

[11] *Mc Donald v Bórd na gCon* [1965] IR 217 set out indicia of judicial power and the list included the imposition of fines.

[12] Art 37 provides '[N]othing in this Constitution shall operate to invalidate the exercise of limited functions and powers of a judicial nature, in matters other than criminal matters, by any person or body of persons duly authorised by law to exercise such functions and powers notwithstanding that such person or body of persons is not a judge or courts appointed or established as such under this Constitution.'

[13] *Melling v Mathghamhna* [1962] IR 1. See further Mary Catherine Lucey, 'Application of EC Competition Law–Some Implications of Bunreacht na hEireann' in Mary Catherine Lucey and Cathrina Keville (eds), *Irish Perspectives on EC Law* (Thomson Round Hall 2003) 79.

[14] Art 38.1 provides '[N]o person shall be tried on any criminal charge save in due course of law.'

[15] Art 38.5 provides that '[N]o person shall be tried on any criminal charge without a jury.'

[16] See further *Purcell v Central Bank and Ors* [2016] IEHC 514.

[17] See further Joe Mc Grath, *Corporate and White-collar Crime in Ireland: A New Architecture of Regulatory Enforcement* (Manchester University Press 2015). Also, see Colin Scott, 'Regulatory Crime: History, Functions, Problems, Solutions' in Ursula Kilkelly and Shane Kilcommins (eds), *Regulatory Crime in Ireland* (First Law 2010) 63.

[18] Robert Baldwin, 'Regulation: After 'Command and Control' in Keith Hawkins (ed), *The Human Face of Law* (Clarendon Press 1997); Christine Parker and John Braithwaite, 'Regulation' in Peter Cane and Mark V Tushnet (eds), *The Oxford Handbook of Legal Studies* (Oxford University Press 2003) 199.

[19] As Colin Scott put it '[I]n the armoury of tools and techniques for regulation licensing has a central place as the exercise of state control seeking to secure particular social and economic outcomes', 'Licensing as a Tool of Regulation and Governance' (2014) 36(2) CASS Journal of Law 35.

faced with corporate wrongdoing. It hopes to contribute to the discussion on the first issue examined by the Law Reform Commission Issues 2016 Paper, 'Regulatory Enforcement and Corporate Enforcement', on achieving a more standardised set of enforcement powers in Ireland.[20] Attention will next be paid, firstly, to settlements and administrative fines and, secondly, to advocacy and transparency initiatives.

Settlements and Administrative Fines

The operation in practice of settlements and administrative financial sanctions in the context of financial services regulation will be contrasted with their operation in respect of competition law enforcement. It will be suggested that the clout of these tools in the hands of the regulator exceeds that which is achievable by the competition law agency.

Settlements and administrative financial sanctions are the primary[21] civil enforcement tools for the Central Bank of Ireland when it suspects, on reasonable grounds, that regulated entity (or individual) is committing or has committed a 'prescribed contravention' of financial services law.[22] Its Administrative Sanction Procedure (ASP) contains a number of stages.[23]

The first phase of the ASP process is designed to allow the ending of the process by entering into a binding written settlement agreement. This facet is regarded by the Central Bank as being 'invaluable.'[24] It is the practice of the Central Bank to promote this option of an early settlement once the ASP commences. The rationale is that this option offers a clear incentive to engage with the Bank at an early stage and, moreover, allows for more efficient use of its publicly funded resources.[25]

Cases where the matter is not resolved by a settlement may be referred to an

---

[20] LRC IP 8-2016, available at <http://www.lawreform.ie/welcome/1-legal-system-and-public-law.378.html> (accessed 30 November 2018). More generally and for international dimension, see Karen Yeung, 'Better Regulation, Administrative Sanctions and Constitutional Values' (2013) 33 Legal Studies 312 and Rachael Barkow, 'Overseeing Agency Enforcement' (2016) 84 Geo Wash L Rev 1129.

[21] Central Bank of Ireland, 'Response to the Law Reform Commission Issues Paper 'Regulatory Enforcement and Corporate Offences'' (December 2017) para 22: 'While retaining its discretion to take summary criminal prosecutions where appropriate, the primary enforcement process …has been the ASP'.

[22] Part III C of Chapter 2, Central Bank Act 1942 and separately Securities and Markets Regulations.

[23] For a fuller account, see: Central Bank of Ireland, Outline of the Administrative Sanctions Procedures (CBI 2014), available at: <https://www.centralbank.ie/docs/default-source/regulation/enforcement/administrative-sanctions-procedure/legislation-and-guidance/outline-of-administrative-sanctions-procedure-2014.pdf?sfvrsn=2> (accessed 1 March 2018).

[24] Central Bank of Ireland, 'Response to the Law Reform Commission Issues Paper 'Regulatory Enforcement and Corporate Offences'' (December 2017) para 12.

[25] Central Bank of Ireland, Outline of the Administrative Sanctions Procedure, (2014) para. 4.2.4, available at: <https://www.centralbank.ie/docs/default-source/regulation/enforcement/administrative-sanctions-procedure/legislation-and-guidance/outline-of-administrative-sanctions-procedure-2014.pdf?sfvrsn=2> (accessed 30 March 2018).

Inquiry.[26] The Inquiry has competence to decide whether or not a 'prescribed contravention' is being or has been committed and to determine appropriate sanction(s). The findings of an Inquiry may be appealed to Irish Financial Services Appeals Tribunal (IFSAT)[27] and, thereafter, to the High Court. For completeness, it should be noted that the Central Bank would welcome the establishment of a specialised appeals body along the lines of the Competition Appeals Tribunal in the United Kingdom.[28]

The current ASP procedure may result in a range of sanctions including financial sanctions.[29] Following the financial crisis,[30] legislation in 2013 increased the level of fines so that financial sanctions on firms may be imposed up to €10m or 10% of firm's turnover.[31] The period from January 2006 to December 2017 saw the conclusion of 116 cases under this mechanism. Financial sanctions on firms (and individuals[32]) in total exceeded €61m. In 2016, in excess of €12m financial sanctions were imposed which amounted to a record annual total since 2006. In the experience of the Central Bank, the ASP has proved to be 'a robust regulatory tool… [which] can be used as part of an overall regulatory response to bad or substandard behaviour.'[33]

While settlements are a relatively long standing feature of competition law enforcement they occur in a different, less uniform and less efficient fashion that under the ASP In practice, there is considerable variation among the arrangements that are agreed in order to conclude competition law proceedings.

---

26 For guidelines on Inquiry, see Central Bank of Ireland, 'Inquiry Guidelines prescribed pursuant to section 33BD of the Central Bank Act 1942', (2014) available at: <https://www.centralbank.ie/docs/default-source/regulation/how-we-regulate/enforcement/administrative-sanctions-procedure/legislation-and-guidance/inquiry-guidelines-2014.pdf?sfvrsn=4> (accessed 30 November 2018).

27 Website of the IFSAT, available at <http://www.ifsat.ie/> (accessed 30 November 2018).

28 Central Bank of Ireland, 'Response to the Law Reform Commission Issues paper 'Regulatory Enforcement and Corporate Offences' (December 2017) para 58. For more information on the Competition Appeal Tribunal, see: <http://www.catribunal.org.uk/> (accessed 30 November 2018).

29 Other sanctions available to Central Bank of Ireland include caution/reprimand, suspension/revocation of authorisation. In the case of a regulated financial service provider (RFSP) it may issue direction to refund /withhold money paid or charged for provisions of a financial service.

30 For reports on the financial crisis in Ireland, the United Kingdom and the EU, see respectively Patrick Honahan, 'The Irish Banking Crisis Regulatory and Financial Stability Policy 2003-2008, *A Report to the Minister for Finance by the Governor of the Central Bank'* (CBI, 2010); Financial Services Authority, *The Turner Review: A Regulatory Response to the Global Banking Crisis* (Financial Services Authority 2009) 36-38 and High Level Group on Financial Supervision in the EU Chaired by Jacques de Larosière, *Report* (European Commission 2009). For an academic's assessment, see: Julia Black, 'Paradoxes and Failures: 'New Governance' Techniques and the Financial Crisis' (2012) 75 Modern Law Review 1037.

31 Central Bank (Supervision and Enforcement) Act 2013 increased financial sanctions and gave Central Bank competence to require redress to customers.

32 Financial sanctions of €1 million are imposable on an individual who is either a regulated financial service provider (RFSP) or a manager of RFSP.

33 Central Bank of Ireland, 'Response to the Law Reform Commission Issues Paper "Regulatory Enforcement and Corporate Offences"' (December 2017) para 10.

In the decades following the Competition Act 1991 a variety of settlement type practices with the Competition Authority and later the CCPC evolved without the benefit of an explicit statutory basis. Eventually, a formal mechanism was introduced by the Competition (Amendment) Act 2012 which allows the CCPC to apply for a High Court order which embodies the terms of a settlement type agreement and the breach of the court order would be punishable as; 'contempt of court'.[34] The mechanism entails a very large number of prescribed steps to be taken over a stipulated time frame.

In order to convey the operational complexity of this mechanism it is essential to set it out in detail rather than offering a summary. First, an agreement must be reached with the undertaking(s) under investigation to either take or refrain from taking specified conduct in return for the competition agency agreeing not to initiate court proceedings alleging an infringement. Then, the competition agency may apply for a High Court order containing the terms of the agreement. Notably, the court may make the order only if it is satisfied that several prescribed steps have been taken. These detailed requirements include: the undertaking having obtained prior legal advice and the competition agency, at least 14 days before making the application, publishing; i) the terms of the agreement on the competition agency's website; and ii) publishing (in at least two daily newspapers) a notice detailing its intention to make the application on a specified date in relation to an agreement published on its website. Moreover, the Act stipulates that an order cannot have effect until 45 days after it is made or, until the final determination is made if an application is made by a third party to vary or annul the order. The variation or annulment order can be made if the court decides that the original order would either: i) effect a breach of contract between the undertaking and the applicant third party; or ii) render a term in such contract with the applicant incapable of performance. If the competition agency wishes to annul or vary the second order, it may make an application to the court only if: a) the other party (i.e. other than the applicant) consents; b) the original order contains a material error; c) there has been material change in circumstance that justified varying the order; and d) the court is satisfied in the interest of justice that the order be varied/annulled. An order may be made for a maximum of seven years' subject to an extension of three years being granted to the competition agency. It seems that this procedure was used in one case[35] but not in subsequent cases which have been resolved outside this bespoke process.[36] Thus, it is fair to cast doubt on its usefulness in practice to the agency.[37]

---

34 Competition Act 2002, s 14B.

35 Enforcement Decision of the Competition Authority (Case coM/ LLloT) Resale price maintenance of FitFlop footwear products (19 April 2013), available at: <https://www.ccpc.ie/business/wp-content/uploads/sites/3/2017/02/E-13-01-FitFlops-Enforcement-Decision.pdf> (accessed 30 November 2018).

36 See, for example, The Competition and Consumer Protection Commission -and-Booking.com, available at: <https://www.ccpc.ie/business/wp-content/uploads/sites/3/2017/02/Booking-comSignedCommitmentsSeptember2015.pdf> (accessed 30 November 2018).

37 See further Mary Catherine Lucey, 'The New Irish Competition and Consumer Protection Commission: Is This 'Powerful Watchdog with Real Teeth' Powerful Enough?' (2015) 6(3) *Journal of European Competition Law & Practice* 185.

Thus, even in the aftermath of the enactment of a specific legislative basis, settlements are not streamlined. Some have occurred directly with the CCPC.[38] However, efficient (from the agency's perspective) resolution occurs only where the corporate entity decides to capitulate at an early stage. As this decision, on the part of the corporate entity, is based on a cost/benefit assessment it must be emphasised that the corporate entity knows it does not face the risk of financial fines being readily and immediately imposed on it. The CCPC (like its predecessor Competition Authority) does not have competence either to make a determination that an infringement of competition law has occurred or to impose any sanction. On this basis, the corporate entity may safely decide not to rush to engage in settlement discussions with the CCPC and, instead. await the next move of the agency. As well placed commentators have observed 'settlement is the CCPC's modus operandi, but often only after legal proceedings have been instituted and/or threatened.' [39]

Where the corporate entity is not inclined to engage in discussions around settling proceedings the only compelling option available to the CCPC is to initiate civil court proceedings seeking a court order in the form of either a declaration and/ or an injunction. It is important to stress that the agency cannot seek a financial sanction in these court proceedings. Fines for competition law violations can only be imposed by courts in criminal proceedings.[40] This leads to the observation that the absence of civil financial sanctions diminishes incentives for corporate entities to enter into settlements and explains the low number that have been concluded without the agency starting legal proceedings.[41]

The number of civil court cases initiated by the Competition Authority/ CCPC is small.[42] Of these a few have been resolved before judgment stage and it is noteworthy that their conclusion has taken various formats. For example, undertakings were given by the Irish Dental Association to the Competition Authority which were read out in the High Court.[43] In 2014, the Irish Medical

---

38 If the corporate entity is willing to offer acceptable promises the CCPC is amenable to rapidly closing a file. In *Irish Property Owners Association,* a press statement of IPOA released in December 2016 triggered the opening of a case by the CCPC which was concluded in January 2017 with undertakings and commitments. See: <https://www.ccpc.ie/business/ccpc-concludes-investigation-ipoa-following-retraction-signed-undertaking/>.

39 Philip Andrews, Paul Gorecki and David Mc Fadden, *Modern Irish Competition Law* (Wolters Kluwer, Law and Business 2015) 171. See also: CCPC, 'Civil Court Cases', available at: <https://www.ccpc.ie/business/enforcement/civil-competition-enforcement/civil-court-cases/> (accessed 30 November 2018).

40 See further Mary Catherine Lucey 'The New Irish Competition and Consumer Protection Commission: Is This 'Powerful Watchdog with Real Teeth' Powerful Enough?' (2015) 6(3) *Journal of European Competition Law & Practice* 185.

41 See: CCPC, 'Civil Court Cases', <https://www.ccpc.ie/business/enforcement/civil competition-enforcement/civil-court-cases/> (accessed 30 November 2018).

42 ibid.

43 CCPC, 'High Court undertakings secured from dentists following collective boycott', available at: <https://www.ccpc.ie/business/enforcement/civil-competition-enforcement/civil-court-cases/dentists-collective-boycott/> (accessed 30 November 2018), alleging boycott type activity.

Organisation (IMO) gave undertakings and commitments to both the High Court and to the CCPC.[44]

Far fewer settlements occur in relation to competition law than under the wholly administrative ASP procedure. The absence of any prospect of a civil financial sanctions for competition law violations means that corporate wrongdoers have far less to fear from enforcement action initiated by the CCPC than ASP proceedings. This is a reality which epitomises the enforcement challenges faced by agencies who are not regulators.[45] Mc Dowell has argued that administrative sanctions may be unconstitutional if they are imposed outside the context of a licencing system which entails a component of agreement.[46]

The (real and perceived) difficulties around extending competence to impose civil financial sanctions to agencies other than regulators should not be underestimated. For this reason, it is apt to recall some of the many unsuccessful attempts, made over several years, to secure the introduction of civil financial sanctions for infringements of competition law.

Civil Fines for Competition Law

In 2006, the then Legal Adviser to Competition Authority proposed the creation of new *sui generis* offences (being neither civil nor criminal) for regulatory law.[47] In 2007, the Competition Authority, in response to a Consultation,[48] proposed that courts have competence to impose fines in civil cases initiated by the agency.[49] The opportunity was taken during the economic crisis[50] to include the matter as part of the Economic Adjustment Programme between Ireland and the Troika.[51]

---

44 CCPC, 'High Court undertakings from the IMO following decision to withdraw services', available at: <https://www.ccpc.ie/business/enforcement/civil-competition-enforcement/civil-court-cases/irish-medical-organisation-high-court/> (accessed 30 November 2018).

45 James Hamilton 'Do we Need a system of Administrative Sanctions in Ireland?' in Ursula Kilkelly and Shane Kilcommins (eds), *Regulatory Crime in Ireland* (First Law 2010) 15.

46 Michael McDowell, 'Non-Criminal Penalties and Criminal Sanctions in Irish Regulatory Law' in Ursula Kilkelly and Shane Kilcommins (eds), *Regulatory Crime in Ireland* (First Law 2010) 129.

47 Noreen Mackey, 'Expanding Civil Penalties Constitutionally: Punishment without Crime? A Reflection on the Constitutional Issues Surrounding the Concept of Civil Crimes' (Competition Press Conference, Dublin, 28 September 2006).

48 The Department of Enterprise, Trade and Employment Public Consultation '*Operation and Implementation of Competition Act 2002*', available at: <http://www.ccpc.ie/s-07-008> (accessed 1 March 2018).

49 See General Proposal 3, paras 5.20-5.25 of the Authority's Submission of December 2007 to the Department of Enterprise Trade and Employment in response to the Department's Public Consultation on the Operation and Implementation of the Competition Act 2002, available at: <http://www.tca.ie/images/uploaded/documents/S_07_008%20Competition%20Act%20200 2.pdf> (accessed 1 March 2018).

50 See further Mary Catherine Lucey, 'So-called 'soft law' Attempts to Achieve Convergent Public Enforcement Tools; Identifying the Achilles' Heel of the Economic Adjustment Programme in Ireland' (2017) 5(1) J Antitrust Enforcement 150.

51 See Cathal Hanley and David Purcell, 'The Memorandum of Understanding on specific economic and competition policy conditionality for granting financial assistance; Irish point of view' e- Competitions No 37521 available at: <http://www.concurrences.com/en/bulletin/news-issues/may-2011/The-Memorandum-of-Understanding-on-37521#>.

Notably, the MoU of December 2010 contained a commitment on the Irish government to provide 'legislative reform empowering judges to impose fines and other sanctions in competition cases with a view to generating more credible deterrence.'[52] But, by April 2011, it was reformulated to a more general promise to make 'effective sanctions' available.[53] In June 2011, a joint paper from Gerald FitzGerald (Member of the Competition Authority) and David Mc Fadden (Legal Adviser to the Competition Authority) proposed that fines be imposable by a court in civil enforcement proceedings brought by the agency.[54] In 2011, the Competition Authority replied to *Consultation on White-collar Crime* proposing supplementing the criminal regime with civil fines so that 'sanctions will be available for those breaches of the law that are either not amenable to criminal prosecution or which simply do not bear the indicia of a criminal offence'.[55] In 2012, regulators and agencies made a submission to Irish Law Reform Commission which, inter alia, warned that the absence of 'fully empowered regulatory regimes comparable with other jurisdictions' may cause other positive improvements to the regulatory landscape to 'lose their value in application.'[56] In 2016, the CCPC made a written response to the Law Reform Issues Paper on *Regulatory Enforcement and Corporate Offences*.[57] Notwithstanding all these endeavours, subsequent legislative reform for competition law has not introduced civil/administrative financial sanctions, thus far.[58]

---

[52] Available at: <http://www.imf.org/external/np/loi/2010/irl/120310.pdf> (accessed 30 November 2018).

[53] It stated 'legislation to strengthen competition law enforcement in Ireland by ensuring the availability of effective sanctions for infringements [of competition law] as well as ensuring the effective functioning of the Competition Authority'. Attachment V MoU (First Update) (28 April 2011) 73. Note also the promise in the accompanying letter from the Irish government stating 'we will also ensure that the competition enforcement regime is reinforced by strengthening the powers of the Competition Authority' in para 27 of Attachment III, both available at: <http://www.imf.org/external/pubs/ft/scr/2011/cr11109.pdf> (accessed 30 November 2018).

[54] Gerald FitzGerald and David McFadden 'Filling a Gap in Irish Competition Law Enforcement; The Need for a Civil Fines Sanction', 3 June 2011 available at: <https://www.ccpc.ie/business/wp-content/uploads/sites/3/2017/05/2011-06-09-Filling-a-gap-in-Irish-competition-law-enforcement-the-need-for-a-civil-fines-sanction.pdf> (accessed 30 November 2018). It explained civil fines as ones imposed by courts according to the civil standard of proof which is 'balance of probabilities' unlike administrative fines which are sanctions imposed by a non-judicial body.

[55] Competition Authority Submission to the Department of Justice and Law Reform: White Paper on Crime Discussion Document No 3 Para 4.7 'Organised and White-collar Crime' February 2011 available at <https://www.ccpc.ie/business/wp-content/uploads/sites/3/2017/05/S-11-002-Submission-on-White-Collar-Crime.pdf> (accessed 30 November 2018).

[56] Submission to the Law Reform Commission Proposed New Programme of Law Reform 2012, para 10 and 12, available at: <https://www.ccpc.ie/business/wp-content/uploads/sites/3/2017/05/S-12-007-Submission-to-Law-Reform-Commission.pdf> (accessed 30 November 2018).

[57] Law Reform Commission Issues Paper on Regulatory Enforcement and Corporate Offences: Response of the Competition and Consumer Protection Commission (CCPC), available at: <https://www.ccpc.ie/business/wp-content/uploads/sites/3/2017/09/2017.09.19-LRC-Issues-Paper-CCPC-Response-FINAL.pdf> (accessed 30 November 2018).

[58] At time of writing the Competition and Consumer Protection (Amendment) Bill 2018 is at First Stage. See Dáil Deb 22 February 2018 vol 965, no 9, available at <http://

For completeness, mention should be made of the on-going EU dimension to competition law enforcement in Ireland. The European Commission staunchly believes that effective enforcement of competition law by national agencies is not possible if they lack competence to impose civil/administrative fines.[59] The lack of civil fines puts Ireland 'out of step'[60] with most EU jurisdictions.[61] As part of a drive towards more convergent enforcement at national level,[62] there have been several EU developments, including consultations,[63] which have culminated in a draft Directive.[64] This Directive may result in the introduction of civil financial sanctions in Ireland for infringements of competition law.[65]

The foregoing examination of the Central Bank's process demonstrates that settlements, when established in a credible context, offer an efficient and pragmatic tool to secure tailored promises which anticipate precise actions in compliance. The operation of settlement type arrangements in the field of

---

oireachtasdebates.oireachtas.ie/debates%20authoring/debateswebpack.nsf/takes/dail2018022200018#Q01200> (accessed 30 November 2018).

59 European Commission, *Ten Years of Anti-trust Enforcement under Regulation 1/2003: Achievements and Future Perspectives* COM (2014) 453, para 35: '[W]hatever sanctions a jurisdiction applies, it is generally recognised that antitrust enforcement cannot be effective if it is not possible to impose deterrent civil/administrative fines on undertakings' and at para 38: '[T]o make enforcement of EU antitrust rules more convergent and more effective throughout the EU, it is necessary to ensure that all NCAs have effective powers to impose deterrent fines on undertakings …. Important aspects in this regard are ensuring that NCAs can impose effective civil/administrative fines on undertakings….'.

60 OECD Competition Committee, Annual Report on Competition Policy Developments in Ireland (2003) para 9, available at <www.oecd.org/ireland/34720597.pdf> (accessed 30 November 2018). See also: Competition Authority, 2003 Annual Report (2004) 5, available at: <https://www.ccpc.ie/business/wp-content/uploads/sites/3/2017/03/annualreport2003.pdf> (accessed 30 November 2018).

61 Mary Catherine Lucey, 'Public Enforcement of EU Competition Law in Ireland: Appraising Divergence' (2016) 12 (1) Comp Law Review 9; Mary Catherine Lucey, '*Ireland: 'Out of Step'- Coping with Constitutional Concerns About Civil Fines*' (2017) Concurrences Review N° 2-2017, Art. N° 84009.

62 There is a view that 'it is therefore quite likely that only a legislative measure (which may take the shape of a Regulation 2) will lead to the convergence that is necessary to make the ECN fully effective.' See: Editorial Comments '*Public Enforcement of EU Competition Law: Why the European Antitrust Family needs a Therapy*' (2015) 52 CMLRev 1191, 1195. Also see: Konrad Ost '*From Regulation 1 to Regulation 2: National Enforcement of EU Cartel Prohibition and the Need for Further Convergence*' (2014) 5(3) Journal of European Competition Law and Practice 125.

63 The CCPC published its submission to European Commission consultation in 2016. See: CCPC, Empowering the national competition authorities to be more effective enforcers, available at: <https://www.ccpc.ie/business/wp-content/uploads/sites/3/2017/05/2016-02-23-Empowering-NCAs-final-uploaded-version.pdf> (accessed 30 November 2018).

64 Proposal for a Directive of the European Parliament and of the Council to empower the competition authorities of the Member States to be more effective enforcers and to ensure the proper functioning of the internal market 2017/0063 (COD) of 22 March 2017, available at: <http://ec.europa.eu/competition/antitrust/proposed_directive_en.pdf> (accessed 30 November 2018).

65 Of course, all depends on what is finally agreed and, additionally, perhaps whether it might benefit from Art 29 of the Irish Constitution. If civil/administrative financial sanctions were 'necessitated', they could not be challenged and struck down as unconstitutional by an Irish court. Art 26.4.6° confers shelter from challenge on the grounds of unconstitutionality to Irish acts or measures which are 'necessitated' by the obligations of EU membership.

competition law provides a telling contrast to those operating as part of the ASP toolkit. The ASP process is structured as a series of escalating stages which can culminate in the imposition of a civil financial sanction by the regulator. It is regarded by the Central Bank of Ireland as an 'adaptive mechanism which facilitates the imposition of a diverse range of sanctions and is an effective escalation tool.'[66]

The mention of a credible prospect of escalation is consonant with the enforcement pyramid model.[67] As Braithwaite recently observed the crucial point is that:

> 'responsive regulation is a dynamic model in which persuasion and/or capacity building are tried before escalation up a pyramid of increasing levels of punishment. It is not about specifying in advance which are the types of matters that should be dealt with at the base of the pyramid, which are so serious that they should be in the middle and which are the most egregious for the peak of the pyramid.'[68]

The kernel of the problem facing the CCPC (and other agencies) is the poor level of dynamism in the context of distinct progressive stages through which escalation towards plausible threat can efficiently occur.

Advocacy and Transparency

Advocacy and transparency measures are key instruments in the civil toolkit of regulators and enforcement agencies whose importance may not always be appreciated. In this author's opinion they deserve to find a core place in the enforcement priorities set by a regulator/agency.[69] They can make efficient and effective contribution to enforcement, especially in respect of deterrence and compliance. The importance of both compliance and sanctions for effective enforcement has long been recognised.[70] Settlements, compliance programmes and administrative financial sanctions can be characterised as advocacy and transparency tools on the basis that they offer an efficient means of increasing

66 Central Bank of Ireland, 'Response to the Law Reform Commission Issues Paper "Regulatory Enforcement and Corporate Offences"' (December 2017) para 10.

67 Ian Ayres and John Braithwaite, *Responsive Regulation: Transcending the Deregulation Debate* (Oxford University Press 1992). For a discussion of the application of the pyramid in Ireland, see Joe Mc Grath, *Corporate and White-collar Crime in Ireland: A New Architecture of Regulatory Enforcement* (Manchester University Press 2015) 150-177.

68 John Braithwaite, 'Types of responsiveness' in Peter Drahos, *Regulatory Theory Foundations and Applications* (Australia National University Press 2017) 117.

69 See Mary Catherine Lucey, 'The Chicken or the Egg?: Dilemmas in Framing Enforcement Priorities' (2018) 13 (1) Competition Law Review 1, 3 . On prioritising project selection by agencies, see: William E. Kovacic, 'Deciding What to Do and How to Do It: Prioritization, Project Selection, and Competition Agency Effectiveness' (2018) 13 (1) Competition Law Review 9.

70 Ian Ayres and John Braithwaite, *Responsive Regulation: Transcending the Deregulation Debate* (Oxford University Press 1992).

the knowledge of those affected by the wrongdoing and the knowledge level of other corporate entities.

The ASP is regarded by the Central Bank of Ireland as an 'effective means of implementing its agenda of credible deterrence.'[71] Public statements on the outcomes of ASP are issued by the Central Bank. The statements intentionally contain significant detail in order to maximise the deterrent effect on poor conduct across the wider industry. Their value, according to the Central Bank, lies in how they engender trust and confidence in the effectiveness of regulatory regimes; facilitate transparency; provide guidance; demonstrate to stakeholders the challenges which they face and how these might be mitigated.[72]

While the financial regulator has competence to establish redress schemes there is no equivalent competence for the CCCP in respect of competition law infringements. In this light it is interesting to note that settlements with the CCPC may contain specific commitments to issue public statements. For example, the recent settlement with a number of Irish universities agreeing to alter their procurement practice regarding tenders for the supply of graduation gowns includes a specific undertaking to state on their websites that students have the option of sourcing gowns from another source.[73] A less obvious cohort, but a more important one from a compliance perspective, which benefits from precise commitments to inform are those who may be somewhat unwitting (or even reluctant) participants in the wrongdoing. Trade or professional associations provide an excellent example. For example, the Irish Property Owners' Association (IPOA) gave undertakings and commitments to write to its members (landlords) stating that decisions on rent are to be made individually (and not collectively). [74]

There is some empirical evidence on the success of compliance programs in respect of obligations under consumer and competition law.[75] The introduction of detailed compliance programmes as part of settlement agreements with the CCPC appears to be increasingly popular and can be regarded as pursuing at least two objectives. The first of these is to efficiently secure future compliance by means of detailed promises to change specified aspects of conduct/practice and the second is to increase transparency and visibility. These twin themes are clearly discernible in cases against associations of businesses where the

---

[71] Central Bank of Ireland, 'Response to the Law Reform Commission Issues paper "Regulatory Enforcement and Corporate Offences"' (December 2017) para 22.

[72] ibid para 14.

[73] Another commitment entailed decoupling the supply of photography services and of gowns. See further: 'CCPC secures commitments in the supply of graduation gowns', available at: <https://www.ccpc.ie/business/ccpc-secures-commitments-supply-graduation-gowns/> (accessed 30 November 2018).

[74] CCPC concludes investigation into the IPOA following retraction & signed undertaking (20 January 2017), available at: <https://www.ccpc.ie/business/ccpc-concludes-investigation-ipoa-following-retraction-signed-undertaking/> (accessed 30 November 2018).

[75] For an empirical survey of Australian businesses see Christine Parker, Vibeke Lehmann Nielsen, 'Do Businesses Take Compliance Systems Seriously? An Empirical Study of Implementation of Trade Practices Compliance Systems in Australia' (2006) 30(2) Melbourne University Law Review 441.

settlement agreements are precisely tailored to ensure that the economic freedom of the individual members of the association is not unacceptably restricted and that the members (and sometimes consumers) are informed of this freedom by the association.[76]

Market Studies and Reports are another example of important advocacy measures which may be usefully undertaken by regulators and agencies. These are popular instruments of the Director General for Competition.[77] Market studies and Reports are almost always the beginning and not the end of the work of the Australian Competition and Consumer Protection Commission (ACCC) in a market. They provide the ACCC with essential knowledge, put an industry on notice and provide a framework for future action. In the words of its Chairman 'we don't write reports to then put them in a drawer.'[78] That said, agencies must be alert to the risk of studies and reports undertaken at the behest of government being viewed as 'long fingering devices'.[79] While the Competition Authority faced criticism for studies that took so long that they lost impact, the CCPC has been praised for prioritising short, sharp and snappy studies rather than encyclopaedic enquiries. [80]

The potential for advocacy and transparency tools to secure effective enforcement should not be underestimated, even if not easily measured. Descriptive statistics, (for example the number of cases concluded) which focus on outputs, reveal very little, if anything, about the impact or effectiveness of a civil enforcement project.[81] More valuable knowledge might be gained through use of reputation measurements such as, for example, a survey before and again after the intervention. Agencies in some other jurisdictions have adopted a very determined and emphatic approach to increasing visibility and transparency

---

[76] For example, the Irish Property Owners Association (IPOA) agreed to introduce a compliance program. See 'CCPC concludes investigation into the IPOA following retraction & signed undertaking' (20 January 2017), available at: <https://www.ccpc.ie/business/ccpc-concludes-investigation-ipoa-following-retraction-signed-undertaking/> (accessed 30 November 2018). Similarly, Independent Nursing Homes Ireland agreed to introduce a compliance programme as part of the commitments recently offered to the CCPC. See: 'The Competition and Consumer Protection Commission and Independent Nursing Home Ireland Company Limited by Guarantee trading as Nursing Homes Ireland Agreement and Undertakings', available at: <https://www.ccpc.ie/business/wp-content/uploads/sites/3/2018/01/CCPC-NHI-Agreement-and-Undertakings-.pdf> (accessed 30 November 2018).

[77] European Commission, Antitrust Sector Inquiries, available, available: <http://ec.europa.eu/competition/antitrust/sector_inquiries.html> (accessed 30 November 2018).

[78] See the speech of the Chairman, Rod Sims, at the launch of the ACCC 2018 priorities, available at <https://www.accc.gov.au/speech/2018-compliance-enforcement-priorities>.

[79] Vincent Power, 'An Analytical Review of the Choices/Priorities made by Ireland's Competition Authority / Competition and Consumer Protection Commission 1991-2016' (2018) 13 (1) Competition law Review 83, 96.

[80] ibid. The same author criticised, for example, the medical profession's report published in December 2010 which had been announced in 2001 and had 'a gestation period longer than that to convert a school leaver into a doctor.'

[81] See ICN Agency Practice Manual on 'Competition Agency Evaluation' (April 2016), available at <http://www.internationalcompetitionnetwork.org/uploads/library/doc1072.pdf> (accessed 1 March 2018).

around their work.[82] For example, the New Zealand Commerce Commission recently published, in one document, its five year vision and strategy for 2017-2022.[83] The Commission believes it is important to set out both its vision and its strategy 'so that all New Zealanders can understand the context for what we are doing, why we are doing it and what we aspire to.'[84] Its strategy specifically includes being trusted, influential and high performing.[85] The Commission recognises that achieving this strategy requires strong relationships with stakeholders in government, business and the community.[86] The Commission reports its progress towards its vision in statements of intent (SoI),[87] annual statements of performance expectations (SPE),[88] annual reports and, every four months, updates on its performance, including enforcement outcomes.[89]

A final remark must be made about the importance of advocacy and transparency initiatives (broadly understood) for enforcement. Such measures permit regulators and agencies not only to develop own capacity by building up expertise and human capital, but, additionally, assist in building support from the community.[90]

Conclusion

The choices made by agencies and regulators when taking enforcement actions affect the quality of what may be termed 'regulatory practice'. According to Sparrow,

---

82 See further Mary Catherine Lucey, 'The Chicken or the Egg?: Dilemmas in Framing Enforcement Priorities' (2018) 1 Competition Law Review 1, 4.

83 Commerce Commission New Zealand, Our Visions and Strategy 2017-2022, available at <http://comcom.govt.nz/the-commission/about-us/#vision> (accessed 30 November 2018).

84 Commerce Commission New Zealand, Our Visions and Strategy 2017-2022, 1, available at <http://comcom.govt.nz/the-commission/about-us/#vision>.

85 Commerce Commission New Zealand, Our Visions and Strategy 2017-2022, 16: 'To achieve our vision we must be a trusted and influential organisation'. Available at: <http://comcom.govt.nz/the-commission/about-us/#vision> (accessed 30 November 2018).

86 Commerce Commission New Zealand, Our Visions and Strategy 2017-2022, 16: 'We want all our stakeholders to be confident we are doing a good job and trust that we act in the best interests of New Zealanders to deliver the best outcomes for the best value. Strong relationships with stakeholders across government, business and in the community are essential for the Commission. We want to be accessible, responsive and easy to deal with.' Available at: <http://comcom.govt.nz/the-commission/about-us/#vision> (accessed 30 November 2018).

87 At least every three years, its work programme for the following four financial years is set out in a Statement of Intent (SOI).

88 Annually it publishes a statement of performance expectations (SPE) which outline its priorities, forecast financial statements, and performance measures for the next financial year

89 Enforcement updates provide information about complaints, investigations, merger applications, regulation determinations and reports. See <http://comcom.govt.nz/the-commission/about-us/performance-updates/> (accessed 30 November 2018).

90 See further: 2017 Global Forum on Competition (8 December 2017), available at: <http://www.oecd.org/competition/globalforum/small-competition-agencies-developing-economies.htm> (accessed 30 November 2018).

> '[T]he nature and quality of regulatory practice hinges on which laws regulators choose to enforce, and when; on how they focus their efforts and structure their use of discretion; on their choice of methods for procuring compliance.'[91]

Some of the tools which may be chosen by a regulator and an agency in Ireland were examined in this chapter with a view to highlighting their operation in practice.

Focussing on settlements and civil fines demonstrated how somewhat similar tools differed in their processes and their application by a regulator and an agency. The presence or absence of the credible threat of a financial sanction affects how settlements function in terms of their operational efficiency and, most likely, effectiveness. This was demonstrated by placing the ASP of the Central Bank of Ireland in juxtaposition with the settlement practice operated in respect of competition law. Where similar types of enforcement tools are applied dissimilarly by regulators and agencies the impact on corporate wrongdoers varies and the overall outcome is a fragmented, disjointed and likely less effective enforcement culture.

It is to be hoped that the fruits of the Law Reform Commission's project on regulatory enforcement will encourage the legislature to fortify the general civil toolkit by broadly conferring stronger civil enforcement competences more broadly on to agencies. Even if, notwithstanding the opportunities available under Art 37 of the Constitution, agencies are not granted power to impose administrative financial sanctions, there are cogent grounds to support the introduction of civil fines by *courts* in civil proceedings initiated by a public enforcement agency.

The other focus of this chapter was on tools of an advocacy nature which enhanced knowledge of and transparency around the enforcement work of agencies and regulators. Deterrence and compliance objectives can be efficiently pursued through various advocacy measures, including settlements (especially if they contain tailored compliance programmes). Market studies and reports play an important role in educating not only (actual and potential) wrongdoers but, also, the agencies/regulators and the community.

The most optimistic view of civil administrative enforcement in Ireland is that it is on the cusp of a new era in which more biting competences, such as administrative financial sanctions, will be conferred more extensively across a range of enforcement agencies tackling corporate wrongdoing. In any event, priority should be accorded by all agencies and regulators to a range of impactful advocacy and transparency measures as part of their civil enforcement strategies

---

[91] Malcolm K Sparrow, *The Regulatory Craft: Controlling Risks, Solving Problems, and Managing Compliance* (Brookings Institution Press 2011) 2.

CHAPTER 8

PROSECUTING COMPANIES AND DIRECTORS

Remy Farrell[*]

INTRODUCTION

It is perhaps to state the obvious to observe that there is a big difference between prosecuting a natural person on the one hand and a corporate entity on the other. The most obvious difference being that the former has a physical existence whilst the latter does not. Or to put it more bluntly, one exists in the real world whereas the other exists only by reason of a consensual imagining. The 18th century jurist Lord Chancellor Edward Thurlow stated the essential conundrum as follows: 'Corporations have neither bodies to be punished, nor souls to be condemned; they therefore do as they like.'[1] Whilst his conclusion that such bodies act with impunity due to their incorporeal nature may seem somewhat harsh, it does highlight a number of issues concerning some of the realities of criminal enforcement against companies. The purpose of this paper is to explore some of those issues. It also explores issues relating to the prosecution of the directors of corporate entities. Many of the issues that are considered below are innately technical in nature and really involve a consideration of the law's response to the fact that a company accused of a criminal offence does not enjoy a physical existence. However, before considering such granular issues of procedure and technical substantive law, it is useful to consider how the incorporeal nature of a company impacts on enforcement decisions more generally.

ENFORCEMENT ISSUES

On 17 July 2012 the *Guardian* published a story under the following headline: 'HSBC 'Sorry' for Aiding Mexican Drug Lords, Rogue States and Terrorists'.[2] The story concerned systemic money laundering engaged in by HSBC over a long period of time. During the course of hearings before the United States Senate, the bank apologised. It subsequently entered into a deferred prosecution agreement with US authorities and paid a fine of almost $2 billion. Notably, neither HSBC nor any of its staff were charged with any criminal offence. The *Guardian* headline is both pointed and pithy as it juxtaposes the conduct of

---

* Senior Counsel.

1 John Poynder, *Literary Extracts Vol. 1* (John Hatchard and Son 1844) 268.

2 Dominic Rushe, 'HSBC 'sorry' for aiding Mexican drugs lords, rogue states and terrorists' *The Guardian* (17 July 2012), available at: <https://www.theguardian.com/business/2012/jul/17/hsbc-executive-resigns-senate> (accessed 30 November 2018).

a major international financial institution with the conduct of drug lords and terrorists. The idea that the latter might escape prosecution for drug dealing, murder, terrorism and so on would rightly be regarded as extraordinary whereas the fact that the former routinely avoid prosecution for assisting in same now seems almost unremarkable. Such a situation highlights many of the specific issues that present themselves in the context of criminal prosecutions against companies.

The first and most obvious of these is that any prosecution against a company results in the punishment of the shareholders as opposed to those who are primarily responsible for the offending behaviour, i.e. the executives of the company. This is for the obvious reason that the primary (and often only) sanction available in a prosecution against a company is the imposition of a fine which primarily impacts shareholder value. Although it might be argued that impacting shareholders in this way will ensure that they are vigilant in ensuring that directors and executives do not contravene the criminal law such an argument is largely theoretical and remote. A related issue is the profile of those within corporate entities who are primarily responsible for offending. Very often such individuals occupy middle management positions and are responsible for the commission of offences by the company involving enormous sums of money in circumstances where the benefit to the relevant individual is modest. This leads to the conclusion that many such offences are best regarded as emergent properties of complex corporate structures rather than behaviour reflecting the will of the corporate entity or those who direct its activities at the highest level.

Another difficulty which can present itself, particularly in the context of very large companies, is the consequence of actually convicting such entities. In much the same way that many large financial institutions were considered too big to fail during the most recent financial crisis it could be said that some are also too big to jail. The HSBC case itself represents a good example. The Chancellor for the Exchequer of the UK prevailed on US authorities not to prosecute HSBC on the basis that it could lead to the collapse of the bank which, in turn might lead to consequences elsewhere in the financial system. Such considerations lead to intriguing moral and political questions which are beyond the scope of this paper. It is sufficient for present purposes to observe that these are considerations that simply do not apply to the prosecution of natural persons.

Finally, it can be said that unlike regular criminal offending the sorts of offences committed by companies fall, as a matter of definition, under the general heading of white-collar crime. The investigation and prosecution of such offences is very different to that of traditional offences, such as murder, armed robbery, terrorism and so on. Specifically, white-collar offences are much more difficult to detect in the first instance — there is often no *corpus delicti*. As such the enforcement of such offences is neither ubiquitous nor consistent. This gives enforcement by way of prosecution for such offences a quality of exceptionality. It follows that one of the primary purposes of such hard enforcement is to signal to the relevant industry or sector of the economy the consequences of wrongdoing particularly in circumstances where there may be some moral ambivalence as to whether the underlying conduct is wrong.

This chapter will set out these observations for the purpose of underlining and emphasizing that prosecuting companies is very different from prosecuting natural persons. This is true not only on the dry level of law and process but also from a moral, ethical and philosophical stand point. It leads to the conclusion that there are certain enforcement goals that are more difficult to achieve by criminal enforcement against companies than as against individuals. In turn, this calls for a consideration of how criminal enforcement action might be taken as against both companies and the individuals who run them.

Investigating Companies – Procedural Rights

Before considering some of the procedural and substantive issues that arise in the context of prosecuting companies, it is first necessary to give some consideration to issues that may arise during the investigative phase. Specifically, the extent to which companies may assert procedural rights. The most important such right that arises in the context of any investigation is the privilege against self-incrimination. This is a right that has its origins in the traditional judicial abhorrence of torture as a means of compulsion. In that sense it can be said that it is a right whose origin is innately tied to the corporeal. It is a somewhat surprising feature of the law in this area that very little attention has been paid to the question of whether companies enjoy the privilege and how it might interact with the various steps taken in an investigation.

Any consideration of international authority in this area gives rise to a somewhat confused picture. In the UK,[3] it has long been the position that companies do enjoy a privilege against self-incrimination whereas in the US the position is the opposite.[4] However, a somewhat more nuanced picture emerges from a consideration of European authorities.

In *OAO Neftyanaya Kompaniya Yukos v Russia* the European Court of Human Rights considered that a company enjoyed a right to fair procedures pursuant to Art 6 of the Convention in civil proceedings.[5] As a matter of logic it would seem to follow that a company ought to be in a position to assert Art 6 rights, including the privilege against self-incrimination, in the context of criminal proceedings. The European Court of Justice appears to have taken just such a view in the context of investigations into breaches of competition law under its administrative sanctions process. In *Orkem SA v Commission* the Court concluded that the Commission had contravened the privilege against self-incrimination by purporting to compel a company to answer various questions put to it in the form of a questionnaire.[6] Although an administrative sanctions

3 *Triplex Safety Glass Co. Ltd v Lancegaye Safety Glass (1934) Ltd* [1939] 2 KB 395.
4 *Hale v Henkel* 201 US 43 (1906).
5 *OAO Neftyanaya Kompaniya Yukos v Russia* App. no. 14902/04 (ECHR, 31 July 2014).
6 *Orkem SA v Commission* [1989] ECR 3282.

process of the sort under consideration in *Orkem* would not be considered to be criminal in the context of Irish law, it would be regarded as criminal for the purpose of the Convention in line with well-established authority.[7] Therefore, the identification by the Court of Justice of a privilege against self-incrimination in the context of administrative sanctions is essentially indistinguishable from the identification of an identical right in a traditional criminal context.

The Supreme Court of Sweden appears to have concluded as much in *Petrolia ASA v The Public Prosecuting Authority*.[8] Whilst the court acknowledged that such a right had not formally been identified by Strasbourg it considered that it must flow from Art 6 given the authorities described above. The court concluded:

> 'In the first place, as previously mentioned, general due process considerations indicate that legal persons are also protected. Secondly, it will in practice always be individual persons who make decisions and act on behalf of the company. It can be alleged that the coercion which the company's representatives are subject to when a company is the object of a criminal prosecution is significantly different to the coercion that a natural person is subject to when the criminal prosecution relates to him/her personally. However, even if the punishment which applies to the company may affect the company's representatives less, the issue is in my view more a question of a difference in degree than a fundamental difference which can provide grounds for legal persons not being covered by the protection against self-incrimination. The company's representatives may in many cases be in a situation in which there is no choice that makes it natural to identify them with the enterprise. One of the considerations behind corporate penalties is exactly to make the company's management act with greater care…'

It is of considerable interest that the judgment seeks, in part at least, to ground the existence of such a privilege in the fact that it will be the human actors within the company that are effectively compelled to make admissions. This gives rise to obvious questions as to whether it is permissible to seek to bypass a company's privilege by simply compelling the directors of the company to make admissions on its behalf. This would be on the supposition that such admissions could either be lead as evidence against the company or the directors called as witnesses against the company. There is no easy answer to such questions and it is beyond the scope of this paper to seek to answer it. Suffice it to note that there is authority both for and against the proposition that to do so would set a company's privilege at nought.[9]

Although there is no direct Irish authority on the question of whether a company enjoys such a privilege, it seems likely that the Irish courts would find the analysis of the European courts compelling. The Supreme Court has in the past been open

7 *Engel v Netherlands* (1976) 1 EHRR 647.

8 *Petrolia ASA v The Public Prosecuting Authority* (Case no. 2011/456) 1 June 2011.

9 *Rio Tinto Zinc Corporation v Westinghouse Electric Corporation* [1978] AC 547 and *Competition Commission v Nutanix Hong Kong Ltd* (CTEA 1/2017) 3 October 2017.

to receiving authority from the courts in Scandinavian Member States which are often published in English.[10] As such the decision in *Petrolia* is likely to be regarded as compelling. If it is the case that companies enjoy such a privilege then this is a matter that may have considerable significance in the investigative stage. This is because many prosecutions against companies are informed by evidence which is in the form of compelled admissions. For example, where a regulator requires a company to provide information to it in the course of a regulatory investigation. There is ample authority for the proposition that such compelled admissions are not actually admissible in evidence against the person (i.e. company) that made them.[11] Although there is a degree of uncertainty as to the law relating to the privilege against self-incrimination as regards companies, it remains somewhat surprising that such an issue as received so little attention in domestic jurisprudence.

Procedural Issues

Although the existence and legitimacy of corporate entities have been acknowledged as far back as the latter days of the Roman republic,[12] the reality is that criminal prosecution of companies only became routine in the 20th century. Another important reality is that the criminal justice system evolved over centuries with a view to prosecuting purely corporeal entities. The primacy of imprisonment as a sanction, deprivation of liberty pending trial, the concept of hard labour and the etymology of such expressions as *habeas corpus* all speak to the underlying assumption that the accused will present in the corporeal form before a court. Indeed, much court procedure requires as much or at least assumes it.

It is hardly surprising then that there are a number of procedural steps in the criminal process that give rise to some difficulties due to the incorporeal nature of corporate bodies. The most obvious such steps are:

- electing for trial on indictment or summary trial;
- receiving the alibi warning on the occasion of being sent forward for trial;
- challenging jurors — although in practice this will be done by the solicitor for the company assuming one is present;
- objecting to the use of 'Section 21 Notices' or certificates under the Criminal Evidence Act;
- Entering a plea of guilty or not guilty.

The difficulties are well illustrated by the case of *The State (Batchelor & Co*

---

10 *Minister for Justice, Equality and Law Reform v Murphy* [2010] IESC 17.

11 *The People (Attorney General) v Gilbert* [1973] IR 383; *Re National Irish Bank Ltd (No 1)* [1999] 3 IR 145; *Dunnes Stores Ireland Company v Ryan* [2002] 2 IR 60.

12 The *societas publicanorum* was an accepted form of public company which could undertake public contracts such as tax collection. Citizens could buy shares in them.

Ireland Ltd) v O Leannain which concerned a prosecution against a company.[13] Batchelor & Co sought to quash the return for trial as the process of taking depositions could not be completed 'in the presence or hearing of the person so accused' as required by s 17 of the Indictable Offences Act 1849 due to the incorporeal nature of the accused. The High Court granted the order and held that the District Justice had no jurisdiction to take depositions in the case of a corporation and as such there could be no return for trial. The effect of the judgment was to render prosecution of corporate entities on indictment impossible given the requirements of indictable criminal procedure at the time.

It is of some note that the Oireachtas did not take any steps to remedy this lacuna until the enactment of s 382 of the Companies Act, 1963 which allowed a *representative* to be nominated to physically stand in and be present for such parts of the criminal process as required the presence of a body. The provisions of the 1963 Act are largely reproduced in s 868 of the Companies Act 2014. It allows for a *representative* to be nominated who can then be present for the necessary procedural steps and who can take the necessary actions such as entering pleas of guilty or not guilty and so on. The manner in which a representative is appointed is relatively informal:

> '(7) A representative for the purpose of this section need not be appointed under the seal of the company.
> (8) A statement in writing purporting to be signed by a managing director of the company or some other person (by whatever name called) who manages, or is one of the persons who manage, the affairs of the company, to the effect that the person named in the statement has been appointed as the representative of the company for the purposes of this section shall be admissible without further proof as evidence that that person has been so appointed.'

All that is required is that there be a written document authorizing the appointment. The authorization does not need to set out in any detail what the representative is authorized to do given the provisions of s 868(5):

> '(5) In this section, 'representative' in relation to a company means a person duly appointed by the company to represent it for the purpose of doing any act or thing which the representative of a company is authorised by this section to do.'

One important limitation as regards the designation of a representative pursuant to s 382 is that it does not confer a right of audience per se on the representative. It does not allow the representative to conduct the defence of the company, unless he or she is also a solicitor or barrister. As such, the dicta in *Battle v Irish Art Promotion Centre Ltd*, would still seem to apply in the context of criminal

13 *The State (Batchelor & Co Ireland Ltd) v O Leannain* [1957] IR 1.The prosecution was brought by one Maureen O'Carroll under the Merchandise Marks Act 1887. She was unhappy with her purchase of a mixture of marrowfat and blue peas to which she contended the false trade description of 'specially selected marrowfats' had been applied.

proceedings — namely, the directors of a company are not entitled to conduct the prosecution or defence of court proceedings on behalf of a company in the absence of a professional right of audience. An authorisation of a representative under s 868 is limited to authorising the representative to carry out a number of defined formal acts in the context of criminal proceedings rather than conferring some general right of audience to plead before a court of trial. The decision in *Battle*[14] was recently considered in *AIB v Aqua Fresh Fish Limited*[15] in which McKechnie J considered that it remained good law albeit that it may be subject to some limited exceptions:

> '45. To conclude on this limited survey of the domestic position regarding natural persons, the related McKenzie situation, and the rule in Battle, can I summarise as follows:-
> ...(iv) A company, or any other artificial or fictitious person with a distinct legal persona, can be represented only by a lawyer duly accredited with a right of audience in our courts.
> (v) There is no right for a secretary, director, shareholder or any other officer to appear in court proceedings on behalf of a company.
> (vi) However, this rule does not interfere with the court's undoubted discretion to permit an individual person to act on behalf of the company where justice so demands.
> (vii) The manner in which this might be done will reflect the presenting circumstances of each particular case, with the courts generally adopting a pragmatic approach to such relaxation on both the personal and corporate side.
> (viii) The existence of such judicial flexibility when the rule might defeat the interests of justice, which is evident in the case law, is not an insignificant factor when the very existence of the rule is under challenge.'

It will be apparent from the foregoing that it will, in general, be necessary for a company that is the subject of a prosecution to be represented by a solicitor at all times. In addition there will be certain occasions whereby a formally designated representative of the company will also have to be present for those steps in the process that presuppose the physical presence of the accused. As a matter of practice and practicality the solicitor representing the company will often be designated as the representative.

Prosecuting Insolvent Companies

The prosecution of insolvent and potentially insolvent companies gives rise to their own specific issues. This is because regard must also be had to the existence of a parallel regulatory regime in the form of the Companies Act 2014. The provisions of s 678 of the Companies Act 2014 (which mirror the provisions of

---

[14] *Battle v Irish Art Promotion Centre Ltd* [1968] IR 252.

[15] [2017] IECA 77.

s 222 of the 1963 Act) seem on the face of them to be broad enough to capture the commencement of criminal proceedings:

> '678. (1) When in relation to a company—
> (a) a winding-up order has been made,
> (b) a provisional liquidator has been appointed, or
> (c) a resolution for voluntary winding up has been passed,
> no action or proceeding shall be proceeded with or commenced against the company except by leave of the court and subject to such terms as the court may impose.
> (2) Subsection (1) shall not apply to the taking of proceedings before the Employment Appeals Tribunal.'

Indeed, it might be observed that the specific ouster as regards proceedings before the Employment Appeals Tribunal gives rise to the implication that the reference to proceedings which would have otherwise captured same is intended to be interpreted in a relatively broad manner.

In *R. v Dickson*[16] it was held that a criminal prosecution amounts to a proceeding within the meaning of the Insolvency Act 1986, which contains a functionally identical provision to s 678.[17] However, it was found that the fact that no leave had been obtained made no material difference to the course of the trial and did not render the conviction unsafe. It would appear that where leave has not been obtained prior to the institution of civil proceedings that it may nonetheless be sought and subsequently granted by the High Court. In her judgment in the case of *In re MJBCH Limited (In Liquidation)*[18] which concerned s 222 of the Companies Act 1963.[19] Finlay-Geoghegan J distinguished the somewhat stricter position under English law on the basis that a restriction on the right to institute proceedings had a constitutional dimension and, as such, any restriction of same should be interpreted strictly. She also identified the purpose of s 222 as not only being the protection of creditors but also the broader purpose of ensuring that all proceedings in relation to a company that was being wound up were subject to the supervision of the High Court. In light of those considerations she considered that it would be permissible to grant leave on an *ex post facto* basis:

> '18. In an Irish context, s. 222 of the Act of 1963 must, of course, be construed in accordance with the ordinary meaning of the words used so

---

[16] *R. v Dickson* (1991) 94 Cr App Rep 7.

[17] In the UK, the equivalent provision is s 130(2) of the Insolvency Act 1986 and it provides that: 'When a winding-up order has been made or a provisional liquidator has been appointed, no action or proceedings shall be proceeded with or commenced against the company or its property, except by leave of the court and subject to such terms as the court may impose.'

[18] *In re MJBCH Limited (In Liquidation)* [2013] IEHC 256.

[19] s 222 provided: 'When a winding-up order has been made or a provisional liquidator has been appointed, no action or proceeding shall be proceeded with or commenced against the company except by leave of the court and subject to such terms as the court may impose.'

> as to give effect to the purpose intended by the Oireachtas. Such purpose is presumed to be one which is consistent with the Constitution. …
> 21. Accordingly, I have come to the conclusion that the Court does have jurisdiction pursuant to s. 222 of the Act of 1963, to consider granting leave for proceedings already commenced and that if such leave is granted, the order will have the effect of retrospectively authorising the commencement and authorising the continuation of the proceedings for the purposes of s. 222 of the Act of 1963.'

The factors to be taken into account when deciding whether a prosecution ought to be allowed or not were considered in *Re Rhondda Waste Disposal Company Ltd.*[20] In that case, it was held that when the public interest requires it, leave should be readily given and that the interests of creditors should not be taken to trump all other considerations.

It should also be noted that the various supervisory powers of the High Court that permit application to be made to stay any action or proceeding against a company (e.g. where a winding up petition has been presented under s 574) would also appear to apply in principle to criminal proceedings. It follows that unlike a prosecution against an individual it may be possible to stay a prosecution against an insolvent company if other rights and interests are likely to be interfered with.

The fact that a prosecutor is obliged to procure the permission of the High Court prior to instituting proceedings against a company in liquidation can represent a significant disincentive to prosecute. It gives rise to the possibility of incurring costs greater than those which might be incurred in prosecuting the substantive case. Moreover, the necessity to obtain permission *prior* to instituting proceedings can give rise to very real difficulties where statutory time limits apply to the institution of summary proceedings.

Most importantly however, such a restriction arguably fails to acknowledge the important signalling effects of prosecution and conviction. To a large degree the ability to collect a fine might well be incidental as compared with the regulatory utility of being seen to pursue a company that has committed regulatory offences. In circumstances where nearly all white-collar prosecutions are brought by statutory bodies the utility of such a restriction might well be open to question.

Trial Venue

A further example of how the procedural machinery of the criminal process has evolved to deal with natural as opposed to non-corporeal persons is to be found in the question of trial venue and jurisdiction. It is a truism that almost all criminal jurisdiction is geographic in nature. This is because criminal charges must first be brought before the District Court, who's jurisdiction is defined by

[20] *Re Rhondda Waste Disposal Company Ltd* [2001] Ch 57.

reference to geography. Charges in a given case may be brought in the District where the accused resides, where the accused was arrested or where the offence was committed.[21] The concept of residence can give rise to difficulties so far as grounding jurisdiction is concerned. Whilst the case of *The State (The Minister for Agriculture) v The District Justice for the District Court Area of Limerick City*[22] would appear to be authority for the proposition that a company can have a residence at a particular place such a determination would seem to be somewhat dependant on evidence to that effect. In particular, it remains unclear whether a company's registered office is properly regarded as its residence. Clearly it is not possible to ground jurisdiction on the basis of the place of arrest as this is an event which cannot occur in relation to a company.

The final basis for grounding jurisdiction, the place of commission of the offence, is the one most frequently cited by prosecutors. However, conceptual difficulties can arise when the offence in question is one of omission. Where can it be said that such an offence occurs? For example where does a failure to file statutory returns occur? There is no obvious answer to such questions.

These issues can often give rise to difficulties for prosecutors who will have to identify some geographic basis on which to ground jurisdiction. It can also lead to the somewhat unusual situation whereby it may not be possible to ground jurisdiction for different co-accused in the same District. In that regard, it is not at all unheard of for a company to be prosecuted in one District whereas its directors are prosecuted for the same offence in another District. This can lead to an otherwise unnecessary duplication of effort.

Prosecuting Directors

As Lord Chancellor Thurlow observed the actions of companies are dictated by different considerations to the actions of natural persons. It is also clear that different considerations inform the prosecution of companies from an enforcement perspective. As a general rule most prosecutors will also seek, where possible, to prosecute the directors or managers of a company at the same time that they prosecute the company itself. This is for a number of reasons.

Most obviously it very substantially raises the stakes so far as the question of penalty is concerned. The harshest penalty that can be imposed on a company is a fine whereas most offences relating to directors and managers can be punished by a significant prison sentence. Additionally it is generally considered that the prosecution, conviction and sentencing of directors or managers will have a much more significant signalling effect from a regulatory perspective.

Nearly all modern statutory offences that are likely to be committed by

---

21 See s 79 of the Courts Act 1924; and Ord 13 of the District Court Rules 1997.

22 *The State (The Minister for Agriculture) v The District Justice for the District Court Area of Limerick City* [1937] IR 692.

companies contain a 'consent, connivance and neglect' provision by which directors or managers of companies can be prosecuted personally. To take an arbitrary example, s 22 of the Criminal Justice Act 2011 provides:

> '22.— (1) Where an offence under this Act is committed by a body corporate and it is proved that the offence was committed with the consent or connivance, or was attributable to any wilful neglect, of a person who was a director, manager, secretary or other officer of the body corporate, or a person purporting to act in that capacity, that person, as well as the body corporate, shall be guilty of an offence and may be proceeded against and punished as if he or she were guilty of the first-mentioned offence.'

Provisions like this create what might properly be described as a form of compound offence or contingent liability. The first element of proof is to show that the company committed the offence. Thereafter, the prosecution must show that it was committed by reason of the consent, connivance or neglect of the relevant director, manager, secretary or other officer.

It is important to understand, however, that this does not mean that there is an obligation to prosecute the company as well. This was made clear in the case of *DPP v Hegarty*[23] when the DPP sought to prosecute a director in circumstances where the company had had a *nolle prosequi*[24] entered against it. The accused argued that any successful prosecution against him was contingent upon the company having committed a particular criminal offence. By a consultative case stated, two questions were raised: firstly, whether it was necessary to also prosecute the company along with the director and, secondly, whether it was necessary that the company be convicted before the director could be convicted.

The prosecution concerned offences under the Competition Act 2002. Section 3(4)(a) of the Act made provision for a consent, connivance, neglect clause in similar terms to that described above. The Supreme Court considered that it was self-evident from the section that before a director could be convicted of the offences charged the prosecution must have established at the relevant time that the company had committed the relevant offence, that the accused was a director of the company and that the acts constituting the company's offence were authorised or consented to by the accused in his capacity as a director. McKechnie J went on to hold that:

> 'There is no reference [in s 3(4)(a)] to a conviction and in my view there is no interpretative basis for importing into the provision such a condition. The Oireachtas could expressly have done so but did not. As previously explained, there may well have been good reason for this. This position becomes clearer when the distinction between a formal conviction and a finding that an offence has been committed, is understood. The former

---

23 *DPP v Hegarty* [2011] IESC 32.

24 A nolle prosequi is no more than an indication by the prosecutor that it no longer wishes to pursue the prosecution. It does not amount to an acquittal and does not preclude prosecution at some later stage.

> needs little attention…what the section requires is a finding of fact by the jury that [the relevant] offence 'has been committed by the undertaking'. Such a finding, if it were to be made, would have the following significant differences than a conviction would have in the process envisaged in the preceding paragraph. These would include the fact that the undertaking: (i) is not on trial or the subject of any charge; (ii) is therefore not an accused person; (iii) is not exposed to any criminal sanction; (iv) cannot have a conviction recorded against it; Moreover, any such finding by the jury:-(v) could not be referred to or relied upon if the undertaking was subsequently charged or became an accused person; (vi) could not amount to an *autrefois convict* or give rise to any form of estoppel if the undertaking was subsequently put on trial; (vii) could not form the basis of either a restriction application under s. 150 of the Companies Act 1990, or a disqualification application under s. 160 thereof. Finally, the undertaking, if subsequently tried, would be entitled to all appropriate rights and safeguards and could challenge any evidence, including that relied upon to obtain any finding in the earlier proceedings. Therefore, it is clear to me that the undertaking is wholly removed from the position it would be in if it was on trial for a criminal offence.'

Accordingly, the court held that the company did not have to be convicted of the relevant offence before the director indicted could be found guilty of the offence. Rather, it was an essential ingredient of the offence as regards the director that the company itself must have committed an offence. This could be established, like all other necessary facts, by placing before the jury such credible evidence as would, when properly charged and directed, enable it to find that the relevant corporate offence had been committed. Such evidence was fully open to challenge by the accused. The jury would approach this task in exactly the same way as all other matters within its purview. In this sense the position as regards a consent, connivance, and neglect clause is broadly analogous to other forms of compound criminal liability such as the liability of an accessory after the fact: whilst it is necessary to show that the principal committed the offence it is not necessary to show that the principal was actually convicted.

This is of particular significance in the context of prosecutions against companies. In many instances the company may no longer be in existence in the sense that it has been wound up. Equally a prosecutor may take the view that there is no point in prosecuting a company that has no assets with which to pay a fine or where the company has been put into liquidation. In such circumstances the directors may find themselves being prosecuted on their own. In *Hegarty* the Supreme Court expressly considered the utility of prosecuting directors and managers in such circumstances:

> 'As natural persons are directly instrumental in the actions of a body corporate, the ['consent and connivance' provision in the Competition Act] also created offences against certain influential position holders within a company, being essentially those without whose involvement the offending conduct could not be endorsed or approved. Culpability in this regard

> was confined to persons with a high level of responsibility for decision making i.e. directors, managers, other similar officers, and those who hold themselves out as such. The result was that, arising out of the same set of circumstances, any one of such persons, if not an undertaking in his/her own right, as well as an undertaking so defined, could each be guilty of a criminal offence. That was the scheme of the Act, with its justification being enforcement driven. If the Act criminalised one player but not the other, responsibility by way of effective sanction and deterrence could be skilfully and freely avoided, or at least substantially diminished, by any number of expedient devices, such as, in the case of a body corporate, liquidation, and in the case of an individual being, impecuniosity. That would not have addressed the weakness mentioned above; it would have made enforcement arduous and it would have made avoidance affordable and undemanding. Therefore, in principle, there is nothing surprising in the concept of both non-personal undertakings and their managers/officers and like persons, being exposed to criminal prosecution arising out of the same abusive conduct. Such persons are separate and distinct legal personalities and therefore no question of double punishment arises.'

Given the prevalence of consent, connivance and neglect clauses in modern legislation the vast majority of prosecutions against directors are brought on this basis. Surprisingly, with the exception of *Hegarty*, there is a marked lack of domestic authority on the meaning of consent, connivance and neglect in the context of prosecutions against directors and other officers of a company.

As a matter of basic statutory interpretation it is perhaps obvious that each of the three concepts must be considered and interpreted separately. However, the concepts of consent and connivance will generally be regarded as cognate terms. Consent arises where a director or officer of the company is aware of the fact that the company is committing the offence and agrees to it whereas connivance arises where a director similarly aware but does nothing to stop the commission of the offence. Both concepts would appear as a matter of definition to require actual knowledge on the part of the director or officer concerned.

The concept of neglect can be somewhat more difficult in that it does not, strictly speaking, require proof of actual knowledge of the commission of the offence by the company on the part of the director or officer. However, the law acknowledges that the many and varying responsibilities that arise in relation to the running of a company and the managing of its affairs can be divided up amongst its directors and officers. In *Huckerby v Elliott*[25] it was held that a consideration of the differing roles and responsibilities of different directors was a necessary element of any analysis of guilt as regards an individual director:

> 'Counsel for the respondent concedes that these words 'attributable to any neglect on the part of the directors' refer to the omission to do something which the director was under a duty to do. It is unnecessary to go through

[25] *Huckerby v Elliott* [1970] 1 All ER 189.

> the cases which deal with what in different circumstances may or may not be the duty of a director, but I know of no authority for the proposition that it is the duty of a director to, as it were, supervise his co-directors or to acquaint himself with all the details of the running of the company. Indeed it has been said by Romer J in *Re City Equitable Fire Insurance Co* Ltd ([1925] Ch 497 at 428–430) that amongst other things it is perfectly proper for a director to leave matters to another director or to an official of the company, and that he is under no obligation to test the accuracy of anything that he is told by such a person, or even to make certain that he is complying with the law. It was pointed out that business cannot be conducted otherwise than on principles of trust, and accordingly as it seems to me on the evidence produced by the prosecution there is disclosed a state of affairs where the appellant left matters concerning the licences to her co-director, Mr Lunn, who was the secretary of the company and fully acquainted with the business. One asks oneself this: has she any reason to distrust Mr Lunn or to feel that he was not carrying out his duty? One finds that she had on the evidence produced no reason to distrust him; indeed as the answer I read out discloses, she knew that he was performing his duty in regard to licences generally, and I can see no further duty on her part to enquire exactly how the £1,600 she referred to had been spent, and whether part of it included a licence for the New Embassy Club in respect of the chemin de fer game. For my part I feel that this is a case in which the prosecution has not proved their case, and accordingly I would allow this appeal and quash the conviction.'

It follows that any assertion of criminal liability on the basis of neglect requires a detailed contextual analysis of the evidence as regards the role of the accused director or officer. In the context of a large company this will require detailed evidence as to the role of the accused and, as importantly, the roles and responsibilities of other directors and officers.

Even in small companies issues may arise. Whilst prosecutions are often brought against both directors, where a company only has two, it may not be immediately apparent that this is always warranted. This is particularly so where one of the directors is a spouse or close relative of the director who is *de facto* the moving force behind the company. The mere fact that a company has only two directors rather than ten cannot lead to the automatic conclusion that both will be responsible for offences committed by the company on the basis of neglect.

Quite apart from the question of any division of responsibility as between directors and the identification of a director or other officer who has responsibility for the aspect of the company's business under consideration, it will be also be necessary for the prosecution to prove that the offence was committed by reason of the alleged neglect. Thus, in circumstances where an employee or manager causes the company to commit the offence in a deliberate manner but conceals same from the directors, it may well be difficult to establish neglect on the part of any of the directors.

In this sense the concept of neglect is also highly contextual and requires to be addressed on a clear evidential basis in any case where the prosecution seeks to rely on it. This becomes relevant when it is considered that regulatory prosecutions are routinely brought as against companies and their directors (particularly where there is only a small number of directors) on the rather simplistic assumption that it is to be presumed that all of the directors are to be regarded as being responsible for the commission of the offence by the company on the basis of neglect. If this were a proper basis alone for proceeding against directors then it would in truth amount to the imposition of strict, or even absolute liability. The authorities make it clear that this is not what is meant by a consent, connivance and neglect clause. Rather liability on the basis of such a provision amounts to a form of contingent liability the scope of which is described by the statutory words themselves. These in turn call for a potentially detailed and contextual evidential consideration of the state of knowledge and assumed responsibilities of each accused director.

Before leaving the question of liability of directors, some mention should be made of the position as regards criminal liability insofar as it applies to partnerships as distinct from companies. The case of *Director of Corporate Enforcement v Gannon*[26] would appear to be authority for the proposition that all partners in a firm will be considered to be criminally liable where one of their number commits an offence in the context of his or her role as a partner. In that case, one of the partners of a firm of accountants acted as an auditor to a company even though he was disqualified. The High Court considered that all of the partners of the firm were criminally liable even though they may not have had any knowledge of the events in question.

Such a conclusion is both remarkable and surprising – particularly in circumstances where the offence in question carried a penalty of five years on indictment. In effect it would appear to establish absolute liability for all partners in respect of a serious indictable offence. In that regard it is difficult to reconcile with subsequent authority concerning offences of strict and absolute liability.[27] As such the correctness of the decision in *Gannon* must be open to considerable doubt.

Conclusion

The foregoing represents but a brief consideration of the difficulties that may arise in prosecuting a body that has no body. One of the remarkable features of our criminal justice process is the extent to which it remains resolutely focused on the prosecution of individuals as opposed to corporate bodies. The procedural machinery that has been put in place to deal with the prosecution of companies is limited in scope and effect. Persistent basic procedural problems remain. This simply underlines the extent to which a prosecution against a company is imbued

---

26 *Director of Corporate Enforcement v Gannon* [2002] 4 IR 439.

27 *CC v Ireland* [2006] 4 IR 1.

with the quality of exceptionality. Given the pre-eminence of limited liability companies as the primary means by which regulated business is transacted it begs the question as to why this should be so — if companies commit most white-collar offences then why does it remain so difficult to prosecute them?

CHAPTER 9

SENTENCING WHITE-COLLAR AND CORPORATE CRIME

Tom O'Malley[*]

No aspect of white-collar crime can usefully be discussed without some initial effort to clarify the definition and scope of the term itself. Working definitions are generally based on the status of the offender or the conduct constituting the offence.[1] Those who undertake empirical or analytical legal research on white-collar crime usually opt for a conduct-based definition, if only for reasons of practicality. Research projects of this nature become more manageable when based on a limited number of clearly defined offences. Reliable conclusions can then be drawn about the recorded incidence of those offences, the way they have been judicially interpreted, the profile of offenders or whatever the object of the inquiry may be. In Ireland nowadays, empirical and analytical studies often take as their starting point some or all of the offences listed in Schedule 1 of the Criminal Justice Act 2011. Similar lists are available in one form or another elsewhere. A status-based approach, by contrast, is less concerned with the legal characterisation of the conduct and more with the attributes of offenders, with special emphasis on any position of power, influence or control they may have exploited to engage in criminal activity. Edwin Sutherland, who is credited with inventing the term 'white-collar crime', defined it as 'any crime committed by a person of respectability and high social status in the course of his occupation.'[2] Notably absent from this definition was any attempt to specify or delineate the nature of the conduct. Both approaches have their strengths and weaknesses.

A conduct-based definition has the merit of precision; it facilitates agreement on the scope of the inquiry being undertaken. However, depending on the nature and range of the selected offences, such an inquiry may ignore or downplay important information about the rank and circumstances of the offenders. A study that treated conduct such as obtaining by deception, stealing from an employer, insurance fraud and welfare fraud as white-collar crime would probably yield a radically different profile of offenders, in social, economic and gender terms, than one concentrating on offences more likely to be committed by persons wielding significant political or economic power or occupying highly-paid positions

---

* Senior Lecturer, School of Law, NUI Galway.

1 Neal Shover and Francis T Cullen, 'Studying and Teaching White-Collar Crime: Populist and Patrician Perspectives' (2008) 19 Journal of Criminal Justice Education 155; David T Johnson and Richard A Leo, 'The Yale White-Collar Crime Project: A Review and Critique' (1993) 18 Law and Social Inquiry 63.

2 Edwin Sutherland, *White-Collar Crime* (Dryden Press 1949) 9. He first used the term in an address delivered in 1939: 'White-Collar Criminality' (1940) 5 American Sociological Review 1.

within organisations.[3] A status-based definition may therefore facilitate a more realistic appraisal of so-called suite crime. But it also risks being either under or over-inclusive in terms of the conduct element. Occasional efforts have been made to marry the two approaches. When Stanton Wheeler and his colleagues undertook their study on the sentencing of white-collar crime as part of the Yale Project in the 1980s, they adopted as a working definition of white-collar crime 'non-violent, economic crimes that involve some level of fraud, collusion, or deception and that are committed by persons in traditionally 'white-collar jobs'.'[4] Among the offences they selected were bribery, income tax fraud, postal and wire fraud, price-fixing, false claims and bank embezzlement. Thus, while they were primarily concerned with conduct, they would also devote some attention to the status of the offenders. Their working definition was arguably preferable to that of Edelhertz, often seen as the main competitor to Sutherland's, which concentrated on conduct alone.[5]

This chapter will broadly follow Wheeler's approach by treating white-collar crime as consisting of economic or business-related offences committed by persons of some degree of affluence or employed in reasonably well-paid positions in the public or private sector. The chapter is structured as follows. Following some preliminary observations about the nature and incidence of white-collar crime about which, in this country at least, we have relatively little reliable statistical data, the general principles of sentencing, particularly as they apply to white-collar offenders, will be described. This will be followed by an analysis of recent sentencing for fraud, probably the most common form of white-collar crime. Two further issues of growing importance in this area, collateral consequences of conviction and deferred prosecution agreements, will then be addressed before finally coming to the sentencing of corporate offenders.

Popular perceptions of white-collar crime are seldom reflected in the concrete circumstances of cases coming before the courts. Public and political protestations about the rarity of prosecutions and the leniency of sentences are often premised on the assumption that this kind of crime typically consists of large-scale fraud within financial institutions or public bodies. The reality is quite different. Most white-collar crime detected and prosecuted in this country is fairly low-level, by international standards at least. Our typical white-collar offender is far more likely to be a person who has stolen money from his or her employer to fund an addiction or an otherwise unaffordable lifestyle than a large-scale fraudster who has deprived individuals, institutions or the State of millions of Euro through some corrupt scheme or enterprise. In the typical

3 For a particularly insightful analysis of this issue, see Kathleen Daly, 'Gender and Varieties of White-Collar Crime' (1989) 27(4) Criminology 769.

4 Stanton Wheeler, Kenneth Mann and Austin Sarat, *Sitting in Judgment: The Sentencing of White-Collar Criminals* (Yale University Press 1988) 5. On the background to the study, see Johnson and Leo, fn 1 above.

5 Herbert Edelhertz, *The Nature, Impact and Prosecution of White-Collar Crime* (US Department of Justice 1970) 3 (defining white-collar crime as 'an illegal act or series of acts committed by non-physical means and by concealment and guile, to obtain money or property, to avoid payment or loss or money or property, or to obtain business or personal advantage').

case, the offences of conviction may not rank very high on the scale of gravity, and there will probably be mitigating or extenuating personal circumstances pointing to a moderate or lenient sentence. In many such cases, sentencing is all that matters because the defendants will have pleaded guilty. Of course, far more serious offences do occasionally come to light, though they are seldom committed in a corporate setting. The white-collar offences for which the heaviest sentences have been imposed in recent years were committed by individuals in the course of their professions or occupations.[6]

The collapse of Anglo-Irish Bank in 2008, with catastrophic results for shareholders, investors and the public at large, prompted renewed calls for a more aggressive approach to the prevention and prosecution of financial crime committed in corporate settings.[7] A few criminal trials did follow, though two of them collapsed almost as spectacularly as the bank itself.[8] What those cases starkly illustrate is the practical difficulty in affixing blame to particular individuals for conduct that was undoubtedly unlawful and injurious to the public but responsibility for which was diffused within the upper echelons of the organisation. This is reflected in the few sentences imposed to date on former Anglo-Irish Bank officials, the highest being six years' imprisonment imposed on the former CEO (Drumm) who was convicted following an 87-day trial of conspiracy to defraud and false accounting in relation to transactions valued at €7.2 million.[9] A former senior executive (McAteer) was sentenced

---

6 Examples include *People (DPP) v Byrne* (Dublin Circuit Criminal Court, 2 December 2013) (a former solicitor sentenced to an effective term of 12 years' imprisonment for a series of theft, deception and forgery offences involving the theft of €52 million from various financial institutions and cheating several clients out of their houses or money); *People (DPP) v O'Brien* [2015] IECA 304 (seven years' imprisonment upheld in the case of a financial consultant convicted of fraud-related offences which caused a loss in excess of €8 million to various individuals); *People (DPP) v Hawkins* [2014] IECCA 38; [2014] IECCA 38 (seven years' imprisonment upheld in the case of a woman who stole approximately €2.8 million from her employer (a member of the band U2) over a period of a few years).

7 See Joe McGrath, *Corporate and White-Collar Crime in Ireland: A New Architecture of Regulatory Enforcement* (Manchester University Press 2015) esp ch 7; Tom Lyons and Brian Carey, *The FitzPatrick Tapes: The Rise and Fall of One Man, One Bank and One Country* (Penguin Ireland 2011); Patrick Honohan, *The Irish Banking Crisis: Regulatory and Financial Stability Policy* (Central Bank 2010).

8 On 23 May 2017, Sean FitzPatrick, former Chairman and Chief Executive of Anglo-Irish Bank, was acquitted by direction on the 126th day of his trial on charges of misleading the bank's creditors and furnishing false information. The trial itself is estimated to have cost the State €3 million and the preceding investigation is estimated to have cost a great deal more (Shane Phelan and Dearbhail McDonald, 'Taxpayer hit for tens of millions as FitzPatrick trial collapses', *Irish Independent* (24 May 2017). On 1 November 2017, Tiarnan O'Mahoney, formerly Chief Operating Officer of the bank, was acquitted by direction on the 21st day of his retrial of all charges which included conspiracy to defraud the revenue and conspiracy to destroy or falsify documents. His original convictions and those of Bernard Daly had been quashed by the Court of Appeal (*People (DPP) v O'Mahoney and Daly* [2016] IECA 111).

9 Dublin Circuit Criminal Court, 20 June 2018. Later he was given a 15-month suspended sentence on pleading guilty 10 counts of authorising financial assistance to various developers to buy shares in Anglo-Irish Bank (Dublin Circuit Criminal Court, 10 July 2018). Other charges against him were dropped at that point.

to three-and-a-half years' imprisonment for his role in the same conspiracy. Two convicted co-accused (Bowe and Casey) were sentenced to terms of two years and two years and nine months respectively.[10] The three last-mentioned sentences were imposed in 2016 and for offences committed in 2008, a time lag that indicates the complexities inherent in the investigation and prosecution of such offences.[11] One of the offenders in question, McAteer, later pleaded guilty to a separate offence of fraudulent trading for which he received two-and-a-half years' imprisonment, but this was ordered to run concurrently with his existing three-and-a-half sentence.[12] An assistant manager at the bank (Maguire) was convicted of conspiracy to defraud the revenue and to commit offences contrary to s 243(1) of the Companies Act 1990. She was sentenced to 18 months' imprisonment, but this was reduced on appeal to nine months with the balance suspended from the date of the appeal decision.[13] There were, it must be said, many mitigating factors in her case. Community service orders were imposed on two former senior officials of the Bank who were convicted of giving illegal loans to developers to buy shares in the bank. The trial judge said it would be unfair to imprison them because the Financial Regulator had led them into error and illegality.[14] The former Chief Financial Officer of the Bank (Moran) was granted immunity from prosecution.

White-collar offenders are sentenced according to the same general principles as apply to all others.[15] As discussed more fully below, the sentence in each case must be proportionate to the gravity of the offence and the personal circumstances of the offender. While the usual range of mitigating and aggravating factors apply, some, as we shall see, are especially salient in white-collar cases. Irish courts have decisively rejected any policy of exceptionalism when it comes to sentencing white-collar offenders. Several recent cases, all involving fairly classic instances of white-collar crime, have confirmed the applicability of standard principles to the sentencing of such crime.[16] A similar policy is applied, here and elsewhere, to other stages of the criminal process. *R v Inns*,[17] in which the English Court of Appeal recently took the opportunity to restate some of the fundamental indicia of a properly conducted trial within an adversarial system, happened to involve a white-collar crime of sorts.

This chapter is concerned solely with the judicial sentencing of individuals and

---

10 *People (DPP) v McAteer, Bowe and Casey* (Dublin Circuit Criminal Court, 29 July 2016).

11 Drumm was sentenced in 2018 but that was largely because he had emigrated to the United States in 2009 and had to be extradited back to Ireland in 2016.

12 *People (DPP) v McAteer* (Dublin Circuit Criminal Court, 23 January 2017).

13 *People (DPP) v Maguire* [2015] IECA 350.

14 *People (DPP) v McAteer and Whelan* (Dublin Circuit Criminal Court, 31 July 2014).

15 *People (DPP) v Begley* [2013] 2 IR 188 provides strong authority for the proposition that there is no parallel set of rules and principles governing the sentencing of social welfare fraud or tax evasion (or, it may be added, any other kind of financial or white-collar crime).

16 *People (DPP) v Begley* [2013] 2 I.R. 188; *People (DPP) v O'Brien* [2015] IECA 304; *People (DPP) v Reilly* [2016] IECA 43; *People (DPP) v Walsh* [2016] IECA 74; *People (DPP) v Maguire* [2015] IECA 350; *People (DPP) v Durcan* [2017] IECA 3; *People (DPP) v Zaffer* [2016] IECA 321; *People (DPP) v Zaffer (No 2)* [2017] IECA 12.

17 *R v Inns* [2018] EWCA Crim 1081.

corporations convicted of economic and business-related offences. It does not deal with civil or administrative penalties although these too, irrespective of how they are legally classified, can be highly punitive in effect.[18] With increasing emphasis on regulation as a means of securing compliance, particularly in the area of financial services, greater attention needs to be paid to the sanctioning powers of regulatory bodies and the manner in which those powers are exercised. The Central Bank of Ireland, for example, in its regulatory capacity, may impose a range of sanctions extending from a caution or reprimand to a financial penalty which, in the case of a corporate body, may as high as €10 million or 10% of turnover.[19] An individual is subjcct to a maximum pcnalty of €1 million. Thcsc powers have so far received little judicial scrutiny. At a minimum, however, regulators should be required to specify exactly how, and in accordance with what principles and criteria, they have calculated any penalties they impose. In *Purcell v Central Bank of Ireland*[20] the High Court held that the Central Bank's power to hold an inquiry when it suspects that a regulated financial service provider is committing or has committed a contravention does not amount to the administration of justice within the meaning of Art 34.1 of the Constitution. It reached this conclusion by applying the test established in *McDonald v Bord na gCon*,[21] and the applicant had accepted that all five elements of that test had to be satisfied. The severity of the sanction imposed or threatened is insufficient in itself to satisfy the *McDonald* test.[22] However, bearing in mind that proportionality is a well-established tenet of Irish constitutional law, as the Supreme Court held in *Rock v Ireland*,[23] civil sanctions, like their criminal counterparts, must be proportionate. Further, in the event that a sanctioned party is later prosecuted and convicted on a criminal charge arising from the same course of conduct, the principle of cumulative proportionality must apply. This is discussed briefly below under 'Collateral Consequences.' Under the jurisprudence of the European Convention on Human Rights, 'criminal charge' is an autonomous concept which means that the legal characterisation of a measure in a member state is by no means determinative for the purpose of deciding if the protections guaranteed by Art 6 of the Convention should apply. According to the *Engel* criteria, other important factors include the nature of the measure and the nature and severity of the penalty.[24] This is clearly a principle to which

---

[18] Andrew Ashworth, 'A New Generation of Omissions Offences?' [2018] Crim LR 354, 361 (noting that in England and Wales court fines may be lower than regulatory penalties). See also Celia Wells, 'Corporate Failure to Prevent Economic Crime – A Proposal' [2017] Crim LR 426.

[19] Central Bank Act 1942, s 33AQ inserted by the Central Bank and Financial Services Authority of Ireland Act 2004. See *Fingleton v Central Bank of Ireland* [2018] IECA 105 (judgment of Finlay Geoghegan J).

[20] *Purcell v Central Bank of Ireland* [2016] IEHC 514.

[21] *McDonald v Bord na gCon* [1965] IR 217.

[22] *O'Connell v The Turf Club* [2015] IESC 57.

[23] *Rock v Ireland* [1997] 3 IR 484.

[24] *Engel v The Netherlands* (1976) 1 EHRR 647. In *Grande Stevens v Italy* (App No 18640/10), 4 March 2014, the Court of Human Rights said (para 94): 'it suffices that the offence in question should by its nature be "criminal" from the point of view of the Convention, or should have made the person in question liable to a sanction which, by virtue of its nature and degree of severity, belongs in general to the "criminal" sphere.' On *Grande Stevens,* see Matteo Gargantini, 'Public Enforcement of Market Abuse Bans.

national authorities should pay close attention when devising regulatory regimes and setting the amounts that may be levied by way of administrative fines.

Distributive Principles of Punishment

Every sentence imposed by a criminal court must be proportionate to the gravity of the offence and the personal circumstances of the offender.[25] This is the overarching distributive principle of sentencing in Ireland where it is now treated as a constitutional imperative.[26] The principle has two limbs and equal attention must be paid to both. First, the gravity of the offence must be assessed. Gravity, in turn, has two ingredients: harm and culpability. Sometimes both ingredients are evenly matched, but there may equally be a significant mismatch between the two. A person who goes out with the intention of inflicting a serious injury on another and succeeds in doing so will have acted with a high level of culpability and caused serious harm. That assault will therefore rank high on the scale of gravity for the relevant offence. However, a person may also cause a high level of harm while acting with a low level of culpability, as in a case of careless driving causing death.[27] Or, a person may act with a high level of culpability and cause very little harm, as in a case of attempted murder. The gravity of an offence can seldom be assessed with any degree of mathematical precision; it is quintessentially an exercise in judgment. Having said that, the present English sentencing guidelines offer considerable assistance in evaluating harm and culpability for the purpose of locating the offence of conviction in the appropriate sentence range.[28]

Once a court has assessed the gravity of an offence, taking account of both harm and culpability, it must then identify a headline sentence. This is the penalty that would be appropriate if it were determined by reference to gravity alone. Thus, the headline sentence for a theft that is deemed to be on the mid-point of the scale of gravity will be in the region of five years, the maximum

The ECtHR *Grande Stevens* Decision' (2015) 1 Journal of Financial Regulation 149; Marco Venturozzo, 'When Market Abuse Rules Violate Human Rights: *Grande Stevens v Italy* and the Different Approaches to Double Jeopardy in Europe and the US' (2015) 16 European Business Organisation Law Review 145.

25 *People (DPP) v M* [1994] 3 IR 306; *People (DPP) v Kelly* [2005] 2 IR 321; [2005] 1 ILRM 19; *Gilligan v Ireland* [2013] 2 IR 745; [2014] 1 ILRM 745.

26 This principle does not apply where an offence attracts a mandatory penalty. However, any mandatory penalty specified by statute must be reasonable having regard to the nature of the offence. See *Lynch and Whelan v Minister for Justice* [2012] 1 IR 1. Murder is, in effect, the only offence that carries a strict mandatory penalty (life imprisonment). Some drug and firearms offences carry presumptive or mandatory minimum sentences.

27 *People (DPP) v O'Shea* [2017] IECA 41; [2017] 2 ILRM 149.

28 On the English sentencing guidelines, see Andrew Ashworth and Julian Roberts (eds), *Sentencing Guidelines: Exploring the English Model* (Oxford University Press 2013); Julian Roberts, 'Structured Sentencing: Lessons from England and Wales for Common Law Jurisdictions' (2012) 14 Punishment & Society 267. The English Sentencing Council has by now produced guidelines for many offences as well as some generic guidelines including *Overarching Principles: Seriousness. Guideline* (2004) (this was actually produced by the Council's predecessor, the Sentencing Guidelines Council).

being 10 years.[29] Consideration must then be given to the second limb of the proportionality principle, the personal circumstances of the offender or, more precisely, those circumstances that may properly be treated as mitigating or aggravating. In fact, the personal circumstances taken into account at this second stage are almost invariably mitigating. Aggravating factors are more likely to be relevant to the assessment of harm or culpability under the first limb of the proportionality principle.

Ever since its establishment in late 2014, the present Court of Appeal has insisted on a structured approach to sentencing.[30] It has expressly rejected the instinctive synthesis approach, which is favoured in some Australian jurisdictions, and which requires a sentencing judge to take a holistic view of the case and come up with a sentence that fairly reflects all the relevant circumstances.[31] Our Court of Appeal, rightly it is suggested, has prescribed a two-stage approach under which a headline sentence is first identified having regard to the objective gravity of the offence, taking account of both harm and culpability, with appropriate adjustments then being made for relevant personal circumstances which, as already noted, will ordinarily be mitigating.[32] Failure on the part of a trial judge to identify a headline sentence will not inevitably amount to an error of principle if the sentence ultimately imposed seems appropriate in light of all the circumstances of the case. The same holds true of an omission to indicate the level of discount being granted for particular mitigating factors. The two-stage procedure certainly encourages more structured sentencing, and it should help in promoting consistency of approach, whatever about consistency of outcome. The Court of Appeal has recently delivered what may be described as guideline judgments indicating appropriate sentence ranges for burglary, robbery and aggravated burglary.[33] This practice, if continued, should help to reduce unwarranted sentencing disparity.

Proportionality is a distributive principle, as opposed to a purpose, of punishment. It does not purport to explain *why* the state is morally justified in punishing criminal offenders. Rather it limits the amount of punishment that may be imposed in a specific case, whatever the animating purpose may be. Proportionality is potentially compatible with any of the traditional purposes of punishment although it clearly sits more easily with some of those purposes than with others. Whether it is to be equated with a desert-based theory depends on the precise formulation of that theory. Some retributivists hold that a penalty

---

29 Criminal Justice (Theft and Fraud Offences) Act 2001, s 4.

30 See, in particular, *People (DPP) v Flynn* [2015] IECA 290; *People (DPP) v Molloy* [2018] IECA 37.

31 *R v Markarian* (2005) 228 CLR 357. For a critical analysis of this approach, see Mirko Bagaric, 'Sentencing: From Vagueness to Arbitrariness: The Need to Abolish the Stain that is the Instinctive Synthesis' (2015) 38(1) Univ New South Wales LJ 76.

32 *People (DPP) v Molloy* [2018] IECA 37.

33 *People (DPP) v Casey and Casey* [2018] IECA 121 (burglary); *People (DPP) v Byrne* [2018] IECA 120 (robbery and aggravated burglary). The former Court of Criminal Appeal had offered similar guidance for the offences of causing serious harm and possessing a firearm in suspicious circumstances: *People (DPP) v Fitzgibbon* [2014] IECCA 12; [2014] 2 ILRM 116 and *People (DPP) v Ryan* [2014] IECCA 11; [2014] 2 ILRM 98.

should be proportionate to the gravity of the offence and to that alone. Others favour a more holistic or inclusive version of retribution or desert that takes at least some offender-related factors into account. In Ireland, as already noted, a sentence must be proportionate both to the gravity of the offence and the offender's personal circumstances. This is broadly, though probably not exactly, equivalent to the more holistic version of desert just mentioned. Other penal purposes can also be accommodated within the confines of a proportionate sentence, bearing in mind that what is proportionate can be expressed only in terms of a sentence range as opposed to a precise penalty. A proportionate sentence may therefore be incapacitating, deterrent or rehabilitative, in addition to being punitive, in its effect.[34] The dominant purpose being pursued will doubtless influence where the sentence for a specific offence is located within the appropriate range. Considerations of deterrence or social protection will ordinarily result in a sentence being located at a higher rather than a lower point within the range. General deterrence is often seen as an important factor in the sentencing of white-collar and corporate crime. It therefore calls for a little more discussion here.

Deterrence

Deterrence is one of the standard justifications for state punishment, but it rests upon two questionable premises, one moral, the other empirical or behavioural. The moral premise is that an offender, irrespective of his or her desert, may be punished to such a degree as will dissuade others from engaging in similar misconduct. By thus allowing individual offenders to be treated instrumentally, deterrent policies run counter to the Kantian precept that human beings should always be treated as ends in themselves and never as means.[35] Punishment, according to Kant, should never be inflicted to promote some good, whether for the offender or for others, but only because the offender has committed a crime. Bentham, the arch utilitarian, championed the opposite view, arguing that all punishment was evil and that it ought to be tolerated only where it promised to prevent some future evil.[36] In other words, it was justified only in so far as it might reduce recidivism and deter others. As Lord Halifax had said a century before Bentham: 'Men are not hanged for stealing horses, but that horses may

---

[34] *People (DPP) v Daniels* [2014] 2 IR 813, 825 where the Supreme Court said: 'A term of imprisonment is not directed solely at the punishment of the offender. It also involves elements such as rehabilitation of the offender, deterrence and the protection of society.'

[35] Immanuel Kant, *Metaphysische Anfangsgründe der Rechtslehre* (1797). See also Immanuel Kant, *Practical Philosophy,* edited and translated by Mary J Gregor (Cambridge University Press 1996); Jeffrie G Murphy, *Retribution, Justice and Therapy: Essays in the Philosophy of Law* (D Reidel Publishing Co. 1979); B Sharon Byrd, 'Kant's Theory of Punishment: Deterrence in its Threat, Retribution in its Execution' (1989) 8(2) Law and Philosophy 151.

[36] Jeremy Bentham, *An Introduction to the Principles of Morals and Legislation* (1789) (Clarendon Press 1907), Ch XIII.2. In *The Rationale of Punishment* (1830), Bentham wrote: 'General prevention ought to be the chief end of punishment, as it is its real justification.' See James E Crimmins, 'Principles of Utilitarian Penal Law in Beccaria, Bentham and Mill' in Peter Karl Koritansky (ed), *The Philosophy of Punishment and the History of Political Thought* (University of Missouri Press 2011) 136 *et seq.*

not be stolen'. However, by eighteenth century standards, Bentham's approach was also an enlightened one in so far as it insisted that punishment should be no greater than was necessary to achieve its utilitarian goal. Useless or ineffective punishments were to be avoided. Specific deterrence, aimed at dissuading the individual from re-offending, may be more compatible with the Kantian imperative to the extent that it remains focused on the circumstances of the person being punished. Modern sentencing codes elsewhere display far more allegiance to Bentham than to Kant because they almost invariably recognise general deterrence (however phrased) as a legitimate penal purpose.[37] The same holds true in Ireland where sentencing principles derive mainly from common law rather than statute. Recently, in *People (DPP) v O'Brien,*[38] the Court of Appeal found itself unable to concur with the former Court of Criminal Appeal that a sentencing court should always accord priority to rehabilitation over other objectives, including deterrence.[39] The Court of Appeal said:

> '[We] prefer an approach in which the correct prioritisation of penal objectives is to be determined by the circumstances of the particular case based on the evidence, [and] we accept that in many cases it may indeed be appropriate to prioritise the penal objective of rehabilitation. There will, however, be other cases in which it may be appropriate to prioritise deterrence, or retribution and incapacitation.'[40]

The behavioural premise underpinning deterrence is that punishment does in fact deter or, as more commonly assumed, that the heavier the punishment imposed, the more effective its deterrent impact will be. No one seriously doubts that punishment deters to some degree. Certain kinds of crime would probably be more prevalent were they not punishable with sanctions that people wish to avoid. But there is little empirical evidence to suggest that an increase in punishment for a given crime will produce a commensurate decrease in the incidence of that crime. It may well result in a marginal reduction, but seldom any more than that. Nor will the heaviest of penalties, even if mandatory, eliminate entirely any form of criminality. A high probability of detection is generally more effective than the threat of a severe penalty.[41] As a penal policy, deterrence assumes that crime is usually, if not invariably, the product of rational choice — that those who are tempted to engage in it will weigh up the benefits or satisfaction they will gain from it compared with the detriment they will suffer if detected, convicted and sentenced. This was the assumption underpinning Bentham's ideas about crime and punishment, but as two critics of his theory once wrote, people are not 'human calculating machines.'[42] Even the most serious offences, including

---

37 Criminal Justice Act 2003, s 142 (England and Wales); Criminal Code, s 718 (Canada); Sentencing Act 2002, s 7 (New Zealand).

38 *People (DPP) v O'Brien* [2018] IECA 2.

39 *People (DPP) v G.K.* [2008] IECCA 110.

40 *People (DPP) v O'Brien* [2018] IECA 2, para 46. See also the Court's more extensive analysis in *People (DPP) v D.W.* [2018] IECA 143.

41 Andrew Von Hirsch, Anthony E Bottoms, Elizabeth Burney and Per-Olof Wikström, *Criminal Deterrence and Sentence Severity: An Analysis of Recent Research* (Hart Publishing 1999).

42 Harry Elmer Barnes and Howard Becker, *Social Thought from Lore to Science* (DC Heath

homicide, are often committed by persons who, at the time, lack the capacity or the inclination to undertake a rational cost-benefit analysis of their impending conduct and its consequences.

Deterrence is routinely mentioned as an important consideration, or even the dominant one, in sentencing white-collar crime, the assumption being that offending of this nature is usually the product of rational choice. It is therefore believed that potential offenders will consider the penalties to which they will be liable, if detected and convicted.[43] Sentences imposed on those who have been convicted should, by this line of reasoning, influence the future conduct of others. Courts across the common-law world (and probably elsewhere) certainly share this view. In *R v Dobis,*[44] a leading Canadian authority on fraud sentencing, the Ontario Court of Appeal, having cited earlier decisions to the same effect, said:

> 'There is a real need to emphasise denunciation and, especially, general deterrence in the realm of large-scale frauds committed by persons in positions of trust with devastating consequences for their victims…'

Likewise, in *People (DPP) v Duffy*[45] McKechnie J, when imposing sentence for cartel-related competition offences, said:

> 'Subject to the stricture that punishment can never exceed that available on the facts and must always be proportionate, both general and specific deterrence have an important role to play in many areas of criminal behaviour, including the examples herein given.'[46]

This probably best summarises Irish law on the matter. Deterrence certainly has a role in the sentencing of white-collar crime generally, although in specific cases its importance may be outweighed by other factors, including the personal circumstances of the offender at the time of sentence. However, even where it is deemed to be a relevant consideration, it cannot trump the overarching principle of proportionality, irrespective of the nature of the offence. In those circumstances, it will justify locating the offence higher rather than lower on the appropriate sentence range.

Mitigating Factors

Mitigation serves to moderate the punishment that would be deserved if sentence

---

1938), Vol 1, 259. See also Gilbert Geis, 'Pioneers in Criminology. VII. Jeremy Bentham (1748-1832)' (1955) 46(2) Journal of Criminal Law, Criminology and Police Science 159.

43 *R v Foran* (1970) 2 OR 52, 53 ('As far as deterrence to others is concerned, the members of the business community should be put on notice that if they break their trust to the public they can expect to receive proper punishment for having done so').

44 (2002) 58 OR (3d) 536, para 42. See also Hession David and Patterson, 'The Prosecution of Complex Fraud: A Fresh Approach' (2016) 63 Criminal Law Quarterly 146.

45 *People (DPP) v Duffy* [2009] 3 IR 613, 630.

46 The examples related mainly to competition offences.

were to be determined solely by reference to the harm element of the offence.[47] Some mitigating factors reduce culpability, thereby influencing the assessment of offence gravity (the first limb of the proportionality principle). In an assault case, for example, factors such as youth, mental disability or provocation, if present at the time of the offence, may reduce culpability. The harm caused or risked must also, of course, be considered before deciding where to locate the offence on the overall scale of gravity. Other mitigating factors are relevant only to the second limb of the proportionality principle which requires consideration of the offender's personal circumstances as they exist at the time of sentence. Those circumstances include the offender's response to the charge. An early admission of guilt and assistance to law enforcement authorities are widely accepted as deserving of mitigation. The range of potentially mitigating factors is quite open-ended. Empirical studies have identified some hundreds of them, although the lists in question reveal significant overlap and, aside from that, only a few such factors will ordinarily be present in a given case.[48] White-collar offenders, as already noted, are sentenced according the same principles as apply to all other offenders. Proportionality remains the overarching distributive principle and the same range of general mitigating factors, whether related to culpability at the time of the offence or personal circumstances at the time of sentence, apply to white-collar offences as to all others that are subject to discretionary penalties. Having said that, certain potentially mitigating factors are more likely to arise in white-collar crime than in cases of 'ordinary' crime, and there may be some difference in emphasis when it comes to considering the more standard grounds of mitigation.

A contested trial usually ends in an unqualified verdict of guilty or not guilty.[49] Discretionary sentencing is intended to mitigate the rigours of that binary choice. Once a person is found guilty, which is a public condemnation in itself,[50] the sentencing judge must embark on the difficult task of measuring the *degree* guilt, as well as taking account of other relevant matters. The circumstances in which the offence was committed may be such that the offender, while legally guilty, acted with a low level of culpability. Manslaughter, to give but one example, is widely accepted as an offence that may be committed in a wide range of circumstances, bordering on murder at one end of the spectrum to little more than accident at the other.[51] The maximum penalty for manslaughter is life imprisonment, but the actual penalty must first and foremost reflect the offender's culpability. Sentencing also provides an opportunity to moderate the impact of

---

47 On mitigation generally, see Julian Roberts (ed), *Mitigation and Aggravation at Sentencing* (Cambridge University Press 2011).

48 Joanna Shapland, *Between Conviction and Sentence: The Process of Mitigation* (Routledge and Kegan Paul 1981) ; Jessica Jacobson and Mike Hough, *Mitigation: the role of personal factors in sentencing* (Prison Reform Trust 2007).

49 A jury, where there is one, may also find itself unable to agree or it may, in appropriate circumstances, return a special verdict of not guilty by reason of insanity.

50 Andrew P Simester, 'Can Negligence be Culpable?' in Jeremy Horder (ed), *Oxford Essays in Jurisprudence, Fourth Series* (Oxford University Press 2000) 85 ('The conviction is a public, condemnatory labelling of the defendant: a finding that she is "guilty" of wrongful, blameworthy, and prohibited action').

51 *R v Hobbs and D.M.* [2018] EWCA Crim 1003.

certain substantive criminal law rules and, occasionally, to compensate for the absence of a defence of ignorance of the law. The last-mentioned considerations often have special relevance in cases of white-collar crime.

Standard Mitigating Factors

All of the standard mitigating factors are potentially applicable in white-collar crime cases, but two call for particular attention: a guilty plea and previous good character.[52] Every person charged with a criminal offence of any description has an unqualified constitutional right to trial in due course of law.[53] A convicted person may never be penalised with a heavier sentence for having pleaded not guilty and opted for trial, but a person who has waived that right, thereby relieving the prosecution of having to prove the charge, is entitled to credit for having done so. The extent of the credit depends on a number of factors including the stage at which the guilty plea was indicated and the length and complexity of the trial that was thereby avoided.[54] English sentencing guidelines specify a discount ranging from 33% to 10% , depending on when the plea was entered.[55] In Ireland, the Court of Appeal has said that the reduction will normally be in the range of 15% to 30%, depending on the circumstances.[56] More recently, it has accepted a 25% reduction as 'common practice.'[57] The complexity of the trial obviated by a plea is especially relevant in fraud prosecutions. Even in a case where a guilty verdict might ultimately seem inevitable, the prosecution will have to prove each element of every offence charged and that, in turn, may require the production and proof of a large volume of documentation and the calling of many witnesses. This would hold true, for example, where the defendant was accused of having committed a series of fraudulent offences against the same person or organisation over a period of years — a not uncommon scenario. A guilty plea will therefore merit a reasonably generous discount in those circumstances, as the courts have consistently acknowledged.[58] A discount over and above the norm will generally be granted where the offender, in addition to pleading guilty, co-operated to a significant degree in the investigation of the offence.[59] Some additional credit may also be due to a person sent forward for trial following a signed plea of guilty in the District Court, as this relieves the prosecution of having to prepare a book of evidence.[60]

Persons convicted of white-collar offences seldom have any previous convictions. In addition, many of them will have been of positively good character in terms

52 Mitigating factors are discussed in more detail in Tom O'Malley, *Sentencing Law and Practice* (3rd edn, Round Hall 2016) ch 6.

53 Constitution of Ireland, Art 38.1.

54 Criminal Justice Act 1999, s 29(1) (in determining credit for a guilty plea, a court may take account of the stage at which, and the circumstances in which, it was indicated).

55 Sentencing Council, *Reduction in Sentence for a Guilty Plea: Definitive Guideline* (London 2017).

56 *People (DPP) v Molloy* [2016] IECA 239.

57 *People (DPP) v T.G.* [2018] IECA 83.

58 See, for example, *People (DPP) v Durcan* [2017] IECA 3.

59 *People (DPP) v Begley* [2013] 2 IR 188.

60 Criminal Procedure Act 1967, s 13(2).

of engagement in voluntary work, having made worthwhile contributions to their local communities and so forth. These factors, while undoubtedly relevant, can complicate the sentencing exercise. This a universal phenomenon; there is nothing peculiarly Irish about it. In *People (DPP) v Zaffer (No. 2)*, the Court of Appeal said:

> 'A feature of these types of fraud cases is often the fact that the perpetrator was previously a person of exemplary character…. Another is the fact that the 'victim' is often a large company reasonably capable of recovering from the event. Invariably also the offender is in a senior position of trust within the organisation…'[61]

Compare this with the observation of Samuel W Buell, a leading authority on white-collar crime in the United States:

> 'It is much easier to say that a relatively faceless class of corporate executives should be subject to long prison sentences than it is to lock away a particular individual who typically stands before the court with a long record of professional success, no record of criminal activity, a history of charitable works, and a story about her ability to contribute in some substantial way to social welfare if spared prison.'[62]

The difficulty in such cases, and it is not an uncommon one in sentencing generally, is that a balance must be struck between two competing sets of values. On the one hand, the penalty must reflect the gravity of the offence and the public interest in ensuring that fraudulent conduct, especially where it has harmed individuals, is adequately punished. On the other, it must reflect the character and circumstances of the offender as well as those of the offence. A similar difficulty occasionally arises at the sentencing of sexual offences, especially in cases of so-called historic child abuse.[63] The offender may have no previous convictions and may have made positive contributions to society, but yet he cannot reasonably claim to be of good character if he persistently abused one or more children over a long period while managing to escape detection. The same applies in some white-collar crime cases. The offence may well be an isolated lapse by a person who has genuinely been of good and commendable character, a factor that can properly be treated as mitigating (as it would be for any offence). However, the absence of previous convictions will count for less, and often considerably less, where there has been a pattern of hitherto undetected offending over a lengthy period. Even where such a pattern is established, the offender may be able to show that he or she has been *otherwise* of good character, and some credit may be granted for that. White-collar offenders can often point to a record of community engagement and charitable work as further proof of good character. But here again, caution is needed. Professional and financial success which is so often accompanied by impressive engagement

---

61 [2017] IECA 12, para 7.

62 Samuel Buell, '"White-collar" Crimes' in Markus D Dubber and Tatjana Hörnle (eds), *The Oxford Handbook of Criminal Law* (Oxford University Press 2014) 837, 860.

63 See discussion by High Court of Australia in *Ryan v The Queen* (2001) 206 CLR 267.

in charitable work may well be owing to the opportunities which a person has had in life and these, in turn, may flow from the good fortune of having been born into an affluent family. For this reason, a sentencing court urged to treat charitable work and the like as mitigating should have regard to the offender's life history and the degree of personal effort or sacrifice reflected in the activities or contributions being relied upon. Some judges and commentators have suggested that good character should count for little in certain white-collar crime cases, such as those involving fraud, 'because it is the same unsullied reputation that the allowed the accused to gain the position from which he could commit the crime.'[64] Undoubtedly, where there is evidence that this has happened, less mitigation may be granted for good character than in the ordinary case. But it would be wrong to hold that the nature of the offence should, of itself, justify withholding mitigation for previous good character.

Aside from a guilty plea and previous good character, other offender-related circumstances existing at the time of sentence may also mitigate. They include ill-health or disability, being a foreigner in the country, having a poor command of English, and having sole or primary responsibility for the care of young children or other dependent relatives. Imprisoning a white-collar crime offender may have serious repercussions for his or her employees if the imprisonment causes the collapse or closure of the offender's business. This may be an influential factor in a cusp case, meaning one that seems to fall just above or just below the custody threshold. In such a case the welfare of others, including family dependants and employees, may justifiably tilt the balance in favour of a suspended or non-custodial sentence.[65]

Ignorance of the Law

There is no formal legal rule in this jurisdiction stating that ignorance of the law is no excuse, but there is a long-standing maxim to that effect which is treated, for all practical purposes, as if it were a binding rule.[66] Adherence to the maxim may be justified on the basis that a person living in a given country is morally obliged to become acquainted with its laws in order to ascertain which conduct is prohibited under the pain of criminal sanction.[67] Cases may, however, arise where mistake of law, while insufficient to exculpate, may be understandable in the circumstances, and therefore justify mitigation at sentencing. Some white-collar and corporate crimes, for example, are so rarely prosecuted that lawyers, let alone lay persons, could be forgiven for being occasionally mistaken as to the range of conduct coming

64 *R v Bunn* [2000] 1 SCR 183, 204 (Bastarache J, dissenting). See also *R v Foran* [1970] 2 OR 52 ('This was a fraud and one who did not have the [offender's] position could not have succeeded in committing it as he did').

65 *R v McLeod* [2013] NSWCCA 108; Tom O'Malley, '"That Measure of Wise Clemency": Defending the Suspended Sentence' (2018) 28 ICLJ 39.

66 In Canada, on the other hand, the Criminal Code (s 19) expressly provides: 'Ignorance of the law by a person committing an offence is not an excuse for committing that offence.'

67 For a critical analysis of the maxim, see Andrew Ashworth, 'Ignorance of the Criminal Law, and Duties to Avoid It' (2011) 74 MLR 1, and reprinted in Andrew Ashworth, *Positive Obligations in Criminal Law* (Hart Publishing 2013) ch 3.

within their definition.[68] The same holds true, in more general terms, of offences created under ancient statutes that remain in force though largely forgotten about.[69] Further, certain theft and fraud offences are so widely drawn that the scope of their application can be unpredictable. For instance, the English High Court has recently held, admittedly in the context of a European Arrest Warrant application, that a person who presented a debit card at an ATM machine to obtain cash when he had neither sufficient funds in his account nor an agreed overdraft to cover the relevant amount could be guilty of theft.[70] In *Idrees v DPP*[71] the same court had no difficulty in holding that a man who had got another to impersonate him to take the theory part of a driving tcst was guilty of fraud contrary to ss 1 and 2 of thc Fraud Act 2006. In Ireland, the offence of making a gain or causing a loss by deception under s 6 of the Criminal Justice (Theft and Fraud Offences) Act 2001 can potentially cover a very wide range of behaviour as illustrated by *Kelly v Ryan*[72] and the many cases and examples cited in academic analyses of the equivalent English provisions.[73] Some who engage in dishonest conduct may not, in fact, know that they are committing a specific criminal offence or indeed any offence. But such ignorance of the law will not necessarily diminish their culpability if they should have known that, by ordinary moral standards, what they were doing was wrong or socially harmful. Mitigation may, however, be appropriate where it can reasonably be concluded that the defendant was genuinely and understandably unaware that his or her conduct constituted a criminal offence.

Compensating for Objective Tests of Criminal Responsibility

Where a criminal offence is so defined that an accused person's guilt must be established by reference to an objective standard, a person may properly and lawfully be convicted even though he or she was not subjectively blameworthy or, at least, not blameworthy to a very high degree. Once again, sentencing, as long as it remains discretionary, can provide some equitable redress. Under English law, a person is guilty of theft if he or she dishonestly appropriates another's property with the intention of permanently depriving the other of it.[74]

68 The defendants in *People (DPP) v McAteer and Whelan* (Dublin Circuit Criminal Court, July 2014) were, by all accounts, the first to be prosecuted for an offence contrary to s 60 of the Companies Act 1963 (which prohibited a company from giving financial assistance for the purchase of its own shares).

69 See, for example, *R v Duncan* [1944] 1 KB 713 where a conviction under the Witchcraft Act 1735 was upheld.

70 *Chodorek v District Court of Kielce, Poland* [2017] EWHC 995 (Admin); [2018] 1 Cr App R 6, 89.

71 *Idrees v DPP* [2011] EWHC 624 (Admin).

72 *Kelly v Ryan* [2015] IESC 69; [2015] 1 IR 360. This case never got to trial, but in the judicial review proceedings the Supreme Court held that there was no evidence or material before the District Court judge who issued the summons to justify a sustainable conclusion that each essential element of alleged offence was present. In particular, there was no evidence that the defendants named in the summons intended to cause a loss.

73 David Ormerod and Karl Laird, *Smith and Hogan's Criminal Law* (14th edn, Oxford University Press 2015), chs 19 and 23; David Ormerod, 'The Fraud Act 2006 – Criminalising Lying' [2007] Crim LR 193.

74 Theft Act 1968, s 1.

Following the decision of the Court of Appeal in *R v Ghosh*[75] dishonesty for this purpose was established by asking two questions:

(1) Was the defendant's conduct dishonest according to the standards of reasonable and honest people?
(2) Did the defendant realise that reasonable and honest people would regard what he or she did as dishonest?

The test posited by the first of these questions was clearly objective while the second was subjective. It was only if both were answered in the affirmative that dishonesty, an essential component of theft, was established. However, the UK Supreme Court has recently held that the second *Ghosh* question need no longer be asked, which means that the test of dishonesty under English theft law is now objective.[76] Admittedly, the *Ghosh* test had long been criticised. As Lord Hughes, who delivered the Supreme Court judgment, remarked, 'the less the defendant's standards conform to what society in general expects, the less likely he is to be held criminally responsible for his behaviour.'[77] A similar objective standard is applied in Ireland in relation to the common law offence of conspiracy to defraud. As the Court of Appeal has said:

> 'All of the jurisprudence relating specifically to this offence seems to us to indicate that it is sufficient for a conviction that the prosecution should prove merely that the accused intended to do the impugned act or to participate in the impugned scheme in circumstances where the relevant act or scheme would attract the value judgment, judged by the standards of ordinary reasonable men *(sic)*, that it was dishonest.'[78]

Although irrelevant for the purpose of establishing criminal liability, a defendant's subjective motivation may be relevant at sentencing which is always concerned with measuring the convicted person's *degree* of blameworthiness. An analogy may be drawn with the defence of duress which has traditionally been governed by an objective test: 'threats of immediate death or serious personal violence so great as to overbear the ordinary power of human resistance.'[79] In fact, some recent appeal court decisions have held that there should be a subjective

---

75 *R v Ghosh* [1982] QB 1053.

76 *Ivey v Genting Casinos (UK) Ltd* [2017] UKSC 67; [2018] 2 All ER 406. This admittedly was a civil case which raised a question about the meaning of dishonesty in relation to cheating. It's status as a precedent for the law of theft may therefore be open to question. See comment by Karl Laird [2018] Crim LR 395.

77 *Ivey v Genting Casinos (UK) Ltd* [2017] UKSC 67; [2018] 2 All ER 406, para 58.

78 *People (DPP) v Bowe and Casey* [2017] IECA 250, para 174. Later, at para 175, the court reiterated: 'It is the conduct which must be dishonest. The motivation of the relevant act is irrelevant to liability. Accordingly, [the phrase] "by dishonestly" [in the definition of the offence] has never been regarded in the context of the offence under consideration as referring to an individual's state of mind, but rather as referring to an objective characterisation of, or value judgment with respect to, the impugned conduct.'

79 *People (Attorney General) v Whelan* [1934] IR 518.

element as well.[80] However, even if the test remains entirely objective, thereby rendering it difficult to establish the full defence, evidence that the offence was committed as a result of threats, pressure or coercion falling short of duress may justify mitigation at sentencing.[81] A similar principle applies where a person has been convicted of an offence the mental element of which is governed by a purely objective test.

Evidence of Diligence

Due diligence, however it may be termed, provides a full defence to a charge in some circumstances. In jurisdictions where a distinction is drawn between offences of strict and absolute liability, due diligence usually provides a defence to offences of strict liability only.[82] It may also operate as a statutory defence to specified offences.[83] Diligent action for this purpose will typically involve taking all reasonable steps to avoid committing the offence. This, in turn, may be achieved by putting in place effective procedures or safeguards to prevent injury to others or to protect the environment. A person who is uncertain as to whether a contemplated course of action will contravene the law may also exercise diligence by seeking advice from an appropriate government official or a lawyer specialising in the relevant area. If a person who, having been assured, though erroneously, by a government official that the proposed course of action was entirely legal, is later prosecuted, he or she may seek to raise a defence of officially induced error. This is a well-recognised defence in Canada and the United States,[84] and it seems to have been occasionally accepted by English courts as well.[85] The purpose of the defence as it operates in Canada was described by McLachlin CJ as follows:

> 'The defence of officially induced error of law is intended to protect a diligent person who first questions a government authority about the interpretation of legislation so as to be sure to comply with it and then

---

80 *People (DPP) v Dickey* (Court of Criminal Appeal, 7 March 2003); *People (DPP) v Gleeson* [2016] IECA 332.

81 *R v Taonis* (1974) 59 Cr App R 160; *People (DPP) v O'Toole* (Court of Criminal Appeal, 25 March 2003).

82 *R v City of Sault Ste Marie* [1978] 2 SCR 1299; *Lévis (City) v Tétreault* [2006] 1 SCR 420.

83 Criminal Justice (Corruption Offences) Act 2018, s 18(2). Other examples include the Intoxicating Liquor Act 1988, s 45.

84 Leading United States authorities include *Raley v Ohio* 360 US 423 (1959) and *Cox v Louisiana* 379 US 536 (1965). See John T Parry, 'Culpability, Mistake and Official Interpretations of the Law' (1997) 25 American Journal of Criminal Law 1; Dean Connelly, 'Bad Advice: The Entrapment by Estoppel Doctrine in Criminal Law' (1994) 48 Univ Miami LR 627.

85 In *Postermobile plc v Brent London Borough Council* (*The Times*, 8 December 1997), the English High Court stayed a prosecution for an alleged planning offence because of officially-induced error. See Andrew Ashworth, 'Testing Fidelity to Legal Values: Official Involvement and Criminal Justice' in Stephen Shute and Andrew P Simester (eds), *Criminal Law Theory: Doctrines of the General Part* (Oxford University Press 2002) ch. 13.

is prosecuted by the same government for acting in accordance with the interpretation the authority gave him or her.'[86]

The defence had been recognised by Lamer CJ in a concurring opinion in *R v Jorgensen*,[87] and it was later adopted by a full and unanimous Supreme Court in *City of Lévis v Tétrault*.[88] Lamer CJ had set out six matters that had to be proved by a person seeking to rely on the defence, including that the advice was sought from an appropriate official and that it was reasonable. These were effectively adopted by the court in *City of Lévis,* although it also stressed that 'it is necessary to establish the objective reasonableness not only of the advice, but also of the reliance on the advice.'[89] This aspect of the question, it held, must be considered from the perspective of a reasonable person in the position of the accused.

The status of officially induced error in Irish law is currently uncertain. It was the subject of some discussion in *People (DPP) v Bowe and Casey*[90] where the Court of Appeal found that it did not arise on the facts. However, the court seemed to accept that it might be available where an accused person '[established] that he expressly or by implication sought information as to the legality of what he was doing and was provided with information that would have entitled him to reach a conclusion that his conduct was legal.'[91] The court further assumed that officially induced error would operate, not as a defence, but as a basis for stopping or prohibiting a trial. This may be a moot point, but it need not detain us here. At sentencing, evidence that the offender had exercised some degree of diligence or conscientiousness, even if not to an extent that would justify restraint of trial or a verdict of acquittal, to avoid committing an offence, should be treated as mitigating. To have taken such steps would reflect well on the offender's character and thus reduce his or her moral blameworthiness. The same applies to reliance on legal advice which will not ordinarily relieve a person of criminal liability.[92]

Occupational Culture

Edwin Sutherland who, as noted earlier, is credited with inventing the term

---

86 *R v Bédard* 2017 SCC 4; [2017] 1 SCR 89.

87 *R v Jorgensen* [1995] 4 SCR 55.

88 *Lévis (City) v Tétreault* [2006] 1 SCR 420.

89 *Lévis (City) v Tétreault* [2006] 1 SCR 420 para. 27. See also *R v Cancoil Thermal Corp.* (1986) 27 CCC (3d) 295 (Ontario Court of Appeal).

90 *People (DPP) v Bowe and Casey* [2017] IECA 250, paras 50-55. The Supreme Court has recently allowed a further appeal to be taken (though yet to be heard) on the question of whether a defence of officially induced error is available in Ireland: *People (DPP) v Casey* [2018] IESCDET 87.

91 ibid, para 50.

92 Exceptionally, in England, the Enterprise Act 2002, s 188B3 provides for a defence of reliance on legal advice in connection with cartel offences. For a critical analysis of the refusal to recognise such a defence generally, see Paul Robinson, *Criminal Law Defences* (West Publishing 1984), Vol 2, §183(c) 1. For further discussion, see Tom O'Malley, *Sentencing Law and Practice* (3rd edn, Round Hall 2016) 552-554.

'white-collar crime', is also acknowledged as one of the leading criminologists of the twentieth century, largely because of his theory of differential association. This was a species of learning theory which, at the risk of over-simplifying, claimed that our behaviour is learned from those with whom we have the closest association, whether in the home, the school, the workplace or elsewhere, but mainly within intimate personal groups.[93] A person's inclination to engage in criminal or deviant behaviour is strongly influenced by exposure to definitions that are favourable or unfavourable to law-breaking. For instance, a person may be more inclined to engage in tax evasion if immersed in an occupational culture where such conduct is routinely condoned or even encouraged. Differential association theory has been criticised for portraying human beings as empty vessels into which values, attitudes and definitions are poured, and which they are incapable of critically evaluating.[94] Yet, it retains some explanatory power for some (though not all) crime committed in an organisational setting. Invocation of organisational culture or practices will not relieve a person of criminal liability. In *R v Hayes*[95] (which arose from the LIBOR scandal in London), the appellant, a trader, was convicted on several counts of conspiracy to defraud and sentenced to 14 years' imprisonment. A central issue for the jury and, later, for the Court of Appeal was whether the appellant had acted dishonestly. As noted earlier, under the first limb of the test in *R v Ghosh*[96] a court must ask if the defendant's conduct was dishonest according to the standards of reasonable and honest people. In *Hayes* the defence contended that when it came to answering that question, 'a necessary contextual factor was the standards of the relevant market at the time and how participants in that market operated.'[97] In other words, the standards of reasonable and honest people should be evaluated by reference to the market and the ethos in which the defendant operated. The Court of Appeal decisively rejected this argument, saying that it was unsupported by authority and that it would be quite harmful if adopted. The court said:

> 'The history of the markets [has] shown that, from time to time, markets adopt patterns of behaviour which are dishonest by the standards of honest and reasonable people; in such cases, the market has simply abandoned ordinary standards of honesty. Each of the members of this Court has seen such cases and the damage caused when a market determines its own standards of honesty in this way. Therefore to depart from the view that standards of honesty are determined by the standards of ordinary reasonable and honest people is not only unsupported by authority, but would undermine the maintenance of honesty and integrity that are essential to the conduct of business and markets.'[98]

The appellant's appeal against conviction was dismissed but his sentence was

---

93 Edwin Sutherland, *Principles of Criminology* (6th edn, Lippincott 1947).
94 Steven Box, *Deviance, Reality and Society* (Holt, Rinehart and Watson 1971).
95 *R v Hayes* [2015] EWCA Crim 1944; [2018] 1 Cr App R 10, 134.
96 *R v Ghosh* [1982] QB 1053.
97 *R v Hayes* [2015] EWCA Crim 1944; [2018] 1 Cr App R 10, 132, para. 17.
98 [2015] EWCA Crim 1944; [2018] 1 Cr App R 10, 132, para. 32.

reduced from 14 to 11 years' imprisonment (though not because of the factor just mentioned).

A sentencing court might legitimately take account of occupational culture, if only to a slight degree, when assessing culpability for an offence committed in an organisational setting. One problem with white-collar crime, as Samuel Buell remarks, is its 'embeddedness', meaning that criminal behaviour is often 'enmeshed within, closely related to, and not readily distinguishable from socially acceptable or even welcome conduct.'[99] The nature of the offence, the age and experience of the offender, the ethos of the particular work environment, the offender's awareness of the illegality of the conduct and the extent to which he or she might reasonably have been expected to refrain from engaging in it are therefore among the factors that might influence a court in deciding if occupational culture should be treated as mitigating. The offender's seniority and income are usually relevant for this purpose. In *Hayes* (above), for example, the English Court of Appeal noted that the appellant had earned as much as £1.54 million in one nine-month period in 2010.[100] Strangely enough, the court cited his 'non-managerial position' as one reason for reducing the sentence. Ordinarily, however, a person with that level of income, and the professional success which it reflects, can scarcely make any credible claim to have been led astray by occupational culture.

Aggravating Factors

Abuse of trust, commonplace and endemic though it may be in fraud-related offences, is usually treated as an aggravating factor. Such a principle is justified where breach of trust is not an essential ingredient of the offence. Theft, for example, sometimes involves a breach of trust, but sometimes not. Courts always take a serious view of dishonest conduct by members of professions in which the public are entitled to place their trust. Misappropriation of client funds by solicitors or accountants amounts to a particularly egregious breach of trust and will be punished accordingly.[101] Where a fraud has been perpetrated over a period of time, the number of transactions and the period during which the offending occurred may be further aggravating factors.[102] An offence or pattern of offending that reflects a sophisticated or careful degree of planning will also be treated as more serious on that account.[103]

---

[99] Samuel Buell, '"White-collar" Crimes' in Markus D Dubber and Tatjana Hörnle (eds), *The Oxford Handbook of Criminal Law* (Oxford University Press 2014) 841.

[100] *R v Hayes* [2015] EWCA Crim 1944; [2018] 1 Cr App R 10, 134, para 101.

[101] *People (DPP) v Durcan* [2017] IECA 3; *R v Cove* (1993) 14 Cr App R (S) 498; *R v Jacob* [1982] Crim LR 135; *R v Miles* [2007] 2 Cr App R (S) 5, 19; *R v Bunn* [2000] 1 SCR 183, 202-203 (Bastarache J, dissenting); *People (DPP) v Byrne* (Dublin Circuit Criminal Court, 2 December 2013).

[102] *People (DPP) v Reilly* [2016] IECA 43. Contrast with *People (DPP) v Walsh* [2016] IECA 74.

[103] This is one of the factors mentioned in the English Sentencing Council's Definitive Guideline on Fraud, Bribery and Money Laundering Offences (London 2014).

Targeting a victim who is vulnerable because of age, disability, isolation or some other factor, is an aggravating factor for many offences. In fraud-related offences, it may become an issue where, for example, an investment broker targeted vulnerable individuals, pressurising them into parting with their money on the pretence that they would profit from doing so, and then misappropriated it. The same applies in so-called tarmacadam scams, where the offenders convince householders (typically elderly persons living alone) that they need to get certain work done, such as resurfacing a driveway, and then charge them extortionate amounts of money.[104]

Previous convictions for similar offences may sometimes be treated as an aggravating factor. This seldom arises in white-collar cases as few offenders have criminal records. Ordinarily, the courts adopt a progressive loss of mitigation approach under which a person with no previous convictions is entitled to substantial mitigation on that account, but to progressively less (and eventually to none) as he or she accumulates more convictions.[105] Treating previous convictions as an aggravating factor is theoretically troublesome, not least because it can amount to double punishment.[106] An offender is being punished more heavily for the current offence because of earlier offences for which he or she has already been punished. Be that as it may, many jurisdictions now have formal provisions requiring previous convictions to be treated as an aggravating factor.[107] Here in Ireland, the present Court of Appeal, while generally adhering to the progressive loss of mitigation approach, has been willing to make an exception where an offender has previous convictions for similar offences, at least where they were reasonably serious in nature.[108] The treatment of previous convictions as an aggravating factor should not, however, lead to the imposition of a disproportionately severe sentence for the offence of conviction. Ordinarily, relevant previous convictions should do no more than justify locating the offence at a higher point within the appropriate sentence range. In an exceptional case, where previous convictions can properly be said to have increased the offender's culpability for the instant offence, they may justify locating the offence in a higher range than would otherwise be appropriate. Needless to say, the maximum sentence for the offence of conviction may never be exceeded.

---

104 In one such case, *People (DPP) v O'Brien* [2018] IECA 85, the Court of Appeal upheld a sentence of three years' imprisonment.

105 *R v Queen* (1981) 3 Cr App R (S) 245 (the leading English authority on this principle).

106 Julian Roberts and Andreas von Hirsch (eds), *Previous Convictions at Sentencing: Theoretical and Applied Perspectives* (Hart Publishing 2010).

107 Criminal Justice Act 2003, s 142 (3) (England and Wales). Grid-based guideline systems in the United States generally impose a significant premium for previous convictions. Under the federal sentencing guidelines, for example, a person with the highest criminal history score qualifies for a prison sentence that is often more than twice as long as the recommended sentence for a person convicted of the same offence but with no previous convictions. See Rhys Hester, Richard S. Frase, Julian Roberts and Kelly Lyn Mitchell, 'Prior Record Enhancements at Sentencing: Unsettled Justifications and Unsettling Consequences' (2018) 47 Crime and Justice: A Review of Research 209.

108 *People (DPP) v Kinsella* [2017] IECA 85; *People (DPP) v Casey and Casey* [2018] IECA 121.

Sentencing Fraud

Fraud, while not a specific offence under Irish law, is commonly used to describe conduct coming within the definition of certain offences under the Criminal Justice (Theft and Fraud Offences) Act 2001, notably making a gain or causing a loss by deception (s 6), false accounting (s 10), forgery offences (ss 24 to 31) and, in some instances, counterfeiting offences (ss 32 to 39). Indeed, it may also consist of theft (s 4) involving a breach of trust.[109] Fraud can take many forms, but it is quite commonly committed by persons who use their occupation or a position of trust to divert to their own use money or other property that rightfully belongs to another. It will often include making false instruments (forgery) and/or using such instruments. Many defendants, by the time they are detected, will have committed many acts of fraud against one or more victims. This, in turn, raises the perennially difficult question of how a court should go about sentencing an offender convicted simultaneously of multiple crimes.[110] Should prison sentences, where they are imposed, be concurrent, consecutive or partly concurrent? There can scarcely be a more intractable question in all of our sentencing law. Not that the problem is in any way peculiar to Ireland; many other jurisdictions struggle with the same issue. Phrased in stark terms, the choice is between concurrent sentences that may be viewed, with some justification, as granting a discount for bulk offending, and consecutive sentences which, even with the application of the totality principle, may result in a cumulative penalty that seems excessive in our legal culture, though not necessarily in that of other jurisdictions such as the United States. Sometimes, admittedly, the answer is quite straightforward. Sentences imposed for offences arising from the same criminal transaction will almost invariably be concurrent.[111] Otherwise, in this country at least, courts have discretion in deciding whether multiple prison sentences should be ordered to run concurrently or consecutively, although there is a general preference for making them concurrent.

In Ireland, as in other common-law countries (apart from some American jurisdictions), the sentencing of multiple offences is approached pragmatically. Courts usually apply a totality principle to arrive at a sentence that seems appropriate in light of the entire criminal conduct reflected in the offences of conviction. They may achieve this by imposing as severe a sentence as proportionality will allow for the most serious offence and order the others to run concurrently. Or they may order two or more of the sentences to run consecutively, making some reduction, if necessary, from the cumulative term to reflect totality. We are referring here to custodial sentences only, but custody will almost inevitably be appropriate for serious fraud offences. Full or part suspension can also, of course, be considered if the circumstances are sufficiently exceptional. Another widely used, though less desirable, strategy is to impose a

---

[109] See, for example, *People (DPP) v Reilly* [2016] IECA 43; *People (DPP) v Hawkins* [2014] IECCA 36.

[110] See Jesper Ryberg, Julian Roberts and Jan Willem de Keijser (eds), *Sentencing Multiple Crimes* (Oxford University Press 2018), an excellent collection of essays on this topic.

[111] See, for example, *R v Robey* [2018] EWCA Crim 906; *R v Greaves* [2010] EWCA Crim 709.

specific sentence for one or more offences and take the others into consideration. As the Court of Appeal recently said, when dealing with multiple offences such as residential burglaries committed as part of a crime spree, the practice of taking offences into consideration is best avoided, even where a court decides to impose a global sentence to reflect the totality of the offending.[112] Apart from everything else, such a practice may give the impression that the offender is being 'let off' for some, perhaps many, of the offences.[113] As the Court of Appeal rightly noted, the Supreme Court (per Finlay CJ), more than 30 years ago, when dealing with a similar situation, had said: 'Appropriate sentence should, in my view, be imposed on all counts in respect of which an accused person has been convicted by a jury.'[114] (The same presumably applies where an offender has pleaded guilty to several offences.) Where several frauds have been committed over a period of time against the same victim, typically by an employee against an employer, the court may treat the total amount taken as if it were the subject of a single offence and sentence accordingly.[115] The sentence will usually be imposed in respect of one specified count. This is one situation where concurrent sentences should be imposed for the remaining counts because the total loss or harm to the victim is reflected in the final sentence.

Certain principles governing the sentencing of fraud may now be deduced from the limited body of modern case law on the topic. Serious fraud, irrespective of whether it involved one or more criminal transactions, will normally merit a custodial sentence. As the Court of Appeal said in *People (DPP) v Zaffer*:

> 'Serious pre-meditated fraud will almost always merit a custodial sentence. The fact that the victim of the fraud is a large corporation rather than an individual may justify a more lenient sentence than would otherwise be the case, but normally, only the existence of exceptional circumstances should result in an entirely non-custodial sentence where there are hundreds of thousands of Euro involved.'[116]

In that case, a wholly suspended sentence imposed on a senior claims officer with an insurance company for a series of well-planned, orchestrated frauds

---

112 *People (DPP) v Casey and Casey* [2018] IECA 121.

113 ibid at para 16.

114 *People (DPP) v Higgins,* Supreme Court, 22 November 1985.

115 This was the approach adopted by the trial judge in *People (DPP) v Zaffer* [2016] IECA 321 and it did not attract any criticism from the Court of Appeal, although the sentence actually imposed was found to be unduly lenient. The same was done in *People (DPP) v Reilly* [2016] IECA 43, discussed below, where a sentence was imposed on the first of 80 counts of theft to which the appellant pleaded guilty, with the remainder taken into consideration. The sentence was upheld on appeal. At the time of writing, a former credit union employee has been charged with 592 separate offences relating to the theft of more than €400,000 from her employer ('Former credit union employee charged with stealing €400k', *Irish Examiner,* 25 May 2018).

116 *People (DPP) v Zaffer* [2016] IECA 321, para 15. Earlier in its judgment (para. 8), the court said that a perusal of its recent decisions 'indicates clearly that an actual custodial term is the common outcome in cases of fraud involving substantial sums of money'. See now *People (DPP) v Maguire* [2018] IECA 116 which deals in considerable detail with fraud sentencing.

which resulted in a loss of more than €200,000 to the company was found to be unduly lenient. The court considered the appropriate headline sentence to be 2½ years' imprisonment but, because of mitigating factors, it suspended all but eight months of that term.[117] Persistence, purpose and impact are among the key factors determining the gravity of fraud offences. Courts are most likely to impose a substantial custodial sentence where there has been a persistent pattern of fraudulent conduct resulting in the loss of a significant amount of money. They also have regard to the purpose of the fraud (e.g. was it to fund an extravagant lifestyle?) and the degree of trust that had been reposed in the offender.[118] The identity and circumstances of the victim may also influence sentence. As in the case of theft generally, a fraud that resulted in individual victims losing money, especially where they could ill afford it, will be treated more seriously than one causing a similar loss to a large corporation. Deceiving individuals or surreptitiously appropriating their property is usually more culpable, in the sense of being more morally blameworthy, than defrauding a corporate entity. Everything, of course, depends on the circumstances. A significant financial loss could cause the collapse of a small or medium-sized business to the great personal detriment of its owners, employees and their families. As noted earlier, a breach of trust, though commonplace in fraud-related offences, is routinely treated as aggravating.

The loss caused by the offence will undoubtedly influence sentence, although it is seldom determinative. Victim impact is equally important. A relatively small loss may have a severe impact on some victims. In *People (DPP) v Reilly,*[119] the appellant, while employed as a tied agent of an insurance company, stole money from clients, the provable loss being well in excess of €800,000. All of the clients were eventually reimbursed by the company which suffered a total loss of more than €1 million. The appellant pleaded guilty and was highly co-operative, and there were further mitigating factors. He was sentenced to four-and-a-half years' imprisonment. As against this, the offences had been committed over a period of 10 years or so. Upholding the sentence, the Court of Appeal said that this was one of those rare cases where something close to the maximum sentence for theft (10 years) would have been appropriate as a headline sentence. Assuming that a reduction of about 50% had been allowed for mitigation, the sentence imposed by the trial judge was appropriate. In *People (DPP) v Walsh*[120] the appellant, on pleading guilty to 75 counts of theft, was sentenced to a total of two-and-a-half years' imprisonment. He was a self-employed agent for a life insurance company and, over a period of about 15 months, he had fabricated policies which resulted in the company being defrauded of €215,000. The Court of Appeal contrasted this case with *Reilly* (above), noting that the loss was much smaller, the fraud was perpetrated over a short period of time, and the offending was not primarily directed at defrauding individuals. There were other mitigating factors as well. The Court therefore suspended the last 10 months of the sentence (although the reduction also included credit for the appellant's

[117] *People (DPP) v Zaffer (No 2)* [2017] IECA 12.
[118] *People (DPP) v O'Brien* [2018] IECA 85, para. 11.
[119] *People (DPP) v Reilly* [2016] IECA 43.
[120] *People (DPP) v Walsh* [2016] IECA 74.

conduct while in custody). *Walsh,* in turn, was used as a comparator in *People (DPP) v Moran*[121] where the appellant pleaded guilty to defrauding his employer (a bank of which he was financial controller) of approximately €283,000. He had no previous convictions. The Court of Appeal considered the three-year prison term imposed by the trial judge to be an appropriate headline sentence but, having regard to the amount of the loss caused (about 25% greater than in *Walsh*) and other factors, it suspended the last 10 months of that term. The appellants in *Walsh* and *Moran* therefore ended up with effective sentences of 20 months and 26 months respectively. Care must obviously be exercised when using comparator cases in this context. For example, the sentences ultimately imposed in *Walsh* and *Moran* were probably consistent with *Reilly* in so far as the amount of loss was concerned (though there were other differences as well). However, if these defendants had been sentenced by reference to the effective term of 12 years' imprisonment imposed by the Circuit Court in *People (DPP) v Byrne*[122] for the theft of €52 million from banks and defrauding 13 clients out of their homes and money, the sentence in each case might have been lower. A comparison with some leading English fraud cases would further underscore this point.[123] This is one area where guidelines could usefully be developed indicating the role to be attributed to loss and, if that is deemed an important factor, further indicating presumptive or recommended starting points depending on the amount involved.

The Court of Appeal has firmly endorsed a principle of parsimony when sentencing first-time offenders of previous good character. A custodial sentence will be avoided unless the nature or gravity of the offence makes it inevitable.[124] In *People (DPP) v Durcan*[125] the court reduced from 12 to six months the term of imprisonment imposed on a former solicitor who pleaded guilty to one count of stealing €260,000 from client accounts over a three-year period. There were several mitigating factors including an early guilty plea, previous good character and the fact that she had fully reimbursed the Law Society Compensation Fund. She was also the mother of five children aged between seven and 13 years who, at the time of sentence, were living with her husband and herself in Brussels where she was teaching English. Having reviewed various Irish and English authorities on the matter, the Court of Appeal said:

---

121 *People (DPP) v Moran* [2016] IECA 215.

122 *People (DPP) v Byrne* (Dublin Circuit Criminal Court, 2 December 2013).

123 In *R v Bright* [2008] 2 Cr App R (S) 102, 578, the appellant was convicted of two counts of conspiracy to defraud which involved losses of about £1 billion and which resulted in about 1,000 employees losing their jobs. The case was described by the Court of Appeal as involving one of the most serious commercial disasters to have occurred in recent years. A sentence of seven years' imprisonment was upheld on appeal. See also *Attorney General's References (Nos 7 and 8 of 2013) (R v Kallakis and Williams)* [2014] 1 Cr App R (S) 26, 140 and the earlier cases cited therein.

124 In *People (DPP) v Moran* [2016] IECA 216, paras 11 and 12, the Court of Appeal said: 'When dealing with first-time offenders… the courts are generally reluctant to impose immediate custodial sentences, and frequently do not do so. This is in the interests of rehabilitation and very much in the public interest. First-time offenders are often deemed unlikely to re-offend in the future…. The exception to this general approach are those cases where the offence is particularly serious and/or where the victim impact is significant.'

125 [2017] IECA 3.

> '[A] judge sentencing a person of previous good character, who has decided that a custodial sentence was necessary and not capable of being avoided, and having decided on what seems an appropriate sentence, should then ask himself or herself whether in fact a sentence less than the one initially contemplated could properly meet the situation.'[126]

As the court noted, there were many precedents to this effect including the well-known statement, which it quoted, of Lawton LJ in *R v Sargeant*: 'We take the view that for men of good character the very fact that prison gates have closed is the main punishment. It does not necessarily follow that they should remain closed for very long.'[127] This principle is potentially applicable to all offences, and not just to those of a white-collar nature. The appellant in *Sargeant* was a nightclub bouncer who pleaded guilty to affray. The offences in the earlier Irish authorities included accepting a corrupt payment[128] and various sexual offences.[129] One factor which will not mitigate is lack of prudence on the part of a victim, whether that happens to be an individual or a corporation. In *Attorney General's References (Nos 7 and 8 of 2013) (R v Kallakis and Williams)*[130] which involved conspiracies to defraud and in which Allied Irish Bank was persuaded to lend more than £743 million, the trial judge held that lack of care on the part of the bank offered no mitigation to the offenders. The Court of Appeal, in increasing the sentences, seems to have endorsed this view. An Irish court would probably adopt the same approach, and all the more so where the victim was an individual as opposed to an institution.

Collateral Consequences

To an increasing extent, a criminal conviction exposes a person not only to the primary punishment, typically a fine or term of imprisonment, specified in the statute creating the offence, but to further penalties and restrictive measures that may, depending on individual circumstances, be quite punitive in effect. Examples include disqualification, forfeiture, confiscation of assets, sex offender notification orders and post-release supervision. All of these measures arise by operation of law. Additionally, a person may suffer many other detriments, including loss of employment and pension rights, adverse publicity, social ostracization and possibly family break-up, as a result of being convicted of a serious offence. The range of ancillary measures potentially

126 [2017] IECA 3, para 21. The court referred to *People (DPP) v Maguire* [2015] IECA 350; *People (DPP) v Doherty* (Court of Criminal Appeal, 29 April 2001); *People (DPP) v Egan* [2001] 2 ILRM 299; *R v Sargeant* (1974) 60 Cr. App. R. 74; *People (DPP) v Prior* [2016] IECA 375; *R v Bibi* [1980] 1 WLR 1193.

127 (1974) 60 Cr App R 74, 77.

128 *People (DPP) v Doherty* (Court of Criminal Appeal, 29 April 2003).

129 *People (DPP) v Mooney* [2015] IECA 301; *People (DPP) v Prior* [2016] IECA 375; *People (DPP) v Egan* [2001] 2 ILRM 299.

130 *Attorney General's References (Nos 7 and 8 of 2013) (R v Kallakis and Williams)* [2014] 1 Cr App R (S) 26, 140. See comment by David Thomas, [2013] Crim LR 776 and Anita Killeen, 'Conspiracy to Defraud: A Clarification of the Sentencing Approach' (2013) 77 Journal of Criminal Law 380.

applicable to convicted persons is constantly expanding. For example, under the Criminal Justice (Corruption Offences) Act 2018 a court imposing sentence for certain corruption offences may order the forfeiture of any office, position or employment as a 'relevant Irish official' (in effect a public servant) held or occupied by the offender. This does not apply to certain office holders such as judges whose removal from office is governed by special constitutional or legislative provisions. Further, a court may make an order prohibiting the offender from seeking to hold any office, position or employment as an Irish official for a specified period not exceeding 10 years (except for membership of the Oireachtas, the European Parliament or a local authority). Such an order may be made in addition to the primary punishment (a fine, term of imprisonment or both) specified for the relevant offence. Disqualification from holding public office, including political office, is widely available to courts in continental European countries.[131] In some American jurisdictions, a felony conviction may result in disenfranchisement, even for life.[132]

There is now an extensive scholarly literature on collateral consequences.[133] In the space available, we shall concentrate on just one aspect of them. This concerns the extent to which collateral consequences should be placed in the balance when determining the primary punishment to be imposed for an offence. The argument in favour of doing so would run as follows. A sentence must always be proportionate to the gravity of the offence and the personal circumstances of the offender. A sentence consists of a punishment imposed for an offence, having regard to all the relevant circumstances. Punishment, in turn, consists of some unpleasant consequence(s) visited upon a person who has violated the criminal law. In many instances, the only such consequence will be a fine or a term of imprisonment. But some offenders will suffer several unpleasant consequences, some arising by operation of law and others (such as loss of employment or public opprobrium) arising, perhaps inevitably, as a matter of

---

131 In 2004, former French Prime Minister, Alain Juppé received a 14-month suspended prison sentence and a one-year deprivation of the right to run for public office on being convicted of paying party activists for doing non-existent jobs in the 1990s. See Philippe Ridet, 'Le 'microcosme français' perturbe la stratégie d'Allain Juppé', *Le Monde* (14 October 2005), available at: <https://www.lemonde.fr/societe/article/2005/10/24/le-microcosme-francais-perturbe-la-strategie-d-alain-juppe_702711_3224.html> (accessed 30 November 2018). At the time of writing, a decision is awaited from the Grand Chamber of the European Court of Human Rights in respect of a similar ban imposed by an Italian court on Silvio Berlusconi (*Berlusconi v Italy* (App No 58428/13).

132 The Sentencing Project, *Felony Disenfranchisement,* available at: <www.sentencingproject.org> (accessed 30 November 2018).

133 See, for example, Nora V Demleitner, 'Collateral Sanctions and American Exceptionalism in Comparative Perspective' in Kevin R Reitz (ed), *American Exceptionalism in Crime and Punishment* (Oxford University Press 2018), ch. 11; Margaret Colgate Love, Jenny M Roberts and Cecelia Klingele, *Collateral Consequences of Criminal Convictions: Law, Policy and Practice* (Thomson West 2016); Gabriel J Chin, 'Collateral Consequences' in Erik Luna (ed), *Reforming Criminal Justice,* Vol 4, available at <www.academyforjustice.org> (accessed 30 November 2018); Michael Pinard, 'An integrated perspective on the collateral consequences of criminal convictions and the re-entry issues faced by formerly incarcerated persons' (2006) 86 Boston Univ LR 632.

fact. It may therefore be argued that some, perhaps all, of these consequences should be given due weight when selecting the primary penalty.

The principle of cumulative proportionality is well established as far as multiple officially imposed penalties are concerned. A criminal court sentencing a person convicted of tax evasion, for example, must take account of any interest and penalties already paid by the offender to the revenue authorities in respect of the same infraction.[134] The same can now almost certainly be said of certain legally mandated ancillary measures, such as sex offender notification orders, which, although avowedly preventative in purpose, may be punitive in effect.[135] Other consequences such as loss of employment, diminished career prospects and reputational damage can undoubtedly flow from a criminal conviction, but the extent to which they should influence sentence is debatable. White-collar offenders are very likely to suffer consequences of this nature, but to give them credit on that account poses ethical difficulties. Should a well-educated, well-paid executive who stole, say, €100,000 from his or her employer or clients be treated more leniently because of loss of employment, social standing and so forth than an unemployed drug addict from a deprived background who stole say, €1,000, but who has nothing else to lose? Certainly, it seems wrong that the white-collar offender should be spared imprisonment for this reason while the other was not. The idea of condemnation without incarceration, which has sometimes been proposed for 'respectable' offenders, is ethically untenable. It has been suggested that being disqualified from exercising a profession, such as that of a solicitor or doctor, should be treated as part of the punishment whereas being temporarily incapacitated through imprisonment from pursuing a trade need not be taken into account. In other words, the convicted solicitor may never practice again, whereas the painter or plumber can resume business on being released from prison.[136] There may be some logic to this. In practice, courts usually give some credit for collateral consequences that have impinged in a real or material way of the offender's life, or are likely to do so in the future. They have particular regard to loss of employment and associated pension rights, the difficulties the offender will have in securing future employment, impact on the offender's family, and adverse publicity.[137] What must be stressed, however, is that these are merely factors that will mitigate sentence to some degree. They will seldom, if ever, save an offender from being sent to prison where the offence itself clearly warrants a custodial sentence, but they may serve to reduce the term that would otherwise be appropriate.

---

134 *People (DPP) v Redmond* [2001] 3 IR 390; *People (DPP) v Hughes* [2012] IECCA 85; *People (DPP) v Begley* [2013] 2 IR 188.

135 *People (DPP) v N.Y.* [2002] 4 IR 309; *C.C. v Ireland* [2006] 4 IR 1.

136 Ellen S Podgor, 'The Challenge of White-collar Sentencing' (2007) 97 Journal of Criminal Law and Criminology 731.

137 *People (DPP) v Lyons* [2014] IECCA 27; *People (DPP) v Walsh* [2016] IECA 74; *People (DPP) v O'Brien* [2015] IECA 304.

Deferred Prosecution Agreements

Deferred Prosecution Agreements (DPAs) provide one means of avoiding collateral consequences of conviction, though they serve other important purposes as well. A DPA is an arrangement whereby a person or organisation believed to have committed an offence is not formally charged but is instead required to fulfil specified conditions. A prosecution may follow if those conditions are not fulfilled. DPAs originated in the United States where they can apply to both individuals and corporations. They were introduced in England and Wales by the Crime and Courts Act 2013, but only in respect of corporate bodies, partnerships and unincorporated associations. DPAs deserve some discussion in a sentencing context because they usually entail the imposition of a financial penalty and often quite a substantial one.[138] Indeed, it is the telling that the final draft of the Model Penal Code: Sentencing adopted by the American Law Institute in 2017 includes a section on deferred prosecution which it describes as being designed 'to facilitate offenders' rehabilitation and reintegration into the law-abiding community and to restore victims and communities affected by crime.'[139] It further says that deferred prosecution is appropriate in order to hold an individual accountable for criminal conduct 'when justice and public safety do not require that the individual be subjected to the stigma and collateral consequences associated with formal charge and conviction.'[140] The use of DPAs in the United States has been strongly criticised as running counter to the rule of law and increasing prosecutorial power which is already, according to many, out of control.[141] Certainly, it is true to say that American prosecutors are very much in control when it comes to choosing the corporations and individuals who are offered a DPA, and also in determining the conditions to be fulfilled. These may include a requirement to make a substantial contribution to a charity or some similar organisation. Quite famously, an agreement concluded with Bristol-Myers Squibb in 2005 required them to contribute $5 million towards the endowment of a chair of business ethics at Seton Hall Law School of which the prosecutor happened to be a graduate, although the idea apparently came

[138] For a comparative analysis of DPAs in the United States and in England and Wales, see Federico Mazzacuva, 'Justifications and Purposes of Negotiated Justice for Corporate Offenders: Deferred and Non-Prosecution Agreements in the UK and US Systems of Criminal Justice' (2014) 78 Journal of Criminal Law 249. On the background to the English legislation, see UK Ministry of Justice, *Consultation on a New Enforcement Tool to Deal with Economic Crime Committed by Commercial Organisations: Deferred Prosecution Agreements* CP9/2012 (London 2012).

[139] American Law Institute, *Model Penal Code: Sentencing* (Proposed Final Draft 2017), §6.02A(2).

[140] §6.02A(2).

[141] Jennifer Arlen, 'Prosecuting Beyond the Rule of Law: Corporate Mandates Imposed through Deferred Prosecution Agreements' (2016) 8(1) Journal of Legal Analysis 191; Jennifer Arlen and Marcel Kahan, 'Corporate Governance Regulation through Nonprosecution' (2017) 84 University of Chicago LR 323.

from the company itself.[142] The US Department of Justice later issued a direction limiting prosecutors' powers to impose such conditions.[143]

The DPA regime introduced in England and Wales in 2013 deserves our closest attention because it is most likely to become the model for any similar system introduced here. Schedule 17 of the Crime and Courts Act 2013 sets out in detail how DPAs are to operate. As noted earlier, they apply solely to corporate bodies, partnership and unincorporated associations. A DPA may be entered only in respect of certain offences listed in the Schedule, and they include many theft, fraud, customs and excise, bribery and financial services offences. The most distinguishing feature of the English system is that DPAs are subject to judicial approval.[144] Before the terms of a DPA are agreed, the prosecutor must apply to the Crown Court for a declaration that entering into the agreement is likely to be in the interests of justice and that the proposed terms of the agreement are fair, reasonable and proportionate. These proceedings are held in private, presumably to avoid the risk of prejudice to the defendant in the event that no agreement is reached and a prosecution follows. If the court makes a positive declaration following that preliminary hearing and the terms of a DPA are agreed, the prosecution must again apply to the court for a declaration in similar terms to the first. If the court decides to approve the agreement, it must do so, and give its reasons, in public. The requirements that may be imposed by a DPA include:

(a) To pay to the prosecutor a financial penalty;
(b) To compensate victims of the alleged offence;
(c) To donate money to a charity or third party;
(d) To disgorge any profits made by the body which has entered into the DPA from the alleged offence;
(e) To implement a compliance programme or make changes to an existing compliance programme relating to the body's policies or the training of its employees or both;
(f) To co-operate in any investigation related to the alleged offences;
(g) To pay any reasonable costs to the prosecutor in relation to the alleged offence or the DPA.

A DPA must specify the date on which it is to expire, although it may be terminated earlier because of a breach. Significantly also,

'[t]he amount of any financial penalty agreed between the prosecutor

142 For a detailed account of the agreement, see Christopher J Christie and Robert M. Hanna, 'A push down the road of good corporate citizenship: The deferred prosecution agreement between the U.S. Attorney for the District of New Jersey and Bristol-Myers Squibb Co.' (2006) 43 American Criminal Law Review 1043. The first author, Christie, was the prosecutor in the case.

143 Albert W Alschuler, 'Two ways to think about the punishment of corporations' (2009) 46 American Criminal Law Review 1359 at 1385, fn 144; Lawrence A Cunningham, 'Deferred prosecutions and corporate governance: An integrated approach to investigation and reform' (2014) 66 Florida LR 1.

144 Michael Bisgrove and Mark Weekes, 'Deferred Prosecution Agreements: A Practical Consideration' [2014] Crim LR 416.

> and P [the body in question] must be broadly comparable to the fine that a court would have imposed on P on conviction for the alleged offence following a guilty plea.'[145]

Obviously, the existence of sentencing guidelines, from whatever source, will greatly assist in this regard. In adjudicating on the three DPAs that have been approved to date, *Serious Fraud Office v Standard Bank plc*,[146] *Serious Fraud Office v XYZ Ltd*[147] and the largest to date, *Serious Fraud Office v Rolls-Royce Plc*,[148] Sir Brian Levenson, President of the Queen's Bench Division, sitting in the Crown Court, referred not only to the Sentencing Council's guideline on bribery offences, which was the relevant guideline in all three cases, but also to generic guidelines such as those on the discount for a guilty plea and taking offences into consideration and totality.[149] He also took account of relevant aggravating and mitigating factors. This is not to say that formal guidelines are essential for the successful operation of DPAs, but it is quite clearly in the interests of justice that a financial penalty, which will ordinarily be only one of several conditions which the corporation must fulfil, should be broadly equivalent to the fine that would be imposed on conviction for the misconduct in question. Having the agreement approved by an experienced judge becomes all the more important in the absence of guidelines.

When DPAs were first suggested in England and Wales, some feared that they would simply allow large corporations to avoid prosecution and conviction, while being of little help to smaller enterprises. Celia Wells initially described them as a form of 'procedural shadow boxing' in the sense that they were prosecutions in everything but name. She also raised the legitimate question of why they should apply to corporations only.[150] However, DPAs are now viewed more favourably and this is probably due in no small measure to the great care Sir Brian Leveson took with the three DPAs he has so far approved. Indeed, he has himself paid tribute to the care and attention devoted to those cases by the counsel and solicitors who dealt with them.[151] From the limited experience in England and Wales to date, DPAs have been anything but a 'let off' for offending corporations, even if one considers nothing more than the agreed financial penalties. In *Rolls-Royce*, for example, where the company, according

---

145 Crime and Courts Act 2013, Schedule 17, para 5(4).

146 *Serious Fraud Office v Standard Bank plc* [2016] Lloyd's Rep. FC 91 and 102. See Nicola Padfield, 'Deferred Prosecution Agreements' (editorial) [2016] Crim LR 449.

147 *Serious Fraud Office v XYZ Ltd* [2016] Lloyd's Rep. FC 507 and 517.

148 *Serious Fraud Office v Rolls-Royce Plc* [2017] Lloyd's Rep. FC 249 (Crown Court at Southwark, 17 January 2017). See Rita Cheung, 'Deferred Prosecution Agreements: Cooperation and Confession' [2018] Cambridge LJ 12.

149 Sentencing Council, *Fraud, Bribery and Money Laundering Offences. Definitive Guideline* (2014); Sentencing Council, *Offences Taken into Consideration and Totality: Definitive Guideline* (2012); Sentencing Council, *Reduction in Sentence for a Guilty Plea: Definitive Guideline* (2017). An earlier version of the last-mentioned guideline was in force when these DPAs were approved.

150 Celia Wells, 'Corporate Criminal Liability: A Ten-Year Review' [2014] Crim LR 849, 875.

151 *Serious Fraud Office v Standard Bank Plc* [2016] Lloyd's Rep FC 102, para 23.

to the court, had engaged in 'egregious criminality over decades', the overall financial penalty was, by any standards, enormous. The company was ordered to pay £497 million in fines and disgorgement of profits as well as almost £13 million in costs. In fact, further payments made in the United States and Brazil brought the total to £671 million.[152] As against this, it should be noted that in 2017 alone, Rolls-Royce had underlying pre-tax profits of £1.1 billion.[153] In *Standard Bank,* the company agreed to pay a financial penalty of $16.8 million as well as compensation of $6 million plus interest. It also disgorged profits on the transaction to the amount of $8.4 million.[154]

As a form of negotiated justice, DPAs allow for compliance measures to be put in place and monitored so as to reduce the risk of re-offending.[155] The threat of a prosecution in the event of non-compliance provides wrongdoers with a powerful incentive to take seriously the obligations they have assumed as part of an agreement. DPAs can save offending corporations (or individuals if eligible for them) from some detrimental collateral consequences of conviction.[156] The collapse of Arthur Andersen, which in turn resulted from the collapse of Enron, is often cited as illustrating the consequence that might be avoided through a DPA. Once Andersen was indicted, it was deserted on a wholesale basis by its clients and it went out of business.[157] David M Uhlmann cautions that this was a special case because Andersen was an accounting firm charged with accounting fraud, and that we should not therefore draw too many conclusions about collateral consequences.[158] That is a fair point in so far as Andersen is concerned. But other cases have shown that highly detrimental collateral consequences can be avoided through diversion from prosecution, whether by way of a DPA or otherwise. State laws, for example, may prohibit the awarding of contracts to companies (or perhaps individuals) convicted of certain offences. In *Rolls-Royce*, for instance, Sir Brian Leveson noted that, for this and other reasons, a criminal prosecution

> 'would have a very substantial impact on the company, which, in turn, would have wider effects for the UK defence industry and persons who were not connected to the criminal conduct, including Rolls-Royce employees and pensioners, and those in its supply chain.'[159]

---

152 Celia Wells, 'Corporate Failure to Prevent Economic Crime – A proposal' [2017] Crim LR 426.

153 Peggy Hollinger, 'Rolls-Royce profits beat expectations despite engine problems' *Financial Times* (7 March 2018), available at: <https://www.ft.com/content/3ec16df8-21e8-11e8-9a70-08f715791301> (accessed 30 November 2018).

154 *Serious Fraud Office v Standard Bank Plc* [2016] Lloyd's Rep FC 102, para 13.

155 On the concept of negotiated justice, see: Francois Tulkens, 'Negotiated Justice' in John R Spencer and Mireille Delmas-Marty (eds), *European Criminal Procedures* (Cambridge University Press 2004), 664.

156 This is often stated as being a primary objective of DPAs. See United States Attorneys' Manual (2009), §9-28.1000 B, and American Law Institute, *Model Penal Code: Sentencing* (Proposed Final Daft, 2017), 6.02A(2).

157 On the background, see *Roquet v Arthur Andersen LLP* 398 F3d 585 (7th Cir 2005).

158 David M Uhlmann, 'Deferred Prosecutions and Non-Prosecution Agreements and the Erosion of Corporate Criminal Liability' (2013) 72 Maryland LR 1295, 1321.

159 *Serious Fraud Office v Rolls-Royce* [2017] Lloyd's Rep FC 249, para 52.

Similar considerations would doubtless arise in many other cases. Ultimately the challenge must be to devise a set of principles that will determine the circumstances in which a DPA is appropriate without at the same time eroding corporate criminal liability and without favouring large corporations at the expense of smaller ones and, indeed, individuals.

SENTENCING CORPORATE OFFENDERS

Two fundamental questions have dominated discussion about corporate criminal liability: (1) is such liability compatible with any acceptable or meaningful notion of criminal responsibility more generally?[160]; (2) If so, how should criminal liability be attributed to a corporate entity? There are some who would answer the first question in the negative, arguing that criminal liability, by its very nature, is contingent on a finding of moral blameworthiness, something that cannot be attributed to an artificial person. Retributivists, in particular, claim that punishment should be reserved for those who are morally culpable of criminal conduct. According to Michael S Moore: '[t]o serve retributive justice, criminal law must punish all and only those who are morally culpable in the doing of some morally wrongful action.'[161] Since a company is 'incapable of acting or speaking or even of thinking except in so far as its officers have acted, spoken or thought',[162] one might therefore ask if it can be morally culpable in the sense that Moore seems to have intended. The question is indeed a difficult one. As Herbert Hart pithily remarked, 'it is not the legal personality but the 'moral' personality of organised groups that perplexes most.'[163] Yet, the argument has been decisively won by consequentialists who have presented a host of reasons, mainly connected with deterrence, public welfare and the promotion of corporate social responsibility, to justify the extension of criminal liability to corporate bodies.[164] The consequentialist triumph is reflected in the judicial acceptance that a corporation might be held liable for crimes involving intention,

---

160 Hugh Collins, 'Ascription of Legal Responsibility to Groups in Complex Patterns of Economic Integration' (1990) 53 MLR 731. On theories of criminal responsibility more generally, see Nicola Lacey, *In Search of Criminal Responsibility: Ideas, Interests and Institutions* (Oxford University Press 2016).

161 Michael S Moore, *Placing Blame: A Theory of Criminal Law* (Clarendon Press 1997), 35. See also G. Robert Sullivan, 'The Attribution of Culpability to Limited Companies' (1996) 55 Cambridge LJ 515; Brent Fisse, 'The Attribution of Criminal Liability to Corporations' (1991) 13 Sydney LR 277; James Gobert, 'Corporate Criminality: Four Models of Fault' [1994] Legal Studies 14; Brent Fisse and John Braithwaite, *Corporations, Crime and Accountability* (Cambridge University Press 1994); Celia Wells, *Corporations and Criminal Responsibility* (2nd edn, Oxford University Press 2001).

162 *DPP v Kent and Sussex Contractors Ltd.* [1944] KB 146, 155.

163 HLA Hart, 'Definition and Theory in Jurisprudence' (1954) 70 LQR 37, 55. This was the first serious attempt to explore the theoretical underpinnings of the liability of companies for offences requiring proof of knowledge or intention in the wake of *DPP v Kent and Sussex Contractors Ltd.* [1944] KB 146.

164 Nicola Lacey, 'Philosophical Foundations of the Common Law': Social not Metaphysical' in Jeremy Horder (ed), *Oxford Essays in Jurisprudence, Fourth Series* (Oxford University Press 2000), 17, 38.

knowledge or some other fault element.[165] It reached its apogee under English law with the recognition of corporate manslaughter, first by the courts[166] and then by Parliament.[167] Irish law has not yet gone that far.

A Hohfeldian concept of the company as nothing more than an association of natural persons conducting business within a particular legal structure might suggest that the law should concentrate on affixing individual directors or members of a company with criminal liability, where that becomes necessary, rather than treating the company itself as a proper subject of the criminal law.[168] After all, one of the favoured means of ascribing criminal liability to a corporate entity is the identification principle, which means that such an entity is deemed to act through those persons who can properly be described as its 'directing mind and will.'[169] It might therefore be argued that responsibility should rest with the 'directing minds' alone. Be that as it may, ever since the landmark case of *Salomon v Salomon*,[170] it has been accepted that a duly incorporated company has a legal personality separate and distinct from the identity of its shareholders. Thus, the company's property belongs to itself and not to the individual shareholders.[171] Moreover, the expansion of the corporation as a legal vehicle for doing business has meant that it now affects all our lives, for better or worse, in myriad ways. In *R v P & O European Ferries (Dover) Ltd*[172] (the Herald of Free Enterprise case), Turner J, having undertaken an impressive survey of the relevant law as it had developed since the mid-nineteenth century, concluded:

---

165 *DPP v Kent and Sussex Construction Ltd.* [1944] KB 146; *Moore v Bresler Ltd.* [1944] KB 551. Contrast with *R v Cory Brothers & Co.* [1927] 1 KB 810 where it was held that an indictment would not lie against a company for a felony or misdemeanour involving personal violence. This, admittedly, was a ruling of an Assize court, and the trial judge seemed to accept that the law could be different.

166 *R v P & O European Ferries (Dover) Ltd* (1991) 93 Cr App R 72.

167 Corporate Manslaughter and Corporate Homicide Act 2007. The Sentencing Council has established sentencing guidelines for this offence: *Health and Safety Offences, Corporate Manslaughter and Food Safety and Hygiene Offences: Definitive Guideline* (London 2015).

168 Wesley Newcomb Hohfeld, 'Nature of Stockholders' Individual Liability for Corporation Debts' (1909) 9 Columbia LR 285 at 319 ('a corporation is simply an association of natural persons organised and doing business under forms, methods and procedures that are *sui generis* [and] all corporate transactions can be adequately understood and stated only in terms of the rights, powers, liberties, duties, liabilities, disabilities, etc. of the natural persons concerned…').

169 *Lennard's Carrying Company Ltd v Asiatic Petroleum Co. Ltd* [1915] AC 705, 713; *Tesco Supermarkets Ltd v Nattrass* [1972] AC 153, 187; *R v St Regis Paper Co. Ltd* [2012] 2 Cr App R 14, 177; *R v A Ltd and Others* [2017] 1 Cr App R 1, paras 26-27.

170 *Salomon v Salomon* [1897] AC 22.

171 *Prest v Petrodel Resources Ltd* [2013] 2 AC 415, para 101, per Rimer LJ ('it follows from the fact of the company's separate identity that its property belongs beneficially to the company itself and in no sense belongs, either in law or in equity, to its shareholders, who have no interest of any nature, whether proprietary or otherwise, in its assets'). See also *Macaura v Northern Assurance Co. Ltd* [1925] AC 619, and Brenda Hannigan, *Company Law* (4th edn, Oxford University Press 2015) ch 3.

172 *R v P & O European Ferries (Dover) Ltd* (1991) 93 Cr App R 72, 83. See comment by Smith [1991] Crim LR 695.

> 'Since the nineteenth century there has been a huge increase in the numbers and activities of corporations whether nationalised, municipal or commercial, which enter into the private lives of 'men and subjects' in a diversity of ways. A clear case can be made for imputing to such corporations social duties including the duty not to offend all the relevant parts of the criminal law. By tracing the history of the cases decided by the English courts over the period of the last 150 years, it can be seen how first tentatively and, finally confidently the courts have been able to ascribe to corporations a 'mind' which is generally one of the essential ingredients of common law and statutory offences. Indeed, it can be seen that in many Acts of Parliament the same concept has been embraced.'

At common law, an unincorporated body was considered incapable of committing an offence, but criminal liability may be imposed on such a body by statute.[173]

The manner in which criminal liability may be attributed to a corporation is not really germane to our present topic, except to remark that the mode of ascription will clearly influence the frequency with which corporations are prosecuted and the range of circumstances in which they come up for sentence. English law adheres generally to the identification principle according to which a company may be convicted of an offence if the person or persons responsible for the relevant conduct represented 'the directing mind and will of the company.'[174] This is a demanding test for the prosecution, and it has been criticised for the extent to which it can allow large companies to escape liability. For example, the person responsible for the offending behaviour may have been a local manager who could not, by any stretch of the imagination, be treated as the company's 'directing mind and will.'[175] In Canada, fault can be attributed to an organisation if a 'senior officer' who was responsible for that aspect of the organisation's activities relevant to the offence departed markedly from the standard of care that could reasonably be expected in the circumstances.[176] A senior officer, in turn, is defined as a:

> 'representative who plays an important role in the establishment of an organisation's policies or is responsible for managing an important aspect of the organisation's activities and, in the case of a body corporate, includes a director, its chief executive officer and its chief financial officer.'[177]

Clearly, therefore, a senior officer need not be the 'directing mind and will' of the corporation, in the sense of being responsible for policy formulation. He or

---

173 *Attorney General v Able* [1984] 1 QB 795; *DPP (Barron) v Wexford Farmers' Club* [1994] 1 ILRM 295.

174 *Tesco Supermarkets v Nattrass* [1972] AC 153.

175 Jeremy Horder, *Ashworth's Principles of Criminal Law* (8th edn, Oxford University Press 2016), 168. See also: Todd Archibald, Kenneth Jull and Kent Roach, 'The Changed Face of Corporate Criminal Liability' (2004) 48 Criminal Law Quarterly 367.

176 Canadian Criminal Code, s 22 (1).

177 Canadian Criminal Code, s 2. See *R v Metron Construction Corporation* 2013 ONCA 541.

she may, instead, be someone with a significant management or executive role of an operational nature.

Irish courts, if presented with the opportunity, might well follow the Canadian approach. In *People (DPP) v T.N.*[178] the Court of Appeal had to decide if a person jointly charged with two companies with an offence under the Waste Management Act 1996 came within the terms of s 9 (1) of the Act which states:

> 'Where an offence… has been committed by a body corporate and is proved to have been committed with the consent or connivance of or to be attributable to any neglect on the part of a person being a director, manager, secretary or some similar officer of the body corporate… that person as well as the body corporate shall be guilty of the offence and shall be liable to be proceeded against and punished as if he or she were guilty of the first-mentioned offence.'

A provision to this effect is, of course, routinely included in statutes imposing criminal liability on corporate bodies. The question in *T.N.* was whether the individual defendant was a director, manager, secretary or a similar officer. Significantly, the Court of Appeal held that the wording of this standard provision must be interpreted in light of the realities of modern corporate organisation. It said:

> '[Nowadays] responsibilities may be distributed in such a way that it would be difficult to say that any one individual was responsible for the management of the whole affairs of the company. However, if the individual's role is a significant one then the fact that there may be some particular areas of the company activity with which he does not have an involvement does not mean that he is not to be regarded as a manager of the corporation.'[179]

Granted, the Court of Appeal was not concerned in this case with the attribution of criminal liability to companies or other organisations. It did, however, refer to *Tesco Supermarkets Ltd v Nattrass,*[180] and it may be inferred from its general observations that it would not necessarily agree with the 'directing mind and will' principle. All of this suggests that the net of criminal liability is being widened for both corporations and senior personnel employed by them. Sentencing courts will therefore find themselves dealing with an ever-increasing variety of corporate offences and offenders.

Proportionality remains the guiding principle for sentencing corporate offenders, although in this instance it derives from the common law rather than the Constitution.[181] A court must therefore begin by assessing the objective gravity of the offence in order to identify a headline sentence, and then make

[178] *People (DPP) v T.N.* [2018] IECA 52.
[179] ibid at para 26.
[180] *Tesco Supermarkets v Nattrass* [1972] AC 153.
[181] *People (DPP) v Cavan County Council and Oxigen Environmental Ltd* [2015] IECA 130;

adjustments to reflect other relevant factors. Both harm and culpability must be considered when assessing gravity.[182] The degree of culpability will depend mainly on the extent to which the corporation's practices or procedures have created a risk of harm or injury to individuals or society at large.[183] For all practical purposes, the only criminal penalties that can be imposed on a corporation are monetary in nature, although some other countries provide for probation as well.[184] The general principles governing the imposition of fines apply with some modifications to corporate offenders.[185] Regard must always be had in the first instance to any maximum fine specified by statute. Once a presumptive fine (effectively the headline sentence under the first limb of the proportionality principle) has been established, account must then be taken of the company's ability to pay and the impact which a heavy fine might have on innocent parties. A court will usually try to avoid imposing a level of fine that might place the viability of the company in jeopardy, the so-called deterrence trap.[186] It will also have regard to the possibility of a 'spill over effect', meaning that the brunt of the fine may eventually have to be borne by consumers, creditors, employees or trading partners. Shareholders may also, of course, suffer although they may attract less sympathy because they do, after all, own the company. The spill over effect may be particularly relevant where the offender is a public body, such as a local authority. Being compelled to pay a heavy fine may genuinely diminish such an offender's capacity to deliver the services for which it is responsible. While courts will anxious to ensure that such bodies obey the law, particularly in relation to environmental protection and health and safety matters, they must also consider how the imposition of a very heavy fine may impact on the delivery of essential services to members of the public.[187] Section 718.21 of the Canadian Criminal Code contains a useful list of the factors to be considered when sentencing organisations. These include the degree of planning involved in carrying out the offence as well as the duration and complexity of the offence, the cost to public authorities

---

People (DPP) v Kilsaran Concrete Ltd [2017] 2 I.R. 510; *People (DPP) v Independent News and Media plc* [2018] IECA 301.

182 *People (DPP) v Roadteam Logistic Solutions (formerly Nolan Transport (Oakland) Ltd)* [2016] IECA 38.

183 Note, 'Developments in the Law: Corporate Crime: Regulating Corporate Behaviour through Criminal Sanctions' (1979) 92 Harvard LR 1227.

184 Under the Canadian Criminal Code (s 732.1), a corporation may be placed on probation and required, as part of the order, to fulfil certain conditions including having to 'establish policies, standards and procedures to reduce the likelihood of the organisation committing a subsequent offence.' In Ireland, a corporate body may be given the benefit of the Probation Act 1907 meaning that, in District Court proceedings, a conviction need not be entered even though guilt has been established. See *Shannon Regional Fisheries Board v Cavan County Council* [1996] 3 IR 267.

185 On fines generally, see Tom O'Malley, *Sentencing Law and Practice* (3rd edn, Round Hall 2016) ch 23.

186 John C Coffee '"No Soul to Damn: No Body to Kick": An Unscandalized Inquiry into the Problem of Corporate Punishment' (1981) 79 Michigan LR 386. Gary Green and Madhava Bodapati, 'The "Deterrence Trap": The Federal Fining of Organisations. A Research Note' (1999) 10(4) Criminal Justice Policy Review 547; Christopher Kennedy, 'Criminal Sentences for Organisations: Alternative Fining Mechanisms' (1985) 43 California LR 443; William S Laufer, 'Corporate Bodies and Guilty Minds' (1994) 43 Emory LJ 647.

187 *People (DPP) v Cavan County Council and Oxigen Environmental Ltd* [2015] IECA 130.

of investigating and prosecuting the offence, any regulatory penalty imposed by another body for the same conduct, the impact which the sentence would have on the economic viability of the organisation, any restitution already made to a victim of the offence, and any measures adopted by the organisation to reduce the likelihood that it will commit a similar offence in the future. Courts in most jurisdictions would doubtless have regard to these factors. Finally, it may be noted that in Ireland, the Companies Act 2014 (s 871) sets out four categories of maximum penalties for offences contrary to the Act itself. Following conviction on indictment for an offence in the highest category, the maximum sentence is a fine not exceeding €500,000, 10 years' imprisonment or both.

Conclusion

The financial meltdown experienced in this country a decade ago had catastrophic consequences for many individuals and families, and indeed for society at large. As the crisis unfolded, it revealed how some individuals, mostly builders and bankers, had ruthlessly pursued personal profit, professional success and self-aggrandisement with little or no regard to the devastating social consequences that their behaviour might, and actually did, bring about. All of this understandably led to pressure for more intense monitoring and regulation of financial institutions, the introduction of further criminal offences, harsher sentences and the creation of specialist agencies to deal with financial, white-collar and corporate crime. Yet, it would be unwise and probably counterproductive to proceed in an empirical vacuum. The need for any such measures must be carefully assessed having regard to the nature of the crime that has so far come to light, the environment and circumstances in which it was committed and evidence-based projections about the nature and extent of the problems we are likely to encounter in this area in the future. Going by our present state of knowledge, it would be far better to strengthen existing institutions, especially by ensuring that police and prosecutors have the expertise and resources to investigate alleged corporate and white-collar crime quickly and effectively, and to bring to justice anyone who has a case to answer. Punishment for those convicted must be proportionate and dissuasive. It is important that sentencing should not be treated as an afterthought, much less ignored, in any law reform exercise. The range and severity of available penalties, and the principles according to which offenders are sentenced may well influence both individual and corporate behaviour. More formal guidance than currently exists would also be welcome, not least because it would increase public confidence in the criminal justice system.

Chapter 10

CONFISCATING AND FORFEITING THE FINANCIAL BENEFIT FROM REGULATORY OFFENCES

Declan O'Reilly[*]

Introduction

The Criminal Assets Bureau (CAB) and the Proceeds of Crime Act are now long established in the Irish legal system.[1] Having been established in 1996, it is perhaps unfortunate to observe that many of those involved in serious organised crime are younger than CAB. Over the intervening 22 years much has been written about the CAB and the associated legislation. This chapter does not intend to cover that well-trodden familiar ground, but rather it will guide the reader to the complex web of interacting legislation that may not be immediately obvious.

All too often, regulatory legislation is read in splendid isolation without having regard to resulting consequences and its interaction with wider legislation. Committing a regulatory offence will most likely give rise to a financial penalty prescribed in that piece of legislation. However, this is not an end to the matter. If the regulatory offence gave rise to a financial benefit in committing same, then any dealing with the financial benefit can amount to money laundering as it is the proceeds of criminal conduct. Furthermore, s 19 of the Criminal Justice Act 2011 places a positive obligation on everyone to report a range of crimes, including money laundering.[2] Failure to do so is a criminal offence of itself. A person may not have a legal obligation to report a crime if that crime falls outside those listed as a 'relevant offence' under the Act, but this does not absolve a person from having to report the secondary offence of money laundering which is a 'relevant offence'.

Similarly, if the person who has failed to report the money laundering under s 19 derives a financial benefit from same, this financial benefit is similarly capable

* Bureau Legal Officer, Criminal Assets Bureau. This chapter was prepared by Declan O'Reilly in his personal capacity. The opinions expressed in this article are the author's own and do not reflect the view of the Criminal Assets Bureau nor the Department of Justice and Equality.

1 The Criminal Assets Bureau Act 1996 and also the Proceeds of Crime Act 1996.

2 s 19 designates 'relevant offences', a number of which include money laundering and related offences as specified under Schedule 1 of the 2011 Act.

of being confiscated.[3] A wide range of regulatory offences do not come within the scope of mandatory s 19 reporting requirements, but once any financial benefit is dealt with, the resulting money laundering offence must be reported.

This chapter will deal primarily with planning law, but only for the reason that this is where the significant case law has emerged. However, it does illustrate well that benefits gained from breaches of planning law are, in fact and in law, the proceeds of crime and are capable of being confiscated.

First Principles

It is perhaps necessary to start at the beginning and on first principles. Why aren't pharmacists simply regarded as 'drug dealers' in the criminal sense of the expression? After all, s 3 of the Misuse of Drugs Act 1977 (as amended) makes it an offence for anyone (street drug dealer and pharmacists alike) to have in their possession a controlled drug. Then why aren't courts and prisons full of pharmacists? Why isn't the Criminal Assets Bureau seizing the homes, cars and bank account of pharmacists? Before reading ahead (no cheating please), take a few seconds to pause and reflect. Ask the simple question: why?

If you've answered something along the lines that one person (the pharmacist) is a good person doing a public service and the other (the street drug dealer) is a bad person doing society harm, then you have somewhat mis-answered and are wrong. The simple answer is that s 4 makes provision for the Minister for Health to make regulations 'so as to secure that it is not unlawful under this Act for a practitioner or pharmacist to have a controlled drug in his possession for the purpose of his profession or business.' Similarly, s 4 makes further provisions for the Minister to:

> 'make regulations enabling any person, or persons of a prescribed class or description, in prescribed circumstances or for prescribed purposes, to possess a controlled drug subject to such conditions (if any), or subject to and in accordance with such licence, as may be prescribed.'

Put bluntly, it's a crime to have controlled drugs unless you are specifically allowed to have them. This is a key concept that must be borne in mind when reading what will follow. Keeping this in mind, we now turn to the UK.

Lessons to be Learnt from the UK

The reason why we will now look at the UK is that their system is highly similar to ours, but also the fact that prosecutors in that jurisdiction have blazed a trail in confiscating the proceeds of regulatory crime. Notwithstanding our similarities, we have our subtle differences. Ireland operates two legislative

[3] Criminal Justice Act 1994, s 9.

schemes to disgorge people of the financial benefits obtained or derived from derived from crime. They are the Post-Conviction Based (PCB) Confiscation scheme operated under the Criminal Justice Act 1994, as amended, and the Non Conviction Based (NCB) Forfeiture scheme operated under the Proceeds of Crime Act 1996, as amended. The UK operates a similar system but both schemes are contained within their Proceeds of Crime Act 2002. This can lead to confusion when comparing systems as both jurisdictions have a 'Proceeds of Crime Act' (sometimes referred to POC in Ireland and POCA in the UK). Ireland's POC is however solely NCB. The UK's POCA is both PCB and NCB.

Felling a Protected Tree

The first case to highlight the far reaching consequences of breaching what might at first blush appear a trivial matter was that of *R v Davey*.[4] The crime at the centre of *R v Davey* was the felling of a 55 year old tree in breach of a conservation order. The felling of the tree gave uninterrupted views out over Poole Harbour from Davey's home valued at STG£725,000. When a planning officer came to inspect the scene of the crime, he found a hot tub and some brand-new sun loungers had been installed on Davey's patio. Davey had been on his honeymoon with his wife in France and it was thought that the tree was felled as a wedding present.[5]

The tree was cut down by Thomas McGuire, a tree surgeon, who claimed he was in Yeovil at the time of the crime. However, following an analysis of mobile phone records McGuire was forced to admit his part in the crime after a mobile phone mast in Poole had recorded his location. The analysis of phone records and locations is something that the wider public might consider reserved for violent or drug related crime, but it shows the seriousness that the UK authorities treated the matter. When Davey was questioned, he initially denied any involvement in the felling of the tree. He later admitted to having engaged McGuire to cut down some branches of a tree on the left hand side of his property.

This case could, on the one hand, be considered a classic white-collar crime, and indeed a victimless crime. Similarly, could this not have been simply regarded as a civil matter between Davey and Bransgrove? The victim in this case could be regarded as the felled tree. This case however, brings to mind the acerbic words of Summer LJ in *Leeds Industrial Co-operative Society Ltd v Slack*[6]:

> 'I doubt whether it is complete justice to allow the big man, with his big building and his enhanced rateable value, and his improvement to the

[4] *R v Davey* [2013] EWCA Crim 1662.

[5] Harriet Arkell, 'Auctioneer who cut down neighbour's tree to improve views from his hot tub ordered to pay record fine of £125,000' *Mail Online* (12 June 2013), available at: <http://www.dailymail.co.uk/news/article-2340354/Auctioneer-cut-neighbours-tree-improve-views-hot-tub-wedding-present-new-wife-ordered-pay-record-fine.html> (accessed 30 March 2018).

[6] *Leeds Industrial Co-operative Society Ltd v Slack* [1924] AC 851, 872.

> neighbourhood to have his way, and to solace the little man for his dark and stuffy little house by giving him a cheque that he does not ask for.'

That case involved a right to light and the adequacy of damages *in lieu* of an injunction.

On the 23 November 2012 at the Crown Court of Bournemouth, both men were found guilty by a jury following a five-day hearing. Davey was convicted of causing or permitting the wilful destruction of the tree, contrary to s 210(1) of the Town and County Planning Act 1990. Judge Peter Johnson said of Davey:

> 'This was a pre-meditated matter, not something spur of the moment. What you orchestrated demonstrated a remarkable arrogance… In order to improve your view you arranged with your co-accused [McGuire] to go around to the tree in the dead of night and cut it down, putting your neighbours' lives at risk.'[7]

McGuire was fined a total of STG£5,515 for his part in the overall scheme. The question that arose is respect of Davey was whether this was merely some small planning regulatory breach or whether this merited a confiscation order under the UK Proceeds of Crime Act. Davey was the directing mind in the crime and the person who benefited from it. But what was this benefit? For the act of having the tree felled, he was fined STG£75,000. This is a very substantial fine by any standards. However, the value of the house was deemed to have increased in value by STG£50,000 by virtue now of having better views. A confiscation order under the UK POCA was made in relation to this proceeds of crime, i.e. the enhanced value. He was also ordered to pay a further STG£14,500 in costs to Poole Council. In coming to the level of the financial penalty, the judge noted that Davey was:

> 'a man of some wealth, which … was obvious to all, and that it had been accepted on his [Davey's] behalf that he would be able to meet any financial penalty imposed by the court. Mr McGuire by contrast was a man of modest means who was struggling financially.'

This case was appealed through the High Court and ultimately to the Court of Appeal where judgment was given on the 11 June 2013. The confiscation order relating to the increase in value was not appealed but rather the fine. This is of itself somewhat telling. In considering the fine of STG£75,000, the Court of Appeal had to consider the nature of the criminal act that had occurred. Similarly, the court had to consider whether the making of the confiscation order under the POCA was of itself a sufficient punishment and thereby remove the requirement

---

7 Harriet Arkell, 'Auctioneer who cut down neighbour's tree to improve views from his hot tub ordered to pay record fine of £125,000' *Mail Online* (12 June 2013), available at: <http://www.dailymail.co.uk/news/article-2340354/Auctioneer-cut-neighbours-tree-improve-views-hot-tub-wedding-present-new-wife-ordered-pay-record-fine.html> (accessed 30 March 2018).

to impose a fine. Was Mr Davey being punished twice for his criminal act? In examining the matter, Mr Justice Edwards-Stuart set out:

> 'The fine was on any view very substantial, but although the confiscation order removed the financial benefit to the appellant, namely increasing the value of this property as a result of the removal of the tree, it did not remove the amenity benefit of the improved view that the appellant will enjoy while he remains in occupation of the property. The fact that this was a significant benefit is demonstrated by the lengths to which the appellant was prepared to go in order to achieve it. Accordingly, that was a factor that the judge would have been entitled to take into account. We do not accept therefore Mr Gau's submission [on behalf of Davey] that this was reflected in the confiscation order. In addition, there was the very serious aggravating feature that the tree was not owned by the appellant. It was his neighbour's tree. Whilst its removal may have advanced the amenity value of the appellant's property, doubtless it removed the amenity value for those other properties for which the tree would have been an attractive local feature and not an inconvenience. There was no evidence before the court as to the appellant's financial circumstances beyond the fact that he was clearly a man of some means. There is no limit to the amount of the fine that the Crown Court can impose. … The facts that we have already identified, demonstrate that this was an offence that was one of the most serious of its type. In addition, we consider that fines for this type of offence must include an element of deterrence. Whilst we consider that the level of the fine was very high, the judge had the advantage of observing the appellant during the trial and was therefore in a position to form a view about his culpability and attitude to the offending in a way that this court cannot. For the reasons that we have already given, the offence called for a very heavy fine. In the absence of any evidence that a fine of this level was disproportionate having regard to the appellant's means, and in the unusual circumstances of this case, we do not consider that it was manifestly excessive.'[8]

A further order for costs was also made against Mr Davey, thereby increasing the financial burden levied on him. And what of the view? The tree was replaced by another maritime pine. It was reported also that Bransgrove was planning a civil action against Davey for the cost he incurred as a result of tree felling.[9]

Park & Ride Car Park Crimes

Many who engage in criminal activity will try to dissuade themselves and courts that their activity was 'merely regulatory non-compliance'. This, however, ignores the reality that such matters are criminal offences. A person who holds

---

8 *R v Davey* [2013] EWCA Crim 1662, para 18-21.

9 Kerry McDermott, 'Wealthy homeowner fined £125,000 after felling neighbour's tree that blocked sea views from his hot tub' *Mail Online* (25 November 2012), available at: <http://www.dailymail.co.uk/news/article-2238252/Wealthy-homeowner-fined-125-000-felling-neighbours-tree-blocked-sea-views-hot-tub.html> (accessed 30 March 2018).

such a regulatory conviction holds a criminal record which may impact on their ability to conduct business, hold certain qualified positions, or indeed freely travel across borders. Certain regulatory offences only receive small fines but offer the perpetrator the potential for substantial financial gain, and as such the temptation for some is to treat the fine merely as a business expense. Those who do so risk considerable losses as the case of *Basso & Goodwin v R* demonstrates.[10]

In June 1999, Timelast Ltd which was owned by Mr Del Basso, made an application for 201 parking spaces on land rented by Bishop's Stortford Football Club. Conditional planning permission was granted but restricted to days when football matches were actually being held at the club. At the time, the football club's success was mixed having bounced around the bottom of the Southern League Premier Division and being eventually relegated back to Division One. The football grounds were, however, located at the end of the runway to London Stansted Airport. Four weeks after planning was granted, a further application was made for a 'Park & Ride' parking facility. The number of match days was at best going to be very limited in comparison to the opportunity presented by its proximity to and thereby earning potential from Stansted Airport. In July 2010, however, the application was rejected, thereby restricting car parking to match days only. Notwithstanding this refusal, Del Basso and Goodwin proceeded with their plan and opened the Park & Ride facility contrary to planning permission. Ultimately, both Del Basso and Goodwin were prosecuted and pled guilty to five and two counts respectively of failing to comply with an enforcement notice contrary to s 179(1) and (2) of the Town and Country Planning Act 1990. In July 2009, Del Basso was fined STG£3,000 and ordered to pay STG£20,000 costs whereas Goodwin was fined STG£5. Were that the end of the matter, the factual position regarding the case would be forgotten. A hearing was held under the POCA 2002 which was conducted initially by the Assets Recovery Agency and latterly by its successor the Serious Organised Crime Agency. For those who are unfamiliar these agencies, their nearest analogy in Ireland is the Criminal Assets Bureau. The ARA was established in 2003 and was largely modelled on the concept of the Criminal Assets Bureau.

Running concurrent with enforcement actions, Del Basso and Goodwin tried to remedy their hand. Back in July 2000, following refusal of the Park & Ride planning application, Del Basso & Goodwin appealed the refusal. In August 2000, the local authority wrote to them stating that planning permission was required and that the unauthorised parking business should cease. This was followed up with repeated warning letters and meetings, all to no avail. The parking continued. In January 2003, the local authority served an enforcement notice. This was appealed to the Planning Inspector, ultimately resulting in the appeal being dismissed following a two-day hearing. The parking continued. A further appeal was brought to the High Court, but in February 2004, permission to appeal was refused. The parking continued. In March 2004, the local authority advised Del Basso & Goodwin that if the operation continued beyond the 11 August 2004, a prosecution would commence immediately. The grounds

[10] *Basso & Goodwin v R* [2010] EWCA Crim 1119.

were inspected by the local authority, and not only had the parking continued, but the area had expanded and no attempt had been made to comply with the enforcement notice. Following Del Basso & Goodwin's conviction, the local authority visited the grounds again. The parking continued. A second prosecution was commenced, at which point the defendants pled guilty again and received nominal fines.

The investigation by ARA/SOCA determined that Del Basso had received a benefit of STG£1,881,221.19 during the period. Altruistic arguments were made that the Park & Ride facility was run to provide an income stream for the football club. The trial judge even concluded that the facility was run on business-like lines: it employed staff, it honoured contractual obligation to employees and third parties alike, and conducted its business in an open manner. However, he concluded that it was nonetheless an illegal operation and both Del Basso & Goodwin had benefited from same and thereby had a 'criminal lifestyle' within the meaning of the UK POCA 2002.[11] He concluded that 'the breach of the enforcement notice rendered the activity itself unlawful, however compliant it was with other legal requirements in the manner in which it was actually carried out.'[12]

The court saw no difficulty in piercing the corporate veils as the benefit accrued to the Del Basso & Goodwin. The Court of Appeal drew on the decision of *R v May*[13] in attempting to understand the scope of calculating the criminal benefit a person derives from the criminal conduct and the meaning of 'confiscation' under the POCA 2002. In *May*, the Appellate Committee concluded:

> 'Although 'confiscation' is the name ordinarily given to this process, it is not confiscation in the sense in which schoolchildren and others understand it. A criminal caught in possession of criminally-acquired assets will, it is true, suffer their seizure by the state. Where, however, a criminal has benefited financially from crime but no longer possesses the specific fruits of his crime, he will be deprived of assets of equivalent value, if he has them. The object is to deprive him, directly or indirectly, of what he has gained. 'Confiscation' is, as Lord Hobhouse of Woodborough observed in In Re Norris [2001] UKHL 34, [2001] 1 WLR 1388, para 12, a misnomer.'

Leveson LJ for the Court of Appeal in *Del Basso & Goodwin* concluded: 'The economic or environmental harm is only one part of the picture: the other is that a requirement to observe the law is imposed on all and Mr Del Basso and Mr Goodwin have only themselves to blame for their persistent failure to do so.' Laws are made to be followed by all, and it is not a matter of people picking and choosing which to follow and which to treat as a mere business expense. This is a basic fundamental principle of equality before the law and to allow

---

11 s 75 of the Proceeds of Crime Act 2002 (UK).

12 *Basso & Goodwin v R* [2010] EWCA Crim 1119, para 15.

13 *R v May* [2008] UKHL 28.

for some deviation that on a childish view that 'it does not apply to my acts' or that 'I am special' is simply wrong.

Leveson LJ entirely agreed with Judge Barker's final concluding remarks:

> 'I conclude with a final observation about the mentality of the [appellants] and other similar law breakers. I have received the strong impression that neither the [appellants] nor … their accountant appreciated fully the risk that the companies and individuals involved in the park and ride operation faced from confiscation proceedings. They have treated the illegality of the operation as a routine business risk with financial implications in the form of potential fines or, at worst, injunctive proceedings. This may reflect a more general public impression among those confronted by enforcement notices with the decision whether to comply with the law or to flout it. The law, however, is plain. Those who choose to run operations in disregard of planning enforcement requirements are at risk of having the gross receipts of their illegal businesses confiscated. This may greatly exceed their personal profits. In this respect they are in the same position as thieves, fraudsters and drug dealers. Although the peculiar facts of the present case have led me to exclude the receipts of the parking company from the confiscation, that is a decision reached very much having regard to the unusual circumstances presented to me. [Counsel for the prosecution's] submission that a defendant should not escape the confiscation consequences of his conduct by the expedient of running his unlawful operation through a company will, I expect, generally carry the day.'[14]

Two points may starkly and directly be drawn from *Del Basso & Goodwin*:

1. Those who commit regulatory offences are the same as thieves, fraudsters and drug dealers: they are criminals;
2. These criminals are liable to have their gross and not just net receipts confiscated.

It is worth pausing at this point. A further point must also be drawn: anyone who deals with money deriving from regulatory offences are potential money launderers. This must serve as words of caution to professionals who are aware that their clients are in breach of regulatory matters. Should those professionals accept payment from those clients it is no different to receiving payments from a thief, from a fraudster, or from a drug dealer. Whilst the two points listed above have been further expanded upon and refined in further decisions, they ought act as a heart arresting moment for all aware of regulatory breaches. Ultimately, the Court of Appeal dismissed the appeal brought by Del Basso & Goodwin.

---

[14] *Basso & Goodwin v R* [2010] EWCA Crim 1119, para 46.

From Stark Clarity to Nuanced Confusion

That is not to say that all regulatory breaches may warrant a confiscation order. Is the conduct prohibited but allowed in licenced circumstances or is the conduct allowed but you are required in addition to hold a licence? This may seem a trivial distinction but it is of crucial importance. This question was considered in *Sumal & Sons (Properties) Ltd v London Borough of Newham*.[15] In that case, a landlord was operating in London Borough of Newham with a turnover of STG£600,000. A licensing scheme came into place on 1 March 2010. This licensing scheme was widely advertised and Sumal & Sons ignored repeated reminders. Ultimately, on the 3 October 2011, Sumal & Sons was convicted, fined STG£2,015, ordered to pay the prosecution cost of STG£3,821.96 and made subject to a confiscation order under POCA to STG£6,450.83. The confiscation order related to the benefit of the rental income obtained from the property whilst it was unlicensed.

Davis LJ on behalf of the Court of Appeal set out that there was a distinction between *Del Basso & Goodwin* to the present case in observing that:

> 'They [Del Basso & Goodwin] had no lawful entitlement to use the land in this way, but instead deliberately flouted the law in doing so in order to secure a profit (benefit). That is in clear distinction from the present case: where the continuance of the letting and the receipt of rent (in contrast with the failure not to have the house licensed) was not made unlawful by the 2004 Act. Putting it in other words, a licence granted under s.88 of the 2004 Act does not operate to confer on a landlord an entitlement lawfully to receive rent which he does not otherwise have.'

The court also noted that a separate confiscation regime exists under s 97 of the Housing Act 2004 in the form of a rent repayment order to an authority following a conviction under s 95(1). The court concluded that this would amount to 'double jeopardy or double recovery.'[16] The court stressed the importance of looking at the underlying behaviour involved in the regulatory offence, and the type of behaviour engaged in. As Davis LJ said:

> 'Whether what may be styled a regulatory offence can, when committed, give rise to the availability of a confiscation order will depend on the terms of the statute or regulations creating the offence, read with the terms of the 2002 Act and set in the context of the facts of the case.'[17]

In essence: it depends. Certainty is something which is something that all would prefer, and in particular in the area of criminal offences. However, it would appear that it is difficult to give a 'one size fits all' answer but instead a detailed examination is required in each instance.

[15] *Sumal & Sons (Properties) Ltd v London Borough of Newham* [2012] EWCA Crim 1840.

[16] ibid, para 41.

[17] ibid, para 30.

The Size of the Confiscation Order to be Made

More nuanced understandings can be gathered from the subsequent Court of Appeal decision in *Sale v R.*[18] This case is one where Sale had pleaded guilty to corruption contrary to s 1 of the Prevention of Corruption Act and also to fraud representation contrary to ss 1 and 2 of the Fraud Act 2006. Sale was deemed to have benefited to the sum of STG£1,918,562.44. What should be emphasised here is not whether a confiscation was to be made, but rather the quantum of same.

The circumstances were that Sale had corruptly bribed an employee of Network Rail. As a result of this corruption, contracts were awarded to Sale. There was no prior business relationship between Sale and Network Rail prior to the corruption. In hearing the appeal, the court noted that apart from the corruption underlying the offence, that the contracts had been properly carried out and given value to Network Rail. Treacy LJ observed that:

> 'The expenses incurred in carrying out those contracts by the company, some ninety percent of the total invoice price, were expenses which would have been incurred in the performance of any legitimately obtained contract. Those expenses represented management, administration, labour, materials, and other ordinary business overheads. Such payments were to be distinguished from the expenses of criminal activity itself, such as the cost of the bribes or favours for which no credit was claimed.'[19]

The court commented that it would be disproportionate to make a confiscation order where the criminal has wholly restored to the loser any benefit he had obtained from his crime. However, that was not the situation in this case:

> '… this is not, in our judgment, a case analogous to one where goods or money have been entirely restored to the loser. True it is that Network Rail received value for money, but Mr Sale had obtained contracts for his company by corrupt means on a continuing basis so that every contract obtained was tainted by it. Moreover, in a case of this nature it is wholly unrealistic to regard Network Rail as the only victim of the crime. Corruption of this nature clearly impacts on others. The company [Mr Sales' company] obtained contracts with a client with whom it had had no previous business relationship. Existing contractors with Network Rail were cheated out of the tendering process. The substantial market in Network Rail contracts of this type was distorted, with the [Mr Sales'] company gaining a market share to the detriment of others. Tendering costs [of Mr Sales' company] were avoided.'[20]

Accordingly, the Court of Appeal concluded that the amount to be confiscated was not gross receipts under the contracts but rather the pecuniary advantage

18 *Sale v R* [2013] EWCA Crim 1306.
19 ibid, para 48.
20 ibid, para 52.

gained by obtaining market share, excluding competitors, and saving on the costs of preparing proper tenders.

A similar issue came before the Court of Appeal in *McDowell & Singh v R* in February 2015.[21] McDowell & Singh arose from two separate and distinct cases but were listed together because they raised the common issues including, *inter alia*, the application of the test whether property was obtained as a result of, or in connection with, criminal conduct. McDowell argued that his criminal conduct comprised trading while unlicensed; Singh that his criminal conduct comprised trading whilst unregistered. Each claimed that his 'benefit' was acquired not from criminal conduct but from lawful trading.

McDowell was the sole director, shareholder and director of a lawful and valid arms dealing company. He had been convicted of being knowingly concerned in the supply etc. of controlled goods with intent to evade the prohibition thereon, contrary to Art 9(2) of the Trade in Goods (Control) Order 2003. McDowell argued he had been convicted of a 'regulatory' offence and that the underlying trading was lawful, but for the absence of a licence. He had applied for a controlled goods licence. However he had engaged in trade before receiving the licence and half of his commission fees were also paid before the licence was granted. His actions before and after the passing of the licence were the same. However, the licence was not retrospective.

On 23 December 2013, in confiscation proceedings, McDowell was found to have obtained benefit in the sum of STG£2,557,826.30. This was the amount he earned in commission before the licence was granted. The available amount was STG£292,499.60 and a confiscation order was made in the latter sum, to be paid by 23 May 2014 with thirty months imprisonment in default. In regard to Singh, he had pleaded guilty to an offence contrary to s 1(1) and (7) of the Scrap Metal Dealers Act 1964. He was sentenced in the Crown Court to a fine of STG£350. However, he was also found to have benefited in the sum of STG£965,838.84, being the receipts of the company during the whole period of trading while unregistered. The available amount was STG£176,218.11 and the judge made a confiscation order in that sum.

Pitchford LJ noted the position in *Del Basso & Goodwin* and also in *Summal & Sons*. He emphasised that finding of Davis LJ in *Summal & Sons* at para 30 (above), the 'it depends test', where no broad statement applies to all legislative licences. In respect of McDowell the court found:

> 'Contrary to the submission made on behalf of Mr McDowell the underlying transactions were, on analysis, prohibited and unlawful. It is, in our view, not arguable that the appellant did not benefit from his criminal conduct.'[22]

[21] *McDowell & Singh v R* [2015] EWCA Crim 173.

[22] ibid, para 50.

The payments he received prior to the granting of the licence were for a prohibited activity notwithstanding the fact that a licence eventually granted. In simple terms, this may be equated to a person drives a car without a car licence. It is an offence to do so. Obtaining a driving licence tomorrow would not free a person from prosecution for haven driven without a licence, as the driving licence is similarly not retrospective. In respect of Singh, the matter is somewhat more nuanced. The initial trial judge had put it in the following terms:

> 'There was no distinction to be made between a scrap dealer trading while unregistered and a drug dealer receiving money in return for the sale of drugs, except in the seriousness of the forbidden conduct. Every transaction was unlawful.'[23]

This would appear similar to *Del Basso & Goodwin*. The Court of Appeal however disagreed with that analysis. The criminal conduct in question here was a failure to register. It was not an offence to deal in scrap metal but rather there is a positive obligation to register if you do. The court again emphasised the necessity to identify the nature of the criminal conduct from the alternative means by which an offence may be committed. The test would appear to be, whether the conduct is one which is prohibited simpliciter but may be carried out subject to licence or lawful conduct for which a licence must be obtained. In the former, the benefit obtained may be subject to confiscation and in the latter no confiscation may be made save for specific statutory schemes. However, matters are somewhat complicated by further judgments of the Court of Appeal given within one day of each other which are hard to reconcile with the above and with each other, namely that of *R v Powell & Westwood*[24] and *R v Palmer*.[25]

Powell was convicted of two counts of consent or conniving as a director in the failure of her company to comply with the condition of an environmental permit and one count of consenting or conniving as a director of a company in the commission of an offence by the company in keeping or disposing of controlled waste in a manner likely to cause pollution. She was sentenced to a 12 months' prison sentence and disqualified as a director for five years. The judge found that she had benefited to the sum of STG£60,000. Westwood pleaded guilty to the same counts and received a 32-week prison sentence and was similarly disqualified for five years. Westwood was found to have benefited to the sum of STG£30,000. The offences resulted in the State having to clean up the site with a cost to the public purse of STG£1.125 million. A confiscation order was made to the sum of STG£200,000 in respect of Powell and to the sum of STG£70,000 as both had personal asset available to that amount. Again it should be noted that a confiscation order was made in addition to a fine. The prosecution however brought an appeal on the basis the judge had refused an application to pierce the corporate veil and trace the benefit into the company. The trial judge had noted that the trial had noted that the purpose of the company was legitimate

23 ibid, para 59.

24 *R v Powell & Westwood* [2016] EWCA 1043.

25 *R v Palmer* [2016] EWCA Crim 1049.

and had obtained the necessary permits. Consultants had been engaged and the company had taken a number of steps involving very significant expenditure to comply with the regulations and permits. It was a lawful operation which had become unlawful through breaches of conditions. The Court of Appeal held that the confiscation orders made against the directors were correct and would not pierce the corporate veil to trace the benefit into the company assets.

A different approach was adopted in *Palmer* where Palmer had been convicted of an offence of engaging in licensable conduct otherwise that in accordance with a licence, namely the operation of a security business. He received a sentence of three months' imprisonment together with a requirement to carry out 100 hours of unpaid work. The trial judge in applying *McDowell & Singh* refused to make a confiscation order on the basis that the conduct was not criminal conduct but only became criminal conduct by virtue of Palmer's failure to obtain a licence. The prosecution appealed the sentence on the basis that a confiscation order ought to have been made. The question that faced the Court of Appeal was whether the legislation created an offence that prohibited and made criminal the activity proved against the respondent (as in *de Basso & Goodwin*), or an offence that comprised the failure to obtain a licence to carry out an activity otherwise lawful (as in *Sumal*). The court found that the legislation criminalised the conduct (subject to licence) and not the failure to obtain a licence. The court also noted that the legislation upon which *Singh* had been decided was now only of historical interest as the legislation had subsequently been replaced. Simon LJ for the court concluded that:

> '... we see no reason in principle why it should make a difference whether an activity is unlawful by reason of a statutory prohibition except in a case of persons who have been granted a licence (on the one hand), or whether an activity which is otherwise lawful is prohibited by statute unless one has a licence (on the other). The result is the same: the activity is prohibited and the conduct is therefore 'criminal conduct.''[26]

Continue to Trade a Business that is in Liquidation

In *R v Neuberg* the Court of Appeal examined whether a confiscation order of STG£100,000 ought to have been made where Neuberg had been charged and convicted of trading under a prohibited style from 19 November 2001 to 14 June 2002.[27] During that period, Neuberg had used the business name 'Neuberg Metal Spiners' where her company had gone into liquidation. It was not lawful for her to trade under that name without leave of the court. What is particularly noteworthy from this case is that the 2016 appeal was the second appeal brought to the Court of Appeal and arose through a reference by the Criminal Cases Review Commission (CCRC). It was believed by the CCRC that the case had been wrongly decided on the basis of *McDowell & Singh* and more particularly that of *Singh*. The Court of Appeal held against Neuberg and CCRC in very

---

26 *R v Palmer* [2016] EWCA Crim 1049, para 23

27 *R v Neuberg* [2016] EWCA Crim 1927.

robust terms, describing the appeal as misconceived and on no less than seven instances and bluntly said that 'it is clear' that finding was correct. Writing the judgment for the court, Thomas LCJ said:

> 'It is clear that the analysis of the offence set out by Elias J was unquestionably correct; the criminal activity was carrying on the business in the prohibited name. On the findings of fact made by the judge, as this court held in 2007, it is simply unarguable to contend that no benefit arose from the criminal activity which comprised the offence. … In simple terms, the illegal use of a name in selling goods is often an activity through which criminals obtain a benefit … it is clear that the appellant carried on the business under a prohibited name and it was the carrying on of that business under that name that gave her a significant benefit.'[28]

Indeed, the court singled out the CCRC for special criticism in bringing the second appeal:

> '… it is clear that this appeal must fail. It is a matter of some regret that the reference was made to the court without a more careful analysis of the basis on which the reference was to proceed ... The result has been the expenditure of the precious resources of the CCRC and of this court to no benefit.'[29]

Many practitioners in the UK await a definitive Supreme Court decision to bring absolute certainty to the position. However, how is the above of assistance to Irish jurisprudence? It must act as strong guidance. Indeed, the above decisions are in concurrence with Irish decisions in parallel issues set out below.

Scottish Corruption

A distinctive approach was, however, taken in the Scottish High Court in *HMA v Weir Group Plc.*[30] Scotland operates a similar yet distinct process in comparison to England and Wales. Weir Group Plc pleaded guilty to two charges of breaching UN sanctions in connection with the 'Oil for Food' programme. In total, Weir Group Plc secured 16 contracts worth STG£34,340,204 by paying kickbacks of STG£3,104,527.[31] On the 15 December 2010 the High Court in Scotland made a confiscation order of almost STG£14m representing the profits the Weir Group Plc had made in Iraq together with a fine of STG£4.5m. The High Court noted that the company had pleaded guilty at the earliest stage of the formal criminal

28 ibid, paras 29 and 30.

29 ibid, para 46.

30 *HMA v Weir Group Plc*, available at: <http://www.scotland-judiciary.org.uk//8/695/HMA-v-WEIR-GROUP-PLC> (accessed 30 March 2018).

31 '"Triumph" for Scottish legal system as Weir Group face sanction-busting fine' *The Scottsman* (17 December 2010), available at: <https://www.scotsman.com/news/triumph-for-scottish-legal-system-as-weir-group-face-sanction-busting-fine-1-1370941> (accessed 30 March 2018).

process and accordingly it was entitled to the maximum one third discount for such an early plea thereby reducing the fine to STG£3m. Commenting on the case George Hamilton, Assistant Chief Constable, Strathclyde Police added:

> 'Just because this case involves a large company does not mean that they are above the law. I sincerely hope that today's result serves as a warning to other companies who may be tempted to think that they can break the law and get away with it. Strathclyde Police will robustly pursue such criminality with all the powers provided under the Proceeds of Crime Act.'[32]

In a sentencing statement made by Carloway LJ the court outlined a range of mitigating factors in favour of the company:

> 'They also include the remorse shown at current group board level in relation to their betrayal of the confidence of the company, its shareholders and the general public. The board has now altered and those involved in the illegal payments have departed from group employment. The particular subsidiary's business has been sold and a large number of new businesses acquired to create a company of a different complexion. The court has been informed that procedures and training are now in place designed to ensure that there can be no repetition of the illegal actings by employees or agents of the group at home or abroad.'[33]

However, this decision is not without criticism. Whilst the board had altered, no director was ever named. As one publication put it:

> 'That does not explain, however, why the names of the men who made the crucial decisions–clearly known to prosecutors–were not included in the Crown Office narrative submitted to the High Court. There is a suspicion in legal circles Weir's guilty plea and co-operation may have come at the price of keeping the identity of the guilty directors secret.'[34]

This, however, must be countered with the stark difficulty that must have faced the prosecutors in obtaining evidence from Iraq. Commenting on the case, John Hillary, executive director of the anti-poverty charity 'War on Want' remarked:

> 'If this marks a new beginning then that's to the good, but I think directors at the top levels of British companies should be held responsible for the

---

32 'Weir Group suffers biggest confiscation order' *The Journal of the Law Society of Scotland* (16 December 2010), available at: <http://www.journalonline.co.uk/News/1009087.aspx#.Wr6W84jwaUk> (accessed 30 March 2018).

33 *HMA v Weir Group Plc*, available at: <http://www.scotland-judiciary.org.uk//8/695/HMA-v-WEIR-GROUP-PLC> (accessed 30 March 2018).

34 "Triumph' for Scottish legal system as Weir Group face sanction-busting fine' *The Scottsman* (17 December 2010), available at: <https://www.scotsman.com/news/triumph-for-scottish-legal-system-as-weir-group-face-sanction-busting-fine-1-1370941> (accessed 30 March 2018).

actions of their companies. What tends to happen is that the sum levied against the companies are easily digestible – they're so small in terms of overall turnover, they can be easily incorporated into their annual profit and loss account, but once you've made it a personal responsibility of the directors it's going to have much more bite.'[35]

Weir Group Plc continues to trade and on the 28 February 2018, the *Financial Times* reported that the Weir Group 'is clearly back on its feet, cranking out a 47% rise in profits for 2017 to [STG]£250m, while revenues also swelled by 28% to [STG]£2.4bn.'[36]

The Importance of Non-Retrospectivity

Whether a licence is retrospective or not is of crucial significance to those who have engaged in regulatory offences. In *McDowell* half of the payments he received related to actions he had carried out before obtaining the licence. These were liable to confiscation. The monies he earned after the granting of the licence were legally earned. This is perfectly sensible. It would be absurd that a person could escape prosecution for possession of drugs on their assertion that one day in the future they will become a pharmacist. This equally applies to planning retention permission. Ireland differs significantly to the UK in planning law in one key area. In the UK a person who carries out an unauthorised development may apply for 'retrospective planning'[37] whereas in Ireland a person applies for 'retention permission'.[38] For the ordinary domestic homeowner, the subtle difference in language causes no concern. However, what of commercial properties? Lodging an application for planning retention for a development that is the subject of enforcement action does not diminish any offence committed.[39] Obtaining retention permission in Ireland does not render that past acts lawful.

Irish Confiscation Orders for Regulatory Offence

Ireland's Post Conviction Based (PCB) confiscation scheme operates under the Criminal Justice Act 1994. It may be broken down into two large categories, under their respective legislative marginal notes:

1. s 4: 'Confiscation orders: drug trafficking offences'; and
2. s 9: 'Confiscation orders: offences other than drug trafficking offences.'

---

35 ibid.

36 Katie Martin, 'Weir Group rides the oil rebound with 47% jump in profits' *Financial Times* (28 February 2018), available at: <https://www.ft.com/content/d73a5064-1c56-11e8-aaca-4574d7dabfb6> (accessed 30 March 2018).

37 Town and Country Planning Act 1990, s 73A.

38 Planning and Development Act 2010, s 32.

39 See further: Department of the Environment, Community and Local Government, 'A Guide to Planning Enforcement in Ireland' (November 2012) 12, available at: <http://www.housing.gov.ie/sites/default/files/migrated-files/en/Publications/DevelopmentandHousing/Planning/FileDownLoad%2C31564%2Cen.pdf> (accessed 30 March 2018).

Caution is urged in reading the above. Sometimes, the unwary practitioner will impute some other drug related offences into s 9. This is incorrect. Section 9 deals with every other criminal offence, regulatory and all. The legislative marginal note is perhaps better understood if read as relating to 'all other offences'. For the purpose of this chapter, the discussion will be limited to s 9 only. However, any practitioner advising in regard to drug trafficking must have proper regard to the extensive provisions of s 4. Similarly, PCB Forfeiture Orders under s 61 of the Act will be omitted from discussion.[40] These PCB Forfeiture Orders relate to things in the possession of the convicted person that have or were intended to have been used for the purpose of committing, or facilitating the commission of, any offence. Forfeiture Orders can of course be applied to money laundering matters where a person is found in possession of, for example, cash, and with a little imagination they can apply to regulatory offences. However, for brevity and clarity they will be omitted. To introduce perhaps some confusion PCB Forfeiture Orders differ to NCB Forfeiture Orders as found in the Proceeds of Crime Act 1996.

In general terms, s 9 provides that where a person has been sentenced for an offence which they have been convicted on indictment (for matters other than drug trafficking), then the DPP may make an application to the court for a confiscation order requiring the person to 'pay such sum as the court thinks fit'.[41] An application may only be made if it appears to the DPP that the person has benefited from the offence of which they are convicted. The application can be made at the sentencing or may be made at a later stage. The amount to be recovered by a s 9 PCB Confiscation Order shall not exceed:

(a) the amount of the benefit or pecuniary advantage which the court is satisfied that a person has obtained, or
(b) the amount appearing to the court to be the amount that might be realised at the time the order is made, whichever is the less.

This is an important distinction. Being financially successful in crime may be figuratively easy; retaining same and wisely investing these ill-gotten gains can be challenging. If the court is satisfied that the convicted person has derived

[40] Confiscation differs to forfeiture, a fact that is a source of great international confusion where in many non-English languages there exists only one word to cover both. The writer has caused much confusion at international conferences where translators are present.

[41] It is to be presumed that the term 'court' does not apply to the Special Criminal Court. In *Gilligan v The Special Criminal Court & Ors* [2005] IESC 86, the Supreme Court examined whether a s 4 PCB Confiscation order could be made by the Special Criminal Court. It concluded that it could not because the Special Criminal Court has limited jurisdiction. s 43 of the Offences against the State Act 1939 provides expressly that the Special Criminal Court has jurisdiction to try and to convict a person lawfully brought before the court for trial. It also provides expressly for an ancillary jurisdiction, such as to enable recognisances be entered into, to admit to bail, to administer oaths, to punish for contempt, and to entreat recognisances and bail bonds. The High Court concluded that '… a confiscation order, is a separate, although possible ancillary, proceeding which could not under any circumstances be said to be the trial of an offence.' The Supreme Court concurred with this view. Accordingly, it would appear that the provisions of s 9 are similarly not available to the Special Criminal Court.

pecuniary advantage as a result of, or in connection with, the commission of the offence the accused is treated for the purpose of s 9 as if he had obtained as a result of or in connection with the commission of the offences a sum of money equal to the value of the pecuniary advantage. It is important to note that whilst a s 9 Order is made in a criminal court, the test applied is the civil standard to proof.

Surprisingly, little academic or other analysis has been carried out in regard to s 9 PCB Confiscation. Much, if not all, of the discussion has focused on the actions of the Criminal Assets Bureau obtaining NCB Forfeiture orders under the Proceeds of Crime Act 1996. An analysis of the DPP's Annual Reports from 2008 to 2011 shows only aggregated figures for s 4 and 9 orders. This was commented on in a paper delivered by Shane Murphy SC at the 12th Annual National Prosecutor' Conference in 2011.[42] He described s 9 PCB Confiscation as '[p]erhaps the most underutilised power of all in the prosecutorial armoury'.[43] He bluntly stated: 'Post conviction confiscation mostly takes place in the field of drug trafficking. In my view this is a mistake.'[44]

In the following years, the DPP's Annual Reports split out s 9 from s 4 figures. The number of orders made under s 9 have been limited. In the period 2012 to 2015, only four such orders were made to a total combined value of €2,069,231.[45] The most recent published annual report indicates that a further two s 9 orders were obtained in 2016 to a combined value of €201,045.57.[46] It is uncertain as to nature of the underlying criminal actions that gave rise to the s 9 applications as no commentary is included on the cases in the DPP's Annual Report. However, the single order from 2013 to a value of €262,404 would appear to relate to an order made by Judge Hogan of Dublin Circuit Criminal Court.[47] This related to a prosecution of Martin Morgan who ran a brothel and prostitution business which had been described previously by the court as 'magnificent operation, highly sophisticated and highly rewarding and not a petty little business working on a shoe string'.[48] Judge Hogan granted the DPP's application for a s 9 PCB Confiscation order and also made an order that Morgan pay the legal costs.[49] This

---

42 Shane Murphy, 'The Trial of Complex Fraud Cases' (12th Annual National Prosecutors' Conference, Dublin Castle, May 2011), available at: <https://www.dppireland.ie/filestore/documents/PAPER_-_Shane_Murphy_SC_280511.pdf> (accessed 30 November 2018).

43 ibid 6.

44 ibid 8.

45 FATF 'Anti-money laundering and counter-terrorist financing measures in Ireland – 2017' (September 2017) 62, available at: <http://www.fatf-gafi.org/media/fatf/documents/reports/mer4/MER-Ireland-2017.pdf> (accessed 30 March 2018).

46 DPP, *Annual Report 2016* (2017) 57, available at: <https://www.dppireland.ie/filestore/documents/AR2016_[eng].pdf> (accessed 30 March 2018). As of writing, the 2017 annual report is unpublished.

47 DPP, *Annual Report 2014* (2015) 59, available at: <https://www.dppireland.ie/filestore/documents/AR_2013_[eng].pdf> (accessed 30 March 2018).

48 'Man jailed for keeping brothel must forfeit €252,000 in assets and cash' *The Irish Times* (29 June 2014), available at: <https://www.irishtimes.com/news/man-jailed-for-keeping-brothel-must-forfeit-252-000-in-assets-and-cash-1.1446926> (accessed 30 March 2018).

49 ibid.

order, however, as of writing, is subject to an appeal to the Court of Appeal.[50] The appeal by Morgan was based on the argument that he had spent the entire benefit realised by him leaving nothing available for confiscation, an assertion which Hedigan J described as 'courageous assertion'. The court has reserved its judgment in the matter.[51] The author believes that this yet to be delivered judgment may be the first published judgment concerning s 9 PCB confiscation and as such is eagerly awaited. However, what appears not in doubt is that s PCB Confiscation orders may be made; the issue under appeal is solely the quantum.

Irish Judicial Guidance

In the absence of s 9 PCB Confiscation judicial decisions, what guidance can we take? Brothel keeping falls outside the traditional definition of white-collar or regulatory crime. How will courts consider any such technical regulatory breaches? Some understanding can be gained from two cases which must be said did not address the issue at all but do give an indication of the Irish courts mind.

The first is that of *Wicklow County Council v Kinsella & Anor*,[52] a case which involved an application by the Council who sought an order under s 160(1) of the Planning and Development Act 200 restraining the Kinsellas from continuing with an unauthorised development on lands where a timber chalet had been erected for residential purposes without planning permission. s 151 provides that a person who carries out unauthorised development is guilty of an offence. On conviction on indictment a person is liable to a fine not exceeding £10,000,000 or to imprisonment for a term not exceeding two years or to both and on summary conviction to a fine not exceeding €5,000 or imprisonment for a term not exceeding six months or both. Ultimately, the matter made its way to the High Court for decision.

In 2007, the Kinsella's sought planning permission for a dormer bungalow and other structures. The Council requested further information and as none was forthcoming, the application was treated as being withdrawn. The Supreme Court highlighted this application as being important as it demonstrated the Kinsellas were well aware of the requirement for planning permission. In August 2012 a planning official found a timber chalet on a concrete plinth had been erected. A warning letter was sent by the Council in September 2012. The Kinsellas were directed to lodge an application for retention within six to eight weeks. They did not do so. A site inspection in December found further work had been

---

50 'Brothel keeper Martin Morgan moves to appeal confiscation order of assets worth €252k' *The Irish Times* (30 January 2018), available at: <https://www.independent.ie/irish-news/courts/brothel-keeper-martin-morgan-moves-to-appeal-confiscation-order-of-assets-worth-252k-36548279.html> (accessed 30 March 2018).

51 Court News Ireland, 'Brothel keeper 'courageously' claims to have spent profits on business expenses' (30 January 2018), available at: <https://courtsnewsireland.ie/brothel-keeper-courageously-claims-spent-profits-business-expenses/2018/01/30/> (accessed 30 March 2018).

52 *Wicklow County Council v Kinsella & Anor* [2015] IEHC 229.

carried out and accordingly on the 19 December 2012 an enforcement notice was served under s 154. When the property was inspected again in April it had been occupied. The Council commenced proceedings to seek an order for the removal of the unauthorised development. An application for retention was eventually made, it was refused, and this refusal was confirmed by An Bord Pleanála.

Kearns P, in giving judgment, considered the vital importance that planning plays in society. Whilst it may be viewed as a regulatory matter, its significance cannot be overstated, nor indeed can a person claim ignorance having regard to the abundance of guidance and warnings available. He observed that:

> '… planning control is an essential environmental necessity in a properly ordered society. Those who propose to engage in development have access to guidance in the form of Government policy directives and development plans, local authority guidance and guidance from the National Roads Authority. They can engage architects and planners who will advise them. Those who ride rough shod over and ignore these requirements take the risk that they will be unable to regularise their position and that they will have to undo what they have done. Indeed the legislature also deems their actions to be criminal offences …'.

An argument was made out that simply not having planning permission was sufficient punishment as it would negatively impact on the value and sale price of the house. Kearns P dismissed this suggestion strongly:

> 'The fact that, in the absence of permission, difficulties in making good title in the event of a sale of property many years later may not have anything like the deterrent effect which he postulated. … This Court apprehends that many developers, including those who have no short term need to sell property on which the unlawful development is located, may … regard flouting the planning laws as a risk worth taking. That would be incredibly destructive of planning law and planning law enforcement in this jurisdiction were it to occur.'

Whilst this case did not involve a PCB Confiscation, it does however demonstrate the approach the Irish courts are willing to take in regard to regulatory matters such as planning permission. Breaches of planning may constitute serious criminal offences.

The Supreme Court has had to consider the range of regulatory offences that arise in the context of enforceability of illegal contracts in *Quinn v. Irish Bank Resolution Corporation Ltd (In special Liquidation) & Ors.*[53] In giving judgment for the court, Clarke J noted the vast range of regulatory offences that may be committed:

---

[53] *Quinn v Irish Bank Resolution Corporation Ltd (In special Liquidation) & Ors* [2015] IESC 29.

> 'At one end of the spectrum, a party may simply not have a licence to conduct a particular activity in circumstances where they were clearly entitled to the licence concerned, and perhaps had held one in the past, where the failure of the relevant party was simply a short term oversight in renewing the relevant licence. Strictly speaking, the carrying on of the activity concerned may well, in those circumstances, be illegal, for the relevant statute may well specify that it is unlawful to carry on the activity concerned without the relevant licence. At the other end of the spectrum, there may be a deliberate and serious breach of important obligations imposed in the public interest by the relevant regime.'[54]

What may be extracted from *Kinsella* and *Quinn* is that where a person commits a deliberate and serious breach of regulatory requirements, that person is unlikely to find any sympathy from the court. Their actions will be viewed as serious criminal offences.

No Conviction does not Mean no Crime

The astute reader will have noticed that confiscation orders in this jurisdiction require one key ingredient: a conviction. If a person is not convicted of a crime, the s 9 Post Conviction Based Confiscation scheme cannot apply. It may be, for example, that the person who committed an offence died before being convicted. The inability to bring a prosecution, however, is not retroactive in making an unlawful act now lawful. Others can still gain from and enjoy the fruits of a deceased's crime.

This is where the reader is directed back to the Proceeds of Crime Act 1996 and to the actions of the Criminal Assets Bureau.[55] The CAB may apply to the High Court for a freezing order[56] over assets which derive directly or indirectly from the proceeds of criminal conduct. The standard of proof is, in common with s 9 PCB Confiscation proceedings, the civil standard. Where a court finds, following an application under s 4 of the Act, that property (including bank accounts) that has been found to be directly or indirectly the proceeds of criminal crime or that the property was acquired, in whole or in part with, or in connection with property that directly or indirectly constitutes the proceeds of crime, then the court may make disposal order in favour of the State.[57]

The Supreme Court has consistently found the Proceeds of Crime Act NCB

---

54 ibid para 6.2-6.3.

55 The reader is also directed to s 16B of the Proceeds of Crime Act 1996 which make provisions for the High Court to make a 'corrupt enrichment order'. However, for the sake of brevity, this chapter shall confine itself to ss 2, 3 and 4 of the Act.

56 s 2 and 3 of the Proceeds of Crime Act 1996 to 2016. s 2 is an ex-parte application, whereas s 3, being the full trial of the action, is on full notice to all parties.

57 A s 4 disposal order operates to deprives the respondent of his or her rights (if any) in property and the property stands transferred to the Minister for Public Expenditure and Reform or to such other person as the court may determine.

Forfeiture features to be fully constitutional. In *Murphy v GM*,[58] the Supreme Court dealt with a constitutional challenge to the Proceeds of Crime Act 1996. In rejecting an assertion of repugnancy to the Constitution, Keane CJ had stated:

> 'This issue in the present case does not raise a challenge to a valid constitutional right of property. It concerns the right of the State to take, or the right of a citizen to resist the State in taking, property which is proved on the balance of probabilities to represent the proceeds of crime. In general such a forfeiture is not a punishment and its operation does not require criminal procedures. Application of such legislation must be sensitive to the actual property and other rights of the citizens but in principle, and subject, no doubt, to special problems which may arise in particular cases, a person in possession of the proceeds of crime can have no constitutional grievance if deprived of their use.'[59]

In *CAB v Kelly & TT* the Supreme Court noted that there is a strong public policy dimension to the Proceeds of Crime Act 1996.[60] That policy is to ensure that persons do not benefit from assets which were obtained with the proceeds of crime irrespective of whether the person benefiting actually knew how such property was obtained with the proceeds of crime. In that case, TT, the wife of Kelly, had sought to stop the forfeiture of a family home to the State which had been found to be the acquired from the proceeds of crime. At the time that the initial freezing order had been made, criminal charges were outstanding before the courts. He had subsequently been convicted but the charges were quashed on technical grounds. He had issued proceedings to restrain further prosecution, this application was rejected, but in any event he was acquitted of any outstanding charges. The Supreme Court found that that could only be seen as being of limited weight in light of concessions made by Kelly and TT regarding the origins of the property.[61] McMenamin J for the court stated:

> 'The Act provides for fair procedures to be observed. It cannot be seen as arbitrary. It is designed to achieve a desirable social objective and be proportionate. It cannot be said to impinge on a right to private property, as the property was acquired unlawfully. One of the facts to be borne in mind is the extent to which, as a result of the commission of crime, persons may directly or indirectly benefit in a way not open to other members of the community, such as living without the requirements of payments of tax, mortgage repayments or rent. These activities are profoundly anti-social and contrary to the common good. The interference with the rights of private property embodied in Article 40.3.2 and Article 43 of the Constitution and Article 8 of the European Convention on Human Rights are, therefore, proportionate and in accordance with law.'

---

58 *Murphy v GM* [2001] 4 IR 113.

59 ibid 153.

60 *CAB v Kelly & TT* [2012] IESC 64.

61 The court went on to clarify 'but subject to whether or not such person may have been a bona fide purchaser for value, where different considerations may arise.' The court held here that the appellant TT was not a good faith purchaser.

Conclusion

As history has shown us, corruption in the planning process appears not to have been uncommon. However, paying a corrupt bribe is risky business as it may be discovered at some point in the future. It requires all parties to keep the secret. It might be viewed as a less risky act to simply ignore planning laws altogether and thereafter seek to regularise matters. In effect, it is easier to seek absolution rather than obtain permission. However, this chapter should caution anyone thinking of doing same as the financial loss may be extensive. It is hoped that this chapter will have opened the reader's eyes to the dangers of reading regulatory legislation in isolation. As a personal observation I might remark that over specialisation of the legal profession is not always a good thing. It creates a blinkered approach when dealing with matters. Too often, solicitors will comment 'I don't do criminal law', oblivious to the reality that they themselves might be committing money laundering offences arising from regulatory breaches. Confiscating and forfeiting the proceeds of regulatory crime is an incredibly new, fast paced and emergent area of law. Those who treat regulatory offences as merely a cost of doing business may one day receive a visit from officers of the Criminal Assets Bureau, amongst others. At that point the die may be cast and the short term financial benefits once gained will be confiscated and forfeited with ignominy. The white-collar perpetrators of regulatory crime will suffer the same fate as thieves, fraudsters and drug dealers.

CHAPTER 11

CONCLUSION: REFLECTING ON PAST AND FUTURE REGULATORY ENFORCEMENT

Joe McGrath

The Irish architecture addressing white-collar crime has changed profoundly since the 1990s, but particularly in the last decade since the financial crisis.[1] This new architecture reflects new ways of thinking about white-collar criminality, new laws to secure accountability, and changed enforcement practices. These matters have been analysed in detail in the chapters of this edited collection. Moreover, the regulatory impulse has not faded; additional broad-ranging reforms are likely. The Law Reform Commission's Issues Paper on Regulatory Enforcement and Corporate Offences in 2016 has canvassed views on a range of related issues of regulatory enforcement, including those relating to the enhanced use of civil and administrative sanctions; the coordination of regulators and the standardisation of their powers; the creation of new offences to address 'gaps' in the criminal law; corporate criminal liability; and deferred prosecution agreements, etc.[2] A report on these matters is expected soon.

Nevertheless, regardless of the specific recommendations advanced by the Commission, and other forthcoming initiatives,[3] it is likely that such reforms will only have traction where they are accompanied by the maintenance of a cultural context which welcomes greater enforcement in the national economic interest. This culture is most likely to support regulatory enforcement where it is recognised that the failure to enforce the law threatens the State's reputation as an attractive place in which to do business. Enforcement of effective regulatory controls must not be perceived as 'red tape' that inhibits risk-taking and entrepreneurship but operates to protect legitimate businesses that comply with the law from those that operate to defraud the market, to protect the public from fraud, and to protect the interests of employees, traders and suppliers that need Irish businesses to remain viable. The paragraphs below offer a reflection on history of corporate enforcement in Ireland, which demonstrates that stringent

---

* Lecturer, Sutherland School of Law, University College Dublin.

1 Joe McGrath, *Corporate and White-Collar Crime in Ireland: A New Architecture of Regulatory Enforcement* (Manchester University Press 2015).

2 Law Reform Commission (LRC IP 8 – 2016) *Issues paper: Regulatory enforcement and corporate offences* (Dublin: Stationery Office, 2016).

3 'Measures to Enhance Ireland's Corporate, Economic and Regulatory Framework' (2017), available at: <https://merrionstreet.ie/MerrionStreet/en/ImageLibrary/20171101_Measures_to_Enhance_Regulatory_Framework.pdf> (accessed 30 May 2018).

laws, without broader cultural support for enforcement, will be ineffective. This reflection is valuable because Ireland must learn from the mistakes of the past or be condemned to repeat them.

On paper, at least, it is arguable that Ireland traditionally had a strong system of enforcing corporate obligations. Obligations in the corporate and financial sectors have long since been underpinning by hundreds of criminal offences in company law and banking law, among others.[4] These laws were often enforced by the ordinary policing and prosecutorial bodies that addressed ordinary crime but more recently have also been enforced by specialist agencies with enhanced powers. Nevertheless, despite addressing corporate wrongdoing with its strongest form of censure, the criminal law, the law was rarely enforced. Various reports, including the Cox Report in 1958, the McDowell Report in 1998, the Honohan and the Regling and Watson Reports of 2010, all detail widespread non-compliance with the law, the deferential approach of regulators to respectable corporate officers and managers, and the chronic reluctance to prosecute corporate wrongdoers who broke the law.[5] The natural question arises, therefore, as to why white-collar crimes were so rarely prosecuted throughout this period? Why were white-collar crimes not considered threats or risks which the State had to address?

It seems likely that the under-policing of and lack of enforcement in the corporate sector persisted because the risks underlying these approaches were underappreciated. The ability to perceive risk is culturally contingent.[6] The risks we identify, and do not identify, reveal as much about society at a given time as they do about hazards in our environment. The socio-economic context in Ireland in the decades following independence was one which had idealised rural living, frugality and isolationism, which had resisted foreign investment and industrialisation as an assertion of sovereignty.[7] Understandably, in this context, white-collar criminality did not animate a State that was largely agrarian in orientation and had low levels of corporate activity. Subsequently, when the state advanced policies which were pro-competition, pro-industry, and pro-European integration, increased corporate activity was often associated with purely positive concepts such as wealth creation, employment, and as a way to escape economic depression.[8] Getting tough on white-collar crimes was clearly not a strategic

---

4 Joe McGrath, 'The Prosecution of White-Collar Crime in a Developing Economy: A Case Study of Ireland in the 20th Century' in Judith van Erp *et al*, eds. *Handbook on White-Collar Crime in Europe* (Routledge 2015) 399.

5 Patrick Honohan, *The Irish Banking Crisis Regulatory and Financial Stability Policy 2003-2008* (Central Bank 2010); Klaus Regling & Maxwell Watson, *A Preliminary Report on the Sources of Ireland's Banking Crisis* (Government Publications Office 2010); Report of the Working Group on Company Law Compliance and Enforcement (Stationery Office 1998); Report of the Company Law Reform Committee (Stationery Office 1958).

6 Mary Douglas, *Risk and Blame: Essays in Cultural Theory* (Routledge 1992). Douglas suggests that social harms must be perceived by individuals to be recognised as such by the community more generally. Harm must be perceived and understood or it will not become politicised in such a way as to mobilise the community to combat it.

7 Joe Lee, *Ireland 1912-1985; Politics and Society* (Cambridge University Press 1989).

8 Diarmuid Ferriter, *The Transformation of Ireland 1900-2000* (Profile Books Ltd 2005).

governance issue when the State was actively courting foreign investment on the basis of its light-touch regulatory regime.[9] This way of thinking may also have supported the routine marginalisation of corporate accountability within the legal system. Friedman states, 'a law which goes against the grain, culturally speaking, will be hard to enforce and probably ineffective'.[10] The criminalisation of the commercial community, bringing jobs and prosperity, went 'against the grain' and had little social or political support in practice. Consequently, corporate enforcement was not resourced or supported and Ireland over-looked the prosecution of white-criminal offences in a way it would never have done with more 'conventional' crime. Ireland exhibited a classic characteristic in the breakdown of the rule of law, identified by Fuller, 'a failure of congruence between the rules as announced and their actual administration'.[11]

As noted throughout this collection, however, the contemporary architecture addressing white-collar crime has changed profoundly since the banking crisis in 2008. Due to the absence of effective regulatory oversight, corporate and financial wrongdoing in the banking sector severely damaged the economy and required the banks to be rescued. People lost their jobs, their homes were devalued, they became more indebted, their taxes increased, and their economic security was jeopardised. If corporate wrongdoing was not pursued in the past because there was no public demand for 'respectable' company officers to be criminally prosecuted like 'ordinary' criminals, then this had changed. It was understood that corporate wrongdoing could damage the security of the State in ways that are at least as harmful as 'street crime'. People wanted accountability and corporate and financial crime became politicised. Politicians stated that white-collar criminals were guilty of economic treason and should be treated like terrorists. The State pledged to be tough on white-collar crime and introduced tougher new laws involving the increased use of strict liability, stronger investigative powers, more stringent accounting rules, increased powers of supervision, greater regulatory accountability, the fragmentation and extension of detention periods, independent verification of legal privilege, confirmation of inroads into the right to silence, and the expanded use of 'information reporters' who must report their suspicions that criminal offences have been committed.[12] There is also more evidence of a more stringent approach to sanctioning white-collar crime. The Central Bank has also drawn more regularly on its administrative sanctions regime to deal with financial services providers and individuals for non-compliance with the law and former directors at Anglo Irish Bank have been convicted on indictment for offences contrary to the Companies Acts, among others. Some of these officers have received significant custodial sentences.[13]

---

9 Joe McGrath, *Corporate and White-collar Crime in Ireland* (Manchester University Press 2015).

10 Laurence M Friedman, *The Legal System: A Social Science Perspective* (Russel Sage 1975) 108.

11 Lon Fuller, *The Morality of Law* (Yale University Press 1969) 39.

12 Joe McGrath, *Corporate and White-collar Crime in Ireland* (Manchester University Press 2015).

13 Joe McGrath, 'Twenty Years since the McDowell Report: A Reflection on the Powers and Performance of the Office of the Director of Corporate Enforcement' (2018) 60 Irish Jurist 33.

These measures suggest that there is an increased willingness to invoke a more stringent approach to corporate and financial wrongdoing, though it may be too early to tell if this approach will be sustained. Nevertheless, a long-term analysis of trends in corporate regulation suggest that regulatory reforms tend to be cyclical such that an economic crash precipitates a greater interest in regulatory intervention.[14] This interest fades as time passes and economic circumstances improve, precipitating another deregulatory or light-touch approach which in turn facilitates corporate irresponsibility and another economic crash.[15] In the current context where Ireland now appears to be exhibiting signs of a strong economic recovery, it is conceivable that the previous philosophy that 'facilitative' or 'light-touch' regulation is good for business, may once again dominate political and social thought, so that the funding and other capacities of regulatory agencies are reduced. Accordingly, caution must be exercised to ensure that the rationales for effective regulatory enforcement and good governance persist in the general consciousness long after the memories of the adverse impacts of economic crimes on the security of the State fade.

[14] Erik F Gerding, 'The next epidemic: Bubbles and the growth and decay of securities regulation' (2005) 38 Conn L Rev. 393.

[15] J Minkes & L Minkes, ed.s, *Corporate and White-collar Crime* (Sage 2008) 40.

INDEX

Bold page numbers indicate figures, *italic* numbers indicate tables.